Priestdaddy

Motherland Fatherland Homelandsexuals
Balloon Pop Outlaw Black

PATRICIA LOCKWOOD

Priestdaddy

A Memoir

ALLEN LANE
an imprint of
PENGUIN BOOKS

ALLEN LANE

UK | USA | Canada | Ireland | Australia
India | New Zealand | South Africa

Penguin Books is part of the Penguin Random House group of companies
whose addresses can be found at global.penguinrandomhouse.com.

First published in the United States of America by Riverhead Books
an imprint of Penguin Random House LLC 2017
First published in Great Britain by Allen Lane 2017
001

Printed in Great Britain by Clays Ltd, St Ives plc

A CIP catalogue record for this book is available from the British Library

ISBN: 978–1–846–14920–7

www.greenpenguin.co.uk

Penguin Random House is committed to a
sustainable future for our business, our readers
and our planet. This book is made from Forest
Stewardship Council® certified paper.

For my family

CONTENTS

PRIESTDADDY

INTRODUCTORY RITES

Before they allowed your father to be a priest," my mother tells me, "they made me take the Psychopath Test. You know, a priest can't have a psychopath wife, it would bring disgrace."

She sets a brimming teacup in front of me and yells, "HOT!" She sets a second one in front of my husband, Jason, and yells, "Don't touch it!" She situates herself in the chair at the head of the table and gazes at the two of us with total maternal happiness, ready to tell the story of the time someone dared to question her mental health.

We are congregating in the dining room of my father's rectory in Kansas City, where I have returned to live with my parents after twelve long years away. Jason presses his shoulder against mine for reassurance and tries to avoid making eye contact with the graphic crucifix on the opposite wall, whose nouns are like a poem's nouns: blood, bone, skin. We are penniless and we are exhausted, and in the grand human tradition, we have thrown ourselves on the mercy of the church, which exists for me on this earth in an unusually patriarchal form. It walks, it cusses, it calls me Bit. It is currently shredding its guitar upstairs, across the hallway from the room where we will be staying for the foreseeable future. Through the east window I can see the same dark geometry of buildings that surrounded me all throughout my childhood: closed school, locked gymnasium, the squares and spires of a place of worship plummeting up into the night.

"Well. You wouldn't want . . . to bring disgrace . . . to the Catholic Church," Jason says, with a diplomacy that is almost beautiful, making a great show of blowing on his murderously hot tea.

"No, you wouldn't," my mother agrees. "They came to the house, because where people are a psychopath the most is in their own homes. And they tried to trap me. They brought all these questions.

"They said, 'Oh, did you ever feel bad when you killed someone? Which drug tastes the best to you? When your dog talks, what does he say? How many times have you been suicidal?' They didn't believe me that I'd *never* been suicidal. *Why would I be suicidal.* I'm in love with life."

She bangs down her rosebud-patterned cup with unexpected force, seized with the sudden urge to backflip through time and attempt a citizen's arrest. "They were using so many double negatives that finally I just lost it. 'You can come back here and give me that test when the questions are in English!' I said, and I chased them away."

"I don't understand how you passed," I say. "From what you're telling me, it sounds like you should have gotten a pretty bad grade. It sounds like you should have gotten the worst grade, actually."

"I passed it by being smarter than the test itself," she says, lifting an aha! finger and touching the tip of my nose with it. "Same way I got the highest-ever score in the history of the SAT."

"I didn't know you even took the SAT."

"The Sears Aptitude Test," she clarifies in ringing tones. "They had never seen anything like it."

"Why would you hang that on your wall," Jason breathes, staring past us at the bloody spectacle of the crucifix, held spellbound by its gore. "Why would you hang that in the room where you eat. It looks like someone screamed into a ribeye."

"They also tested you," my mother continues, "to see if you were a psychopath. But you were young enough that nothing showed up, thank God."

"Your dad gets an F," Jason says, looking up the questions on his phone and motioning us to be quiet. "Listen."

I was a problem child.
>   True
>   False

I am neither shy nor self-conscious; I speak with authority.
>   True
>   False

I am not or would not be proud of getting away with crimes.
>   True
>   False

I can hear my father's objections now: who wouldn't be proud of getting away with crimes? Who wasn't a problem child? When your dog talks, doesn't he tell you that you're a champion? Mom can't remember if he took it at all, but if he did, Jesus must have appeared at the last minute and filled out the answers for him, because he was allowed to walk through the doors of the priesthood freely, as upright as sanity itself, while his sane wife and sane children watched sanely from the pews.

Jason continues to scroll through the test, growing more and more horrified as he goes. When he reads, "'I often get others to pay for things for me, true or false,'" he clutches at his heart. "We're psychopaths," he says mournfully. "We're being psychopaths right now, in your dad's holy rectory."

"I told you it happens at home," says my mother.

WE TAKE OUR TEACUPS into the living room and curl up on the couch together looking at family pictures. There are hundreds and hundreds of them, almost none of them fine except the sunsets over flat scalloping water and beaches of crushed mussel shells. There is my mother in a Playboy Bunny T-shirt my father gave her for her twenty-second birthday—that was before he found God. My mother in a library, with long carved carnelian hair, smiling in front of shelves of red-and-gold encyclopedias. There is my father on a five-week "biblical archaeological dig," wearing white short shorts and his whole body the color of wet sand, searching for the door of the First Temple. There he is standing on the spot where the herd of demon swine were driven squealing into the Sea of Galilee.

"Should we see if Dad wants to come down?" I ask, but he's never found the family saga as compelling as the rest of us do. Once, when we were going through the slides from that aforementioned dig with him, he was somehow able to tell us his exact geographical coordinates in the Holy Land and every detail of every last stone in the excavation sites, but when the first baby picture popped up, he didn't know which of his five children it was.

There I am, sluglike and drooling, unwilling to close my mouth until my first words arrived to me. "You were the kind of baby I could set down on a blanket and then come back three hours later and you hadn't moved," my mother tells me approvingly. "That's how I knew you were a thinker." There I am, held in a pair of black-sleeved arms, a white rectangular collar floating over my head, not like a halo at all, but like the first page of an open notebook.

My father in a tight, appalling sailor suit. My father dressed as a pro-life Dracula. My father wearing a Speedo at the lapping edge of a picturesque lake, between two buff buttocky dunes. "There's no in-between with him, is there," Jason says. "He's either buck nude or he's in a little outfit."

My father propping my boneless, footie-pajamaed form up on the back of a chrome-and-lipstick motorcycle. My eyes full of unshed tears, because I am thinking of accidents and crashes, of the inherent dangers of going vroom-vroom. My father lying on his back and pretending to eat my cheeks, ears, hands. My father reclining spread-legged in the sunlight while terrier puppies romped over his lap.

"Is he wearing anything at all on his lower half?" Jason cries, as if in supplication to heaven.

"Underwear," answers my mother, turning her head sideways and squinting. "Just . . . underwear."

"You came out of that," Jason says, indicating the white triangle at the center of a whirl of dog-fur. "*That's* where you came from." I close my eyes to shut out the image. I like to think I sprang from a head; I like to think the head was mine.

A picture of my father standing at the altar in a lamb-white robe, ready to accept an unseen blessing and enter his life as I have always known it: as an oddity, an impossibility, a contradiction in terms. Catholic priests, by definition, aren't allowed to be married, but my father snuck past the definition while the dictionary was sleeping and was somehow ordained one anyway. An exception to the rules, before I even understood what the rules were. A human loophole, and I slipped through him into the world.

"Just look at him," Jason says, with something approaching awe, all five of the journalistic *W*s present in his eyes, plus a single shining *H*. But faith and my father taught me the same lesson: to live in the mystery, even to love it.

SOME MEN ARE so larger-than-life that it's impossible to imagine them days-old and diapered, but I've always found it the easiest thing in the world to see my father as a baby, lolling on his back in the middle of fresh sheets, smoking a fat cigar to congratulate himself on his own birth, stubbing out the cigar—with great style—in the face of his first teddy bear.

He suffered, or did not suffer, from congenital naughtiness. He was either the favorite child or else the sort of person who would claim to be the favorite child when he wasn't. In even his earliest pictures, he grinned with the huge, hand-rubbing glee of a cartoon villain, as if he just watched the photographer trip and fall into an open sewer. His hair curled upward, dark and frizzed, like the smoke of an illegal bonfire. He was cherubic, satanic, dressed in scandalously short pants. Myopic in a way only I have inherited—even back then, his lenses were thicker than the glass in the popemobile. Propelled forward by his wants, which were enormous. When he was little, he used to creep into his mother's cocktail parties and eat all the shrimps off the silver platters and then run away giggling. My grandmother would shake her pink fist, which generally gripped a gin and tonic. She would chase and try to catch him, but you can never catch my father. The element of surprise is forever on his side.

Instead of being fascinated by trains, as more orderly boys might have been, he was fascinated by cement mixers, whose job it was to perpetually stir.

I believe he itched against the way things were. I believe he grew toward heaven only because it was not possible to grow toward hell, inching taller and weedier to the Cincinnati sky. Before long, he had turned into a smirking teenage atheist, whose only religion was rock and roll, tight jeans, and making rude comments to authority figures. He played the guitar upside down and set off cherry bombs in the school toilets. He was the first boy in school to grow his hair—out in a cloud, not down to his shoulders—and when they tried to kick him out for it, he just laughed.

He first encountered my mother in 1968, when she was sent to his freshman algebra class on a hall monitor assignment. It has always given me considerable pleasure to imagine this scene. "Some people in this school," my little mother might have announced, "are not disposing of their gum properly, and the rest of us are paying the price." My father looked up from his desk and was thunderstruck. Like all contrarians, he felt a secret longing to live with the rules and to love them. He wanted to sleep tucked into the rulebook, where he would feel safe. She stood in the doorway of the classroom with her beautiful boundaries shining all around her—yes like a halo this time—and he decided he would marry her. He pursued her and he pestered her; he followed her home and threw rocks at her. He pelted a single question persistently at her window: will you marry me?

A picture of my mother holding my father's hand, the very essence of oval-faced, madonna-blank loveliness, with something mischievous about her left canine. "Why did you say yes?" I ask her, but I already know the answer. My mother loves to argue, and love is the only argument you can win by saying yes.

"He was pretty bad at that time," she reflects, "but I knew I would make him a Catholic eventually, because the really bad ones always convert sooner or later. The worst bad boy of all was St. Paul, and he fell off his horse and ended up in the Bible."

I am long and fatally lapsed in the tradition, so the time I feel most Catholic is when I think about how many Irish people had to have sex before I became a statistical possibility. My mother was the last in a staggering line of them—the second of six children, raised up in a neighborhood that had a St. Something-or-Other on every corner, a handful of beads in her cardigan pocket. When it came to the athleticism of religion she was a natural. She didn't have to think about it; her body thought for her. She crossed herself and folded her hands because those were the movements her body liked best, the way a hurdler's likes best to leap. She said yes to my father, rejoicing in her heart that she had won the debate at last, and they stood at the altar together when they were just eighteen.

She attended church every Sunday, which my father thought was "just so damn hilarious." *He* was not going to be shut up in small spaces and forced to do tricks on command. Instead, he joined the Navy and plunged into the ocean in that smallest and most obedient space of all: a nuclear submarine called the USS *Flying Fish*. And it was here, in the middle of perfect claustrophobia, that a moment of his life split open and spilled the nuclear green glow of infinity all over him, and became his origin story. It occurred during a late-night viewing of *The Exorcist*. The room was dark and that eerie, pea-soup light was pouring down, and all around him men in sailor suits were getting the bejesus scared out of them, and the bejesus flew into my father like a dart into a bull's-eye. He saw the little girl's head spin around to consider the hidden half of things and his head spun around likewise. Over the course of that patrol, the men watched *The Exorcist* seventy-two times, and on the very next patrol, my father converted.

Put yourself in his place. You're a drop of blood at the center of the ocean, which plays a tense soundtrack all night long, interspersed with bright blips of radar. Russians are trying to blow up capitalism and you're surrounded by dolphins who know how to spy and the general atmosphere is one of cinematic suspense. All of a sudden you look up at a screen and see a possessed twelve-year-old with violent bedhead vomiting green chunks and backwards Latin. She's so full of a demon that the only way to relieve her feelings is to have hate sex with a crucifix. You would convert too, I guarantee it.

Down in the amniotic sea, and ready to be born again. Later, he always called it "the deepest conversion on record," which just goes to show we like a nice way of saying things.

When I think about his time in the Navy, there is a certain unreality about it, as there is with anything underwater. I picture a little toy submarine, sleek and bobbing in the bath, but I know there must have been more shape and dimension and metal guts to it than that. It must have been such a place to him. He must have had such affection for its physical workings, and such a private knowledge of them. When he fell down an open submarine hatch and broke his back, it must have been like falling down a channel of his own self—and when he felt the pain, he must have felt it in the whole ship, vastly and beyond him.

Rearranged in both body and beliefs, he returned home to my mother, who was wearing an I-told-you-so face so triumphant it was never able to return to its former configuration. He now counted himself a Christian, and he disappeared for a few years into books and study. He could argue the numbers off a clock and the print off a newspaper, and now he argued himself into orthodoxy. He had decided he was meant for the Lutheran ministry. Why he chose Lutheranism I cannot say, but I suspect he was attracted to the glamour of its founder: a snout-faced man who spewed insults from every orifice and believed he had the power to fart away the devil.

My mother, not wishing to let Ireland down, now turned her attention to the all-consuming art of procreation. There are two facts of our ancestry she frequently mentions, believing they apply to me: my great-great-great-aunt was excommunicated from the Catholic Church for practicing witchcraft, and my great-grandmother was a corset model. The great-great-great-aunt was known far and wide for telling fortunes, administering potions, gazing deep into the eyes of potatoes, and just generally giving the pope a hard time. The great-grandmother who modeled corsets was spoken of in the same tone of disapproval, as if somehow they were in league with each other across centuries—this one stirring the cauldron, that one bouncing in slow motion through a field of daisies. No surprise at all, then, when I emerged from my own mother in the form of a tiny psychic covered with tits.

"An old soul," said the nurse, but everyone saw through her tactful euphemism to the truth: I was a sport, an abomination, a monstrous hybrid of high and low. A voluptuous scent of sulfur attended me. I rolled toward the doctor and made an obscene gesture that no one had ever seen before.

"She looks just like me," my father said.

My parents joined hands and named me after a nun in an attempt to alter the course of my destiny, but there was no turning back and they knew it. The nurse covered me with ink and stamped me.

We all lived together in a trailer while my father dove into his books and stayed under, under, until finally he was ready to be ordained. He put on his first white collar, which it would be my mother's responsibility for the rest of their marriage to keep clean, and we moved from the trailer into a parsonage. If I have any memories of this time, they are of castle walls and chocolate-brown pews and bright banners hanging in high places. Lutherans have a passion for banners that approaches the erotic. They are never happier than when they are scissoring big purple grapes out of felt and gluing them onto other felt. I can picture a few members of the congregation, who were square-faced and blue-eyed and gently brimming with pie filling. I also recall consuming an enormous quantity and variety of mayonnaise salads, which Lutherans loved and excelled at making. If Jesus himself appeared in their midst and said, "Eat my body," they would first slather mayonnaise all over him.

Against this pastoral, God-fearing backdrop, I exhibited my first signs of blasphemy. At a funeral in that solemn, banner-hung church, I turned to my mother and demanded, "WHERE'S YA NIPPLE, MOMMY?" She clapped a hand over my mouth and carried me out amid a loud chorus of Lutheran gasps. I could not see why. My yearning for the invisible was just as legitimate as theirs. It would not be the last time I tried to locate a nipple in church, but it would be the last time I announced it.

They were homey people, but somehow my father was not at home among them. The sermons he gave stretched themselves more and more away from Martin Luther and toward something else, but at that point, only my mother knew what it was. My father, she knew, was becoming Catholic. He was tired of grape juice. He wanted wine.

Here is how it works: when a married minister of another faith converts to Catholicism, he can apply to Rome for a dispensation to become a married Catholic priest. He is allowed, yes, to keep his wife. He is even allowed to keep his children, no matter how bad they might be. The Vatican must review his case and declare the man fit for duty. (My father's paperwork was approved by Joseph Ratzinger, later to take the name Pope Benedict XVI, later to resign the papacy and become an enigma in fine elfin shoes wandering through private gardens, his eyes among the bushes like unblinking black roses.) Once he has received this approval, the man can enter training for the priesthood and be ordained, but only after every member of his immediate family passes the Psychopath Test.

At his ordination, he lay flat on the floor, and I felt a moment of brief concern that someone was going to stomp on him. The ceremony lasted as long as what it promised us: an eternity. I was wearing my itchiest dress, the color of bad weather, and I wriggled in my seat the entire time, which later came to seem significant. My mother sat next to me, and I understood that she was what made him different from the other priests, and that I was what made him different from the other priests. After it was all over, everyone had to call him Father, but I called him that anyway, so it made no difference to me. All fathers believe they are God, and I took it for granted that my father especially believed it.

There was always a certain stoniness to his pronouncements, as if he had come down off the mountaintop holding tablets, even when he was saying things like "GAD" and "NAW" and "JIMINY CHRISTMAS." I inherited this too, and I thank him for it.

MY FATHER'S HEAD appears in the doorway like a planet of much higher density than ours. Tucked under his arm is a thick book about false popes, of which there must have been a great many. Our glasses flint and flash against each other, shortsightedness against short-sightedness, and I regard him with a complex fondness. I remember a sermon he once gave about me called "The Prodigal Daughter," soon after I first ran away with Jason at the age of nineteen. I had returned for a brief visit and was singing cantor with my older sister in a side alcove of the church, next to the wheezing old organ and a choir of votive candles. I listened with my head bent down—I have memorized the floors in all my father's churches. The sermon was about me being the bad pig-keeping son who runs away from home and then has to oink back on all fours when his money runs out. At the time my reaction alternated between embarrassment and amusement, but now I see it must have been prophetic. All these years I have been tending the pigs of liberalism, agnosticism, poetry, fornication, cussing, salad-eating, and wanting to visit Europe, but I am back home now, and the pigs can't come with me.

My father greets us with his usual largesse, disparages the president in passing, expresses a belief that the Cincinnati Bengals are going to "win it all this season," yells out "Hoooo-eee!" for no particular reason, tells my mother to wash a jumbo load of his underwear, and then pops back into the kitchen and begins to cook one pound of bacon.

"Dad," I call to him, "did you ever take this test Mom was telling us about?"

"I took it twice," he answers. "The first time I got angry, because they asked every question four different ways, trying to mess you up. So I resented it, and I answered every question wrong on purpose, and it came back that I was one hundred percent a psychopath."

"And the second time?" I venture.

"Oh, the second time I just took it normally."

My mother nods along to this shocking confession with a "hell yeah" expression on her face. An overwhelming feeling of *Who ARE these people?* washes over me, but in fact I know exactly who they are, and they make more immediate sense to me than people who grew up going to the ballet and getting *The New York Times* on Sunday and passing personality tests with flying colors. The sizzling scent of my former life wafts out from the kitchen, and I breathe it along with the air.

A book doesn't ask to begin, any more than a baby asks to be born. But still, best to begin at the beginning.

1

MEETING OF THE MINDS

At nineteen, I ought to have been in college along with the rest of my high school class, gaining fifteen pounds of knowledge and bursting the sweatpants of my ignorance. What else did people do there? Changed their names to Patchouli, became vegetarians, grew out their leg hair for the first time, got so caught up in their studies of ancient Greece that they murdered a farmer while worshipping the grape-god in the countryside. It seemed the very act of stacking boxes in a second-hand car and driving away with your childhood home in the rearview allowed you to be born again in whatever form you chose, and I could hardly wait. I had applied and been accepted, and was all set to start attending a Great Books college in the winter of 2001, but the night before Christmas—two weeks before I was supposed to depart for Annapolis—my father called me into his study for a talk.

The orotund, indignant sound of Rush Limbaugh was blasting from a radio in the corner, and the drunken leprechaun sound of Bill O'Reilly was blasting from the television. It was my father's pleasure to listen to the two men simultaneously, while emitting the occasional "hoo-HOO" of agreement. He was wearing his most formal boxer shorts, the ones you could almost not see through. He patted a spot next to him on the overstuffed leather sofa. (It was one of his personal commandments that a couch must absolutely always be made of leather. If your couch was made of chintz or something, go live on Fairy Island.) I sat down, averting my eyes, staring past the curve of his cheek and out the window, where the upper feathers of a pillowfight swirled between us and the school next door.

"We can't do it, Bit," he said, shaking his curly head kindly, as if it couldn't be helped. "The money just isn't there," he explained, which made me think of a smoke-and-mirrors trick: poof, and the pile of money is gone, the pile of textbooks, the pile of bricks that would have been college.

"Okay," I said, automatic, from a body that didn't seem to be mine. I didn't ask a single question. When I remember this, the urge to fly back and shake my young self by the shoulders shakes my present self to the point of pain. What I knew about the world was from books; what I did not know about the world is that *there are ways*, there are ways in, through, above, and around it. I accepted the statement as a mountain, a fact on the face of the earth—as final as if he had told me I would not be going to heaven. Suddenly out the window, the pillowfight ceased and the snow flew in long white strikeouts.

"Of course," I thought, actually blushing at my stupidity. There was a reason we hadn't bought any supplies, any notebooks or highlighters or beanbag chairs for my dorm room. There was a reason I didn't have a framed poster of *The Kiss* or *The Starry Night* all ready to hang—

or at the very least one of Francis Bacon's screaming popes, to remember the family by. There was a reason my mother changed the subject when I brought up my departure, now one day nearer, now one more. The entire East Coast began to float out to sea. The chamber behind my eyes felt hot. I thought, "Why would I ever think I could go."

The same thing had happened to my older sister, Christina, who had a soprano so lovely it sounded like the pure concentrate of a hymn. She had planned to study singing at Washington University in St. Louis but had had to drop out at the last minute, for reasons that remained foggy and unexplained. Something about a FAFSA, something about my mother's inability to ever file our taxes on time. Perhaps she had been called in for a similar talk and had accepted the verdict without question. A brief, tumultuous year later, she was married. But somehow, even after all that, I had not foreseen it happening to me.

My father's left hand dangled in a green Tupperware bowl full of homemade pickles, which were the only vegetables he ever ate willingly. The bowl was gargantuan, easily large enough to baptize the infant Taft. He lifted one transparent circle out of it, set it on his tongue, and crunched happily. The signs of his consecration were everywhere.

I lingered a bit longer, in a room filled with gleaming guitars on stands, candy-apple red, spruce green, lake blue and carapace black. They wailed a little in the silence. Soon he would acquire another guitar, more costly than all of these, a lefty that had originally been made for Paul McCartney. When Paul decided he didn't want it, my father snapped it up and showed it to us with the lavish, loving gaze he reserved for colorful, well-oiled, and obedient machines. Later, I would take a detached literary pleasure in the notion that higher education had been unwittingly robbed from me by a Beatle.

. . .

ADRIFT, I MOVED from the rectory of my father's church in Cincinnati to the abandoned convent next door. The convent looked out on a petroleum plant, and just beyond that, the polluted, hellbender-colored Ohio River. The sisters had fled long ago and now the building was used for church business during the daytime; I heard the ceaseless counting of collections while I hid upstairs reading books on an old futon. But when the sun sank down and was replaced by an artificial orange somehow brighter than daylight, I tiptoed downstairs and took refuge in a place of living, moving, breathing text, a book that continually wrote itself: the internet.

The room had the scent of office supplies. Stacks of paper, adding machines, cups of pens, a folding table that stretched across a whole wall. In the corners were the narrow starved bookcases you see in church places, that have never held a copy of *Jane Eyre*. Often there would be a pewter medal of the Virgin lying forgotten in the dust of one shelf, like pennies in other houses. The scene was familiar, but there was a difference now. There was a portal in the corner and I could reach my hand in and get any information I wanted.

I sat in the computer chair and spun myself around once, twice: the child's gesture of sudden and unsupervised freedom. Across the front lawn I saw blacktop, then the road, then the train tracks, then the tanks, then the river, then Kentucky. It looked like the seamed side of something—of the country, of industry, of American progress. Old modes of communication raced across the view, old ways of eating the miles. I turned the computer on and listened to the tower rev and wheeze. The monitor was capacious enough to hold a human head. I lifted my hands to the keyboard and opened up a window. I took a breath and eliminated the distance between two points.

"I wrote a poem today," I typed to Jason, a total stranger who lived in Fort Collins, Colorado. We had met by chance, on a bulletin board devoted to the discussion of poetry, and were now in the grip of a fevered correspondence. "It's about Billie Holiday giving herself an abortion in a hot bath."

"I wrote a poem today too," he responded, not five minutes later. "It's about the splendor and the majesty of the tetons."

The feeling of getting an email! As if the ghost of a passenger pigeon had flown into your home and delivered it directly into your head, so swooping and unexpected and feathered was the feeling. How suddenly full you felt of white vapor. How you set your fingers on the keyboard to write back, and your fingers disappeared almost up to the first knuckle in those clattering beige keys—so much more satisfying than the shallow keys that came later, or the touchscreens that came even after that. The story of any courtship is one of ephemera, dead vehicles, outdated technology. Name cards, canoes, pagers. The roller rink, telegrams, mixtapes. Radio dedications. The drive-in. Hotmail dot com.

"Send me yours," I wrote him, at the exact moment he responded to tell me to send him mine.

Most of my poems were about mermaids losing their virginity to Jesus (metaphor), and most of his poems were about the majesty of canyons, arroyos, and mesas. The West had infected him with some sort of landscape mania—these were essentially poems a cartoon roadrunner would write, after retiring from a career of anarchy. He had, however, written one good image, which stays with me even now: "the milk bottles burst like scared chickens." It might strike you as irresponsible, to fall in love on the strength of one image about chickens bursting, but this was a different time. I didn't even know what he looked like. He was under the mistaken impression that I was "fifty years old and Latina." We were all made up of words.

We progressed from typing to the phone. I would lie on my back on the floor of the convent with my bare feet up against the wall, and talk quietly so as not to disturb the shapes of the absent nuns, which still seemed to flock in their black-and-white forms through the rooms. It surprises me sometimes to think that I was never frightened to sleep there alone, but then I remember that I stayed up in the glow all night talking. Sometimes I would doze off for a minute and wake to a seeming sunrise out the window, trumpets and banners and streaming incandescence, but no, it was only that cloud of radioactivity across the street. When I woke, either his voice or his silence was still going on the other end. And then deep in the valley between two hours, a train would roar and rumble: wheels could roll away from these places, wheels did.

WE HAD CERTAIN THINGS in common. His father was a Baptist preacher who was saved after a dream about flying an airplane over a landscape of erupting volcanoes. A wall of flame appeared in front of him and he opened the door and jumped. He felt himself drifting softly, safely, toward earth and he looked up and saw that Jesus had him by the hands and *was using his own sacred body to parachute him down*. This seems like a specifically Baptist dream. Catholic dreams haven't caught up to airplanes yet. The dream that converts a Catholic is more likely to take place in a medieval prison, or on a slave ship in the days of Ben-Hur, or in a sinister outhouse filled with red light.

After his father converted, he went to Bible school and became a missionary in Southeast Asia. That meant Jason was born in Thailand, among the splash of flowers, clear water and caressing air, the rainbow all fallen out of its stripes. It was like living at the firm center of a fruit. He loved it there. He ran around wearing a diaper and no shirt, much to the curiosity of the Thai babies, who wore shirts and no diapers. He had the same birthday as the king, and every year there was a parade of elephants, and every year his parents said it was for him. When he found out the truth, he turned his back on kings forever. He clenched his small fist, bellowed his rage to the heavens, and resolved to never again recognize the authority of any man on earth.

Catholicism, he saw at once, had more kings than he could ever keep track of. "What did those people teach you?" he asked me one night, mystified. "What exactly do Catholics believe?"

I'd been preparing my whole life for this question. "First of all, blood. BLOOD. Second of all, thorns. Third of all, put dirt on your forehead. Do it right now. Fourth of all, Martin Luther was a pig in a cloak. Fifth of all, Jesus is alive, but he's also dead, and he's also immortal, but he's also made of clouds, and his face is a picture of infinite peace, but he also always looks like one of those men in a headache commercial, because you're causing him so much suffering whenever you cuss. He is so gentle that sheep seem like demented murderers in his presence, but also rays of sunlight shoot out of his face so hard they can kill people. In fact they do kill people, and one day they will kill you. He has a tattoo of a daisy on his lower back and he gets his hair permed every eight weeks. He's wearing a flowing white dress, but only because people didn't know about jeans back then. He's holding up two fingers because his dad won't let him have a gun. If he lived on earth, he would have a white truck, plastered with bumper stickers of Calvin peeing on a smaller Calvin who is not a Catholic."

Jason was aghast. "Thorns?" he whispered. "But that's the most dangerous part of the rose."

MOSTLY, THOUGH, WE TALKED about things we liked. All the things we liked and listened to and read fanned out behind us like peacock plumage—or the bursting milk of scared chickens, I guess. We were composed of conversation, so it didn't matter where our hands and lips and heads were. The legs we walked on were the long and shifting lists of what we loved, what we had discovered, what we could not live without.

Writers like being bodiless. Two people who have collectively lived in twenty different cities across the world don't consider their feet rooted to any particular ground. As we talked, the shape of a future gradually resolved. He would drive out to meet me in Ohio. I would return with him to Colorado. I had visited a place in Colorado once called Purgatory, and now I intended to see the rest. I am not sure why it was so fast, so extreme, so precipitate, but nothing less would have worked. A cliff had presented itself as we were walking along together, and it called for a leap.

Had I really thought it through? you ask. Ridiculous question. I had never really thought anything through, except perhaps Wallace Stevens' "Anecdote of the Jar"—a poem about the landscape licking up to a portal, in love. Were we crazy? We were nineteen.

I KNEW IF I TOLD my parents I wanted to move to Colorado with someone I had never met, they would figure out a way to stop me, so I decided to begin by telling them only that I was meeting a boy from the internet. Even this was a delicate proposition. It was 2002, and back then, everyone believed the internet was a country where murderers lived. "He's from the poetry internet," I reassured them, "where everyone just argues about sonnets all the time, and whether endings are Earned," but it didn't seem to penetrate.

"Who knows what a freak might do," my mother hissed, which sounded almost like a philosophical koan. Who DOES know what a freak might do. Could God make a freak so big even he didn't know what it might do?

"Tricia, I've built computers," my father said. "I've built computers with my bare hands. These guys get on the web . . ."

"What they want to do is *cyber*," my mother broke in. "They'll tell you anything, if it means they get to cyber." I took a moment to wonder what constituted my mother's understanding of "cybering." Hackers in black leather gloves, giving each other handjobs in space, while glowing green numbers streamed through the air?

"They'll tell you they live in Tucson when they live in Pittsburgh. He says his name is Jack, but actually it's Dave."

"And he'll kill you," my mother said, making what she considered to be a logical leap. "He'll do it without a second thought, and we'll read all about your body in the newspaper."

"What a tangled web, bay-bee," my father sighed, shaking his head. "What a tangled web we weave."

WE WERE STANDING in a triangle in the living room of the St. Vincent de Paul rectory, which was so ancient, stony, and capacious it had actually been used as a stop on the Underground Railroad. The river waited a sprint away, ready to carry or be crossed, and the house itself was rumored to be full of secret passages, which my siblings and I were too stupid to find. The drama of the scene ought to have been tense and throbbing, but it was undercut somewhat by my mother's decorating, which ran heavily to bowls of gold balls. Still, we played our parts: every once in a while my father would bang down his fist while looking patriarchal, and my mother would turn to stare out the window while looking powerless, which contributed to the overall impression that we were participating in a Tennessee Williams play where "the internet" was being used as code for "homosexuality."

"Why should I trust the internet?" my mother asked. "It gets into my house and I don't know how."

"Well, so does electricity," I pointed out.

"Which has fried many children in its day," she said significantly. "Put your finger in the wrong hole and face the consequences."

"What your mother is trying to say," my father interrupted, "is that if you go through with this, anything could happen to you, anything at all."

My heart caught the air like a parachute—if I looked up, I knew I might see Jesus, spiriting me away to another place. Why else would I be doing it?

ONLY MY LITTLE SISTER, MARY, dribbling a soccer ball in and out of the room as we talked, seemed unconcerned. "We are the ones who are not normal," she said as she passed, her shin guards flashing. "How bad can a guy named Jason be?"

"I am so much more likely to murder him," I said, trying to put their minds at ease. "He wouldn't even see it coming. I would wait till he was asleep . . ."

"I did not raise you to murder," said my mother. "Others, however . . ."

"He's from Colorado, Mom. All people do in Colorado is get high, think about the mountains, and try to feel their white dreads growing."

"If he has dreads I will put my foot down," she declared. "You know how I feel. It's not a mistake that it is called a Dread."

"Disintegration of the family unit!" my father shouted, apropos of nothing—I suspected he hadn't really been listening—and then disappeared upstairs to fondle his guns and drink cream liqueurs in secret, which was his way of dealing with grief. I fled back over to my room at the convent and began to bundle up my worldly possessions, which included eight androgynous sweaters; two pairs of cascading jeans; various immortal manuscripts, no longer extant; a selection of electronic music that sounded like robots making up their own religion from scratch; four hundred books I needed to live; and deodorant.

Nuns pass their time in a hopeful way, waiting for the man who might be good. On the morning Jason was due to arrive, I woke early, showered, dressed, sat cross-legged on my uncomfortable futon, and joined in their tradition. Above the ambient sound of the tank farm came the crunch of a car rolling up the steep entrance of the parking lot. I took a moment to compose myself and then walked out to meet him. He emerged from his seafoam-green Mercury Mystique—the car NO woman can resist—and waved a shy hello. There was something in the composition of his face that meant he could never look angry; the proportions didn't allow for it. He had the small, neat, unjudgmental ears of a teddy bear. He unfolded his long arms and legs as he walked, until he stood as straight and easy as a set of chimes, and when he reached the bottom step he took my hand. "The woman in my dream!" he gasped, before he said anything else. He had dreamed of me the year before, when he lived by himself in an apartment in St. Petersburg,

Florida, overlooking the water. "You were a witch or something, very beautiful but also very evil, and I never forgot your face." The romance could not have begun any other way.

My father, who has a sixth sense for other cars driving onto his property, exploded in slow motion out the door of the rectory and toddled over to us with as much speed as he could muster. "Gimme your license!" he yelled to Jason. "I got cop friends!" Jason obligingly handed over his license, and my father took it away to have it checked, or just to stand with it inside for a threatening period of time while watching us from behind the gold drapes.

"Do you have a criminal record?" I asked him. It had never occurred to me to wonder. I had never even run a stop sign, or stolen a lipstick, or torn one of those tags off a mattress. I realized for the first time that I knew very few facts about him, only feelings.

He cocked his head to one side. "No, but the FBI once barged through my front door when I was fifteen years old because they thought I was a genius hacker."

I remembered the leather gloves and the streaming green numbers, and the sound of the word "cyber" in my mother's mouth. "WERE you a genius hacker?"

"No, but one of my friends was. He had been stealing people's credit card information and using it to buy climbing gear. When they caught him, he gave them my name."

"That's the most Colorado crime I've ever heard of."

"He works at MIT now. Anyway, they took my computer away and searched it and found nothing but hundreds of guitar tab websites."

"Your secret shame!"

"When they burst in shouting, 'WE KNOW WHAT YOU'VE

BEEN DOING!' I thought, 'Oh my god, the feds know I've been trying to learn the chord progression to "American Pie" for months now.'"

My father strode back across the blacktop twenty minutes later and returned the license to him with the news that he was all clear. We stood there looking at each other for a minute. I asked my father if we were allowed to go for a drive and he said guardedly that we were, but that we had to return to the rectory in an hour so we could hold a family council. If we had been a truly rebellious teen couple, we would have fled the city limits right then, but our "family councils" were such breathtaking spectacles that I thought it would be better to let Jason witness one before he was tied to me for eternity. Dad turned on his heel—the Achilles had been bothering him for a long time—and left us alone together.

"HERE, I'LL SHOW YOU around the convent," I said, not shy exactly, but feeling new.

The appearance of it seemed to confuse him. "I thought it would be like the one in *Sister Act*," he said, squinting, "where the nuns sang all day and were girlfriends at night. This is just a regular house." Perhaps it was the mental image of that towering and gargoyled place that had led him to suspect I was locked up in here, somehow, that I could not leave whenever I wanted, though I had never told him anything of the kind.

We tiptoed upstairs to my spartan little room. When we kissed, perhaps because we had so many teeth, it was exactly like two birdcages touching together. We laughed quietly, almost into each other's mouths, and slipped out again to explore the neighborhood. Conspiracy had arrived to us, whole, intact, and just large enough for two people.

. . .

AN HOUR LATER, we convened again in the living room. My father sat in a brocade chair, as richly embroidered as the Sun King's underwear. He adopted his most lordly and intimidating position, with his thighs spread so wide it seemed like there might be a gateway to another dimension between them. Jason unconsciously adopted this position also. A person looking down from space might have thought they were having a squat contest.

My mother and I sat next to each other on the couch, leaning into the softness of each other's shoulders, and watched the interrogation. She has ultimate trust in tall men, and Jason was six-two with two additional inches of millennial hair, so she no longer suspected he might be a murderer. "He seems so . . . calm," she told me in an undertone. "Maybe too calm." Indeed, his eyes looked like lotto balls floating on currents of air, and he exuded the trippy peacefulness of a psychoactive toad. He never wasted a movement, and exhaled quiet wafts of new age music. He seemed to actually soothe all people within a six-foot radius of him. I had never been so intrigued.

"Do you think he's sick?" she asked. We contemplated him in unison. My father was asking him what he was going to do with his life, and Jason appeared to be answering that he was the lizard king, who slept in a pyramid every night and meditated by counting all the grains of sand in the universe.

"He probably just needs some iced tea," I said.

"We should get some dinner," said my mother, who believed if you stuffed people's faces full enough, they would stop arguing with each other. "Let's go out to Don Pablo's and talk. We can continue the family council there." Don Pablo's was a fake Mexican restaurant that prided itself on the sizzlingness of its food. Why would you want food that sizzled only a little bit, when you could have food that sizzled so loud it sounded like the screaming of souls in hell? "Greg? Do you want to go to Don Pablo's?"

My father's face lit up at the suggestion, but then he turned wary. Was my mother trying to use food to trick him into accepting a chat-room bastard into his family? Don't even try it, woman. "Let me just . . . get ready . . . for the meal," he said craftily, and then came downstairs with a gun tucked into his priest pants.

WE CLIMBED INTO THE CAR and began to drive down River Road. "Put on your seat belt, Greg," my mother said automatically—the latest sally in a war that had lasted the whole duration of their marriage.

My father has never willingly put on a seat belt in his life. He has always found the very idea of "safety" to be ridiculous. Why would he ever want to be safe? What was he, a little girl? A miniature woman? A babylady? John Wayne, Clint Eastwood, huge hairy Samson from the Bible—those men didn't wear seat belts. If they needed a seat belt, they tore off a man's arm and laid it across their lap.

"No!" he shouted. Like all men of enormous personal appetites, he loved to shout the word "no" at other people.

"If we get in an accident, you will go headfirst through the window and your children will wake up tomorrow morning without a father."

"Sounds like a personal problem," he said, and chuckled quietly to himself. "Sounds like a personal problem" was one of his stock responses, along with "What's this 'we' business, white man?" He used each of them about a dozen times a day; they never lost their freshness or their wide applicability.

He took a moment to savor the seat belt victory, then turned back to Jason and glared. "If you try anything at the Don Pablo's, you'll have to answer to me," he told him, and tapped the gun.

I'm not sure why I chose this moment to inform him of our actual intentions. Perhaps it was the same instinct that had once caused me to throw a lit firecracker directly at the face of my sister Mary while yelling, "GET OUT OF THE WAY!" It wasn't the imp of the perverse, exactly. It was just knee-jerk panic.

I asked my body whether it was brave. It said no, but I forged on anyway, filling my lungs and straightening up in my seat. "Mom, Dad, I have to tell you something. I'm going back to Colorado with Jason."

"NAW!" my father erupted, louder than I had ever heard him. The problems with me going to Colorado were too many to name. For starters, that was where all the hippies lived. My mother said nothing, but she closed her eyes briefly, having a blood-red vision of Colorado legalizing marijuana ten years in the future.

"Colorado?" she repeated. "But where will you live?"

"Oh, we'll live with my roommates," Jason said. "We have a house in Fort Collins." The only thing I knew about these boys was that they ate steak every day and were in a terrible band called Flush. They had tried out a lot of names, Jason told me, but when they hit on Flush, they knew it was the one. Since we had just emerged from the great golden age of toilet bands, this didn't faze me a bit. And if my dad had known about them eating steak every day, he would have been won over to their side instantly, recognizing them as essentially honorable fellow cavemen. He didn't give me a chance to tell him that part, however.

"You're not going anywhere," he said. "Where I come from, people get married instead of driving across the country to go live with each other."

"Ah!" said Jason, seeing an opening. "Don't worry, Mister . . . Father."

I worried for a second he might lose his head and call him Your Holiness. "If that's what you're concerned about, then I want you to know that I proposed to your daughter earlier, in the parking lot of the grocery store."

"The Kroger's," I added, as if that were the most matrimonial of all grocery stores.

We were telling the truth. When we were cruising around the neighborhood on our own that afternoon, in the single hour allotted to us, Jason had been overcome by a sense of destiny and pulled into the nearest parking lot. He contorted his body down onto the floor of the driver's seat, gazed up at me like a hunchback in love, and proposed. This additional information should have made my announcement more acceptable, but somehow it didn't.

"Turn this car around," my father told my mother, spitting the words like bullets. "If I have to go into a Don Pablo's right now, I don't know what I'll do." Murder Don Pablo himself, perhaps, just to relieve his feelings. My mother turned the car around.

THE REMAINING THREE OF US weren't particularly hungry after that, but we went on to the restaurant anyway. The Don Pablo's in Cincinnati was a large converted factory, so it looked vaguely like a nightclub where people went to have wrong ideas about Mexico. In the corner, a fake cactus threw up its helpless arms, as if my father were holding it at gunpoint. My mother had not yet reached the stage of her journey where she realized margaritas were a medicine that could relax you, and drank so much iced tea that by the time our food arrived, mariachi music was coming out of her eyes. Jason stared down at his dead fajita, horrified. It had once, in the West, been a majestic animal.

. . .

WHEN WE CAME HOME LATER, my father was wearing his most transparent pair of boxer shorts, to show us he was angry, and drinking Baileys Irish Cream liqueur out of a miniature crystal glass, to show us his heart was broken.

I cannot overstate how tiny the sips he was taking were. He looked like a gigantic brownie drinking drops of dew. He would screw up his mouth into a rosebud, and *siiiiip*, inhale the smallest amount of Baileys possible. Greg Lockwood, thank goodness, was never much of a drinker—though he did get so drunk at his own bachelor party that he was still drunk the day of the wedding and almost fell asleep standing up in his sailor suit in the middle of the ceremony. Perhaps that experience taught him a lesson.

I do not mean to make light of his shock. He recognized what I did not: that I was running away. I had never been much interested in story, so I had yet to realize I was participating in one: that I would see rising action, twists, and climax; that there would be conflict, revenge, and resolution; but above all, that I was the engine powering it forward. The landscape slid past me because I was moving. I was keeping the I upright.

Jason went up the great staircase to try to talk to him. He found him sitting in silence, practically nude, and surrounded with gun parts like a deranged warlord. This was at the height of his gun craze, when he used to make the whole family go to the shooting range and compete with each other for accuracy. Whenever he didn't like people, he cleaned his guns in front of them. Part of me found this habit appalling, but the other part of me respected his flair for high theater. If I wanted to frighten off a chat-room bastard who was trying to be monogamous with my daughter, what better way than to lure him into my rec room and put together the world's most deadly jigsaw puzzle right in front of his face?

"Your father has had too much Cream," Jason whispered to me when he came back down. "He's had too much Cream and it's gone to his head. Do you think he'll try to kill me?"

"Did you give him any indication that you were a pacifist or an intellectual, or that you liked abstract art?"

"Hmmmm, I don't think so," but his *hmmmm* had the quality of a yummy sound, like he found the act of thinking itself to be delicious. This was a bad sign. If he had let a *hmmmm* slip in front of my father, that might have been enough to do it. We decided we had better leave that night, just to be sure.

WE WALKED HAND IN HAND back to the convent, just as the clouds were beginning to ignite. "Oh my god," he said, flinching at the sight of the river, which must have been the place where mud was invented. "You can practically see the three-eyed fish." I nodded. If I developed a psychic tumor in my sixth decade, both of us would know why. A beautiful backdrop is an aesthetic luxury, same as shelves of books and music lessons and trips to museums on weekends. It is green, green money to roll in.

Far in the west, the sun was a malignant pearl. Next to the convent was a little anemic wood, and above its scrabbling branches, the sky was a blood transfusion. My view was stunning too, but in a way that would eventually produce mutants. My sister's words floated back to me: "We are not the normal ones. A guy named Jason is probably fine."

He was whistling, with a sound as full and fibrous as a violin. He contained a wide and wandering spaciousness, in the same way I contained a cloister. His eyes always seemed to be registering great distances. He cast them over the blunt cliffs of the petroleum tanks and turned back to me. "They remind me of the mesas," he said.

"ARE YOU REALLY LEAVING?" my mother asked. The car was packed, and my father was nowhere to be seen. She reached through the passenger window and pressed money into my hand. A mother, as I understood it, was someone who was always trying to give you sixty dollars. Extremity had brought her over to my side.

I told her I was. I was wonderful at endings, I thought. I found an artful and unexpected one every time. Endings sprang out of the tip of my pencil like bouquets: they were magic; they were silk and illusion; they were not earned.

"Please be safe," she said, her mouth pulled down at both corners like a genius clown's, a clown known worldwide for her ability to turn human tragedy into facial expressions. My mother understood the fundamental facts about me. She knew that I would always prefer to eat with a tiny spoon rather than a regular one, that I was an excellent Thing Finder because I was always looking down at the sidewalk, that I wanted to recite spells, live in a nutshell, play a gold harp. That I had a house in my head that was far away. But it did not seem plausible, yet, that she and her pain had actually produced me.

I would be fine, I felt. I would be better. I would be free.

"Are you sure you have everything?" she asked as Jason started up the

engine, and he smiled and gestured to the piles of my books in the backseat. We pulled out past the sign that said GOD ANSWERS KNEE-MAIL and
drove away from the church and the rectory, the convent and my stifling
upstairs room, the inexplicable thousand-pound statue of a gorilla in the
neighbor's front yard. All of it grew small behind us; I watched it grow
small. The stars came out one by one, and the moon: I saw a hinge and
a doorknob on the sky.

2

LOW COUNTRY

After we were married—by my father, in the same church where my parents were wed—we moved from city to city, restless and never settling. We dragged a red line behind us across the map and we did not stop. My family had moved so often during my childhood that this did not seem strange to me; in fact, the belief that people should stuff all their possessions into a U-Haul and move kit and caboodle to a different state every few years seemed to be the only similarity my husband shared with my father. We lived in Hebron, Kentucky, near where they had just begun to build a Creation Museum full of apelike mannequins of Methuselah and Moses interacting with the noble triceratops, and we lived in Keene, New Hampshire, where the LIVE FREE OR DIE license plates paraded up and down quaint Main Street, and we lived in Colorado Springs, where I could see the jagged quartz tip of Pikes Peak from my study, and we lived in Stuart, Florida, which made the dubious claim of being the Sailfish Capital of the World. Finally we ended up in Savannah, Georgia, which is the first place that ever felt like home to me.

It looked like an enlightened underwater city with all the water gone, and seaweed still hanging in the middle of the air. Great mermaids flowed through the streets: southerners. The sun shone down because it was a blonde. The cobblestones were the former ballast of ships and the town was famous for its graveyards and every gate was topped with an iron pineapple. The Cathedral of St. John the Baptist was across the street from us, and I was amused to see that my old senses were still in tune: I could feel it whenever the bishop was there.

At one point a second cathedral grew up around it, made of scaffolding, and construction workers sat there and ate their bagged lunches and swung their legs. No one knew what they were doing, and it seemed to go on forever. The Flannery O'Connor house stared suspiciously at them all day. She had been a child in that house, with boiled-clear eyes and a watery chin. She had been briefly obsessed with the Dionne Quintuplets. She had a chicken that she taught to walk backwards. The little-leafed vines that climbed up the side of her school had fine penmanship; so did she. She would grow up, and leave, and keep peacocks. Her lipstick would always be the wrong color, but her ink would be fine: black. The sea that had been removed from the city was a force, was full of pronouncement, was equally capable of religious calm. You could feel it, you could still feel it. And over it all, anchored equally in time and eternity, the beautiful laboring sound of the bells.

IN FLORIDA, I HAD WAITRESSED at a Key West–themed diner that had coarse fishing nets and tangled buoys hung on the walls, and where I was required to wear loud tropical shirts that made me look like Jimmy Buffett's illegitimate son. The owner was a handsome, compact Greek man who combed his black hair back and had a fetish for smashing pies in women's faces—though perhaps he didn't know it was a fetish, since he refused to ever use the internet. "The porn is there," he said witheringly, every time it came up in conversation. "Disgusting." Whenever customers slowed to a trickle, he would stand by the dessert refrigerator and flirtatiously lift pies in my direction, a hopeful arch in his eyebrows. When my first poem was published in *The New Yorker*— plucked out of the slush pile somehow, a miracle—I brought a copy to work and watched him puzzling over it throughout my shift, with the expression of someone trying to decode a magic trick. On my last day, he asked if he could throw a whole pie at me, but then someone ordered a piece of it and his dreams were dashed.

Those afternoons of legitimate employment often drifted back to me as I worked in our large, lazy apartment in downtown Savannah, in a building erected sometime around the end of the Civil War. It echoed because we couldn't afford to fill it with furniture, and the echoes were slower-moving than our voices, somehow drawling. The windows sorted and poured light like prisms, and patches of clarity fell everywhere onto the floor. I had decided not to take a job right away, but to keep concentrating on the strange bundle of poems I was writing, ones that revealed my most hidden preoccupations: sex, gender, animal puberty, bizarre fetishes and the Midwest, the Loch Ness Monster despairing of ever being able to leave her remote silver-skinned lake and get an education. I was never sure whether these long stretches of refusing to draw a paycheck were a mark of my entitlement or the only act of rebellion available to me. My flaming certainty that I was born to write books dovetailed so neatly with Jason's belief that he was destined to be a sort of Leonard Woolf figure, helping to usher female thinking into the world, that mostly we accepted our pinched circumstances as foreordained.

It was the first place, too, where I didn't feel alone in my ambitions. Diapered, moody horses clopped by at all hours pulling carriages of kindhearted tourists, which is as good a metaphor for writing as any I can think of. One of my friends had a job at the local art college where she was required to do things like come up with synonyms for "spritz" all day, and another friend had been writing a novel about loons for five years, or something like that, which struck me as the upper limit for how long a person could write about loons, but maybe it was a masterpiece. Two poets up the street ran a reading series, which meant every month we all got drunk on cheap whiskey while listening to traveling poets read, then walked home shoulder to shoulder swaying like long grasses. Sometimes on the mornings after the readings, after we had eaten hungover eggs and salami at a nearby diner, we went to Bonaventure Cemetery out near the islands, which was supposed to be full of ghosts. I'm not sure whether it was named after St. Bonaventure or not, but that would have been apt—St. Bonaventure was said to have continued his memoirs *even after his own death*. The only surviving relics of him are the arm and hand he wrote with. That seems exactly like God, doesn't it, to kill a man and then make his hand keep writing his books.

There was a poet buried in that cemetery, too: Conrad Aiken, who once said that poets "really stink. Especially in large numbers, when herding." This was a slander, in my opinion. Before I met any other poets, I worried that they were the sort of people who said "lo" in conversation and were constantly forcing you to play games of exquisite corpse, but that hadn't turned out to be the case at all. These poets were normal; they even knew their own phone numbers. I was getting to herd for the first time, and I was happy among the other ruminants.

During the day, though, I kept to myself. I liked being able to walk to the river, where ideas swam in the water, firm as the backs of terrapins.

If I had a few dollars, I would get a baguette and a cup of coffee and ride the ferry back and forth just like Edna St. Vincent Millay, and then walk home after a while in a cloud of no-see-ums and contemplation— not sweating, exactly, but working up a higher shine.

JASON WORKED AT THE NEWSPAPER: editing and designing pages and following the exploits of the local politicians, who all had names like "Saxby Chambliss." He entertained himself by slipping increasingly outrageous puns into the copy, which culminated in a headline about a dachshund race that read, "All Wieners in the Long Run." He was so pleased with himself over that one he brought home a bottle of champagne that night. "To the wieners," he toasted, "and to their long lives."

He always answered the phones during his shift, and every night an old woman called, recited three random news sound bites in a row, and then hung up the phone. "GEORGE BUSH. NUCLEAR HOLO-CAUST. HORSEMEAT IN HAMBURGERS." She repeated the phrases three times, waited a beat, and then commanded him gracefully, "Put it in print." She gave the impression of having been doing it for decades. "MOON LANDING. STOCK MARKET CRASH. THE REDCOATS ARE COMING." Perhaps she was the news itself. And at the end, always, "Put it in print."

"Yes, ma'am," he would say with relish, and she would hang up the phone with a satisfied click: a citizen who was simply performing her duty. If it hadn't been for her, the flow of reliable information would have ceased. I imagined my mother would take up a similar hobby in her twilight years, and I looked forward to her contributions.

He liked that job better than any he had ever had. He took me to see the press once, where people still lost their fingers even though this was the twenty-first century. There was a sign announcing how many days had passed since the last workplace accident, which made me think of the unlucky employee who had to climb up on a ladder the next morning and flip the number back to zero with a maimed hand. It was navy blue outside, past midnight, and we stood looking at the galloping press from above. The front pages shot out the mouth of the machine: fresh, up to the minute, blazing with something terrible. Put it in print.

BACK WHEN I WAS WAITRESSING at the diner, Jason had often told me my tropical shirts looked nice, which had been my first clue his vision was going. I sent him off to the local mall, which was offering free checkups, and he came back with a pair of glasses from an optometrist in tight disco trousers whose septum had been almost entirely worn away by cocaine use. After a few months at the *Savannah Morning News*, he realized the glasses weren't helping anymore and went to visit a more respectable doctor, one whose pants would presumably not melt and fuse to his body in the event of a fire. Halfway through his examination, the man murmured, "Wait a minute," which is never a good sign, and zoomed in for a closer look.

He had, it turned out, a rare type of cataracts, and he needed double lens replacements. The doctor had no idea why he had developed them, since they were most frequently seen in the elderly or children who lived in the developing world; he had never encountered them in someone under the age of thirty. He told Jason that without surgery, the cataracts would mist over his natural lenses until he was blind.

Empedocles wrote that the eye was fire set in a lantern, which poured out to illuminate mountains and forests and the face of the beloved. Other Greek philosophers believed sight was water. Either way, it was an element, capable of flaming or flooding if it was let loose from its delicate pen, of sending mountains and forests and the face of the beloved up in smoke, or else surging them away till they were gone.

I couldn't make myself understand it—it had come out of the clear sky. It was even more shocking because the color of his eyes was so extraordinary: the purest sea-glass green, with crystals of blue and black in a ring around the pupil. They should have lasted longer than other eyes, I thought irrationally. They should have been indestructible. They should have had deep and anchoring reserves of vision under the surface like glaciers, the same cool colors and going nowhere.

THE COST OF THE SURGERIES would be astronomical. Our meager health insurance covered only a small portion, and the rest needed to be paid in advance. The doctor gave us a stack of literature, and later we pored over brochures of silver foxes peering sightfully at old hotties across candlelit tables. *You might even be able to read the menu in a romantic restaurant,* the brochures claimed. Indeed, the people in the pictures were laughing out loud in pitch-black steakhouses while toasting each other with glasses of white wine that represented the perfect acuity of their vision. We lived on very little, though, and had for a long time. We couldn't afford to go to romantic restaurants, let alone pay for the cyborg technology that would allow us to see each other in them. Money was as far away as the moon.

"Ten thousand dollars?" my mother gasped, when I called to break the bad news. "What are you going to do?"

I would return to waitressing or get work at a bookstore, I told her, but nothing I did would really matter in the short term. "We have to come up with the money in the next few weeks," I said. "The longer we wait, the riskier the surgeries will be."

Even over the phone, I could hear her mind begin to whir. She was trying to figure out how to scoop out her own kidneys, sell them on the black market, and have the money to me by tomorrow.

"People on Twitter have been asking if they can help," I continued. "They want to hold a fund-raiser."

I had unthinkingly started a Twitter account in the spring of 2011, when Jason had surprised me with my first-ever cellphone. Free in the knowledge that no one was listening, I mostly used it to tweet absurdities like "'Touch it,' Mr. Quiddity moaned. 'Touch Mr. Quiddity's thing,'" and "2 Predators f'ing in the trees. The girl is on her period and their intercourse is glowin like a rave. Arnold pops an X and begins to climb." These penetrating insights had swiftly found me a number of friends there, and soon after that, an influx of followers completely unknown to me, who seemed to be general connoisseurs of filth and nonsense. Yet connections forged in filth and nonsense are strong.

"What, those internet addicts?" she asked in disbelief. She had progressed from believing the internet was a country where murderers lived to believing the internet was something you could inject into your veins, and she had fondled a special hatred of Twitter in her heart ever since she had stumbled upon a user who called himself satanic_cumlord.

"Tweeting is an art form," I told her. "Like sculpture, or honking the national anthem under your armpit."

"It's not art if it's evil," she said.

"It's *only* art if it's evil, Mom."

The internet addicts somehow banded together and raised the money in less than twelve hours. Their sense of humor had not abated. They gave in increments of $4.20 and $6.66 and $69.69, and they gave under usernames like gilled_burpito and PLEASURE_STEPDAD. The jokes were gifts too. Everyone gave, students and rich people, a man who had written a television show about an island and a dancer called Bubbles who donated all her tips from that night and a comedian whose chest hair looked like three otters engaging in a leisurely orgy while floating up the river of his torso. It was people I knew and people I didn't know. It was so total and unexpected I couldn't look at it directly, as if generosity itself had opened up its trench coat and flashed me. Jason shook me awake that morning to tell me to call off the fundraiser, we had raised enough. It was his thirtieth birthday, and he was crying.

JUST AS THAT CHAOS was dying down, my mother arrived for a visit. "I came as soon as I could," she said, and hugged us both with the force of someone administering the Heimlich. She had come to revive us.

"Mom, you must be so tired," I said, though that was just a formality. In fact she resembled a supernatural monster who hadn't slept for a thousand years, had caffeine instead of blood, and ate high-powered insomniacs for all its meals. She had driven ten hours over the course of a single day. How could she still be standing?

"No I'm NOT tired. I'm on a huge dose of steroids," she asserted. It was dusk, and romantic seniors with flawless vision stopped in their tracks and stared at us. We were walking to The Olde Pink House, to eat she-crab soup dotted with sherry and black pepper in its jazzy underground bar. "I'm getting very strong on them. They're making me very powerful."

"Why are you on steroids?" I asked.

"The doctor thinks I might be ALLERGIC to your FATHER," she said, her words ricocheting down a picturesque alley. "Ha ha ha. It would serve him right."

Already, just looking at her, Jason seemed less blind. She whirled on him with the concern of a lunatic nurse. "Tell me about your disease," she said.

He explained the surgeries to her as simply as possible. It was best not to give her too many gory details that she might stay up imagining later. "The surgeon will slice open the surface of my eye, and they'll use a little jackhammer to blast apart the old lenses so they can insert the artificial ones."

Jackhammer? I mouthed at him. Why not just tell my mother a miniature construction worker was going to swing a wrecking ball straight into his face?

"You know, Mrs. Ford had that," my mother remembered. "She can see her pie recipes just fine now." Mrs. Ford was one of my parents' friends, who lived out on the gated islands. She was approximately eighty years old. Her husband was a retired general who was a convicted Latin Mass goer, and he was always trying to persuade my father to move down South where all the shrimps were. The general was the source of numerous startling quotes. He had once frightened Jason badly by placing an iron hand on his shoulder and whispering to him, *"I've never felt closer to God than I do in the churches of Poland."* Another time he told us a story about an airplane hangar in an "all-black city" that became filled with escaped monkeys during Hurricane Andrew. The story was long and rambling and somehow involved the National Guard, and at the end of it, he peered at us with a weird triumph and delivered the unforeseeable punch line: "And you know what? Every single one of those monkeys had been injected with AIDS."

"Tricia, are you going to be able to drive him home from the hospital, while he's all doped up and wearing an eyepatch?"

I'd been wondering the same thing myself. In my carefree youth, I had been so traumatized by my mother's driving lessons, which had generally found me rolling at a crawl through local cemeteries while she shriekingly entreated me not to crash into various mausoleums and somehow kill the occupants a second time, that I drove now only in the worst of emergencies. "I'm going to try. It's only two miles—nothing could happen in just two miles, could it?"

"Well, I don't need to sleep anymore, so if you need me to do it, just let me know and I'll be down here in ten hours. Nine. Eight hours." Passing a darkened shape teetering on the edge of a curb, she gasped suddenly, "Oh my god, it's a double amputee!"

"Mom, no. It's a trash can."

"Oh."

We descended the stone steps and ordered drinks. Immediately a man at the other end of the bar began beaming at my mother like a lustful moon. I nudged her. "Don't look now, but that man is hitting on you."

She flipped her hair like Miss Teen Texas. "I get it all the time, Tricia. Cougar."

"What will you do if he comes over here?"

"Off with his penis. Just . . . kick it off." She crossed her arms dramatically in front of her chest to indicate a karate stance. Despite the fact that he could see only the bare outline of this, Jason nearly collapsed with appreciation. Again and again, my mother proved herself to be the person you wanted with you in a crisis. She was someone who willingly went down into the underworld and came up again as pure levity.

. . .

THREE WEEKS LATER I sat in the chill waiting room, picked up one of those magazines that are always telling you how to "surprise your man" during sex—as if what the volatile male animal needs is to be surprised while he's inside you—and looked at a perfume ad of a sparkling white horse appearing to make love to a woman on the beach. Such wonderful art was everywhere in the world. What if the surgeon cut wrong and Jason could no longer see it? Then it would be my job to describe it to him, the same way Laura Ingalls had to describe the prairies to her blind sister, Mary. I peered closer at the picture and began to practice. *The horse is an erotic moonbeam, trampling across the shore of infinity. He's eating the woman's neck with arousal. She smells so good that the horse thinks he is a man. He wants to conceive a pearl with her and watch her give birth to it in the sea.* I was good, maybe too good. But what if I had to describe something that wasn't an ethereal horse, something he actually wanted to look at? Oh my god, was I going to have to learn how football worked?

They pumped him full of Valium during prep, which made him feel that "presidents were negotiating peace treaties in his mind and heart," but he was awake for the procedure itself, a detail we both found frightening. At the moment they began to break apart his lenses, he saw a fractured kaleidoscope and a spreading light, rose windows and stained glass, and when he emerged from the operating room, his mind had been expanded almost past the point of no return. His pupils, from the eye drops, were as large as portals, and he was smiling like a baby who had achieved enlightenment. "I'm riding the train!" he cried joyfully as I helped him hobble up the stairs into our apartment, feeling proud and capable because I had managed not to destroy us on the way home.

"I think you mean *riding the dragon*," I told him, hauling the dead weight of his legs up onto the couch.

"Please give Jackie Chan a message for me," he murmured as I tucked a blanket over him. "Please tell Jackie Chan . . . that he is my boy." He folded his hands on his chest with the solemn exaggeration of a dracula. Then he closed his eyes, with their fluttery black lashes, and slept for a long time.

THAT SHOULD HAVE BEEN the end of the story, but something went wrong with the first surgery. When he woke up and the fog cleared, we saw the right eye had gone into Wonderland. Distances folded up and sprang out again at will, coiled themselves and then struck, were wild. Color was different, and everything had halos. The city turned into a painting before the invention of perspective. The news receded until he could not touch it; the headlines fled. Sitting across the table from him, I was no longer in his range of vision. I thought of the sexual old people in their restaurant, laughing with bionic giddiness, reading the menu out loud to each other as a kind of foreplay. My face began to feel insubstantial, to dissipate into a mere haze that smiled and spoke. He could not see me.

He described his new sight to me, to try to make me understand. He said it was like water flowing away from him relentlessly and stopping only when it slammed up against dams. The only place he felt relief was at the top of tall buildings, where the view went on and on, where he could let his eye go until it emptied into the Savannah River like a small mad tributary.

Something, the doctor determined, was wrong with that lens, or else with the way his brain reacted to it. He removed it and implanted both eyes with a different kind, which worked better, but the valley between what he saw before and what he saw now was too wide. It was like waking up in the morning to find that English had rearranged itself, or that all pretty women had been scrambled into Picassos. It was not even remotely funny, unlike the vast majority of things that had ever happened to us—we had been lucky, of course we had been lucky. But now some distance had been put between him and the world, and I could not help him bridge it.

ALL THE WHILE I walked more than ever. I walked past Flannery O'Connor's house and I thought about her grotesques and her misfortunates, and I wondered, as I always did, where the mercy was located in her stories. They seemed so pitiless, as pitiless as reality, but somehow the mercy was there. Suddenly I thought, "It is located in *us*, it is external, she shows us the sores of the world and we are filled with a great raw feeling for them." I should not have been thinking of literature at a time like that, but I was. Across the street, bells rolled and rolled as if they were speaking, and uselessly the old words came into my head:

> *Go and tell John what you hear and see: the blind receive their sight and the lame walk, lepers are cleansed and the deaf hear, and the dead are raised up, and the poor have good news preached to them. And blessed is the one who is not offended by me.*

The words rang with meaning, because I had been raised that way. That is the vestigial organ of religion—the voice that speaks, the hand that reaches out to hold.

. . .

HE TOOK A LEAVE of absence from his job, and then he resigned. We would be all right for a few months, we calculated, once unemployment came through—but then it never did. My mother sent money, my older sister sent money. We couldn't afford proper groceries, so our poet friends made us vegetable pizzas and chicken thighs and drank cheap red wine with us in the park, the kind that tastes like the points of rusty nails, and we sat together in the sort of dire silence poets find very companionable, swatting away the swarms of no-see-ums. Despite all of that, our sight was long gone, sprinting into the distance, vanishing into a point on the horizon. We would have to leave this place. We had always come from elsewhere, and in the end we would always go there again. That was our real hometown.

We had just a few hundred dollars in our bank account, a handful of dwindled zeros that would not last us the month. "Come home," my mother told me on the phone. "Your father says it's all right, you can stay with us as long as you want. Come home."

3

BABIES IN LIMBO

id I ever tell you that before we got married, your dad took me aside and told me you were insane, and that I would have to take care of you for the rest of your life?" Jason asks me.

We are driving out of Savannah through tunnels of moss-dripping oaks, with filigreed sun and shadow racing over the windshield and boxes of our belongings once again piled high in the backseat. The cat's carrier is wedged between my feet on the floor, and it occasionally mews to ask where we are going. Next to it is a short stack of books and my tarot cards—though I don't know why I brought them along, since all I ever draw these days is the Hermit and the Devil. I've had to leave the majority of my treasures, including my collection of powerful stones.

But now that we have left everything behind, now that the city is diminishing behind us, Jason feels relief. He can rest from the front page for a month or two, adjust to the new apparition of the world, the cardboard trees and haloed streetlights and the farness of my face, and then begin searching for a new job. He has carried such weight for so long, and now his shoulders straighten. The heavy, humid climate still surrounds us in the car, but I know it will dissipate as soon as we step out.

I burst into laughter. "No, but if that's all he said, you're lucky. Before my brother-in-law got married to my sister, my dad took him out to a nice dinner and confessed to him that he had a Hot Prostate. We looked it up later, and it turns out it doesn't exist."

"I'll never forget it. We were hanging around in the church parking lot after Mass—I think you had been cantoring that day—and he put a hand on my shoulder and sighed and said, 'She's always going to be an albatross around your neck, J.'"

I laugh a little again, to myself. We treasure these sayings of my father's, we store them up and polish them. Through long retelling, they take on the sheen of crazed pearls. "Well, he wasn't wrong, either. When I left home, I *was* insane. I used to lie down on the floor next to my boombox, press my ear against the speaker, and pretend I was listening to the fetal heartbeat of music itself."

"Oh, I remember," he says, giving a long, low whistle—not the kind you use to tell a woman that she's hot, but the kind you use when a woman rips off her wig and reveals to you her gaping head wound.

"I wouldn't have blamed you at all if . . . did you ever think of not marrying me?"

"Of course," he says, and I feel the jolt you feel when alternate universes, which usually run parallel and unseen alongside you, leap out of black water and crisscross like dolphins over your trajectory. When you realize it might have been different. "But I decided it didn't matter if you never got better. If I had to take care of you, I would take care of you." Then he lets loose a loud, wild caw. "Besides, I thought it might be cool to have a bird tied around my neck for the rest of my life."

"Strange that my dad likes you so much now," I ponder, "even though you're a member of the media."

"I can pinpoint the exact moment it happened," he says, through a mist of nostalgia. "It was just before we all left for a big family vacation, a year or two after we were married. Your mom had finished packing and was trying to herd everyone into the van, and the dog was barking at the top of her lungs, and one of your little brothers was peeing into a pile of clean laundry, and the rectory was just in total chaos. In the middle of all this, your dad called me into his room, handed me a crisp twenty-dollar bill, and said, 'J, I need you to go to Arby's *and get me as many Beef 'n Cheddars as this will buy.*' I didn't ask any questions. I just went and did it." He stops to remember. "It took me a long time, actually, because to Arby's credit, the Beef 'n Cheddars are always made fresh."

"And after that, he liked you."

"After that, I think he loved me."

The road hums along under the wheels. Jason swerves to miss a shadow in the shape of a squirrel. "Besides," he says, "the craziness was *in the house*. It was like a weather, or an endless guitar solo, or a radio broadcast that never stops playing. I knew once you left, it would be all right."

Ten hours later, a squat brick institution rises up in our sight, crowned with a tall stone cross. Jesus, unhappily nailed there, has a childish roundness to his arms and legs that suggests he is made of endless breadsticks. A brick house with shutters the color of fiddlehead ferns waits just around the corner, with an American flag dangling down one side of the door and a Marine Corps flag dangling down the other. Electric candles glow their invitation in every window. We have arrived.

THE FIRST GLIMPSE I get of my father he's spread out on a leather couch in a pair of tighty-whities, which reassures me that nothing significant in the Lockwood household has changed since my departure twelve years ago. "I know so much about him," Jason whispers over my shoulder. "Every time I'm in a room with your father, I feel like I'm supposed to be sketching his thighs." It's true. My childhood was one long life-drawing class where Santa posed for us, stripped naked and loudly challenging us to add more detail to his jelly.

I submit that every man of God has two religions: one that belongs to heaven and one that belongs to the world. My father's second religion is Nudity, or Underwear, to be more precise. There are some men who must strip straight down to their personality as soon as they walk through the door of their castle, and my father is one of them. I have almost no memories of him wearing pants, and I have a lot of memories of him sitting me down for serious talks while leaning forward on his bare haunches. He just never wore pants on principle. We saw him in his collar and we saw him in his underwear, and nothing ever in between. It was like he couldn't think unless his terrier could see his belly button. In the afternoons, he reclined brazenly on leather couches and talked to Arnold Schwarzenegger while he shot up the jungle, and every time Arnold made a pun about murder, he laughed with gratification. As far as I could tell, he thought movies were real. He watched them in a state of alarming physical receptiveness, with his legs so completely open toward the television that it seemed possible he was trying to watch it with his butt. His default position was a kind of explicit lounge, with one leg up and the other leg extended, like the worst kind of Jazzercise stretch you could possibly imagine.

Whenever we brought a friend home to study, we called through his closed door, "DAD, ARE YOU DRESSED?" and he would call back, "OF COURSE I AM DRESSED," and then later he would forget and enter a room resplendent in only his underwear, which perhaps because of his commitment to honesty seemed more transparent than other underwears, and he would catch the eye of the burning Jennifer at our kitchen table and then smack his forehead and yell, "OH, GAD!" He was surprised every time, and every time he yelled, "OH, GAD!" With tremendous nude dignity, he would take hold of a bag of pork rinds and then excuse himself from our presence, disappearing to a place where a man could eat pork rinds with his boobs out like God intended without any Jennifers trying to look at him. He was, after all, a decent man.

"BIT!" HE CRIES HAPPILY, gnawing a rope of jerky that looks suspiciously as if it might have come from the pet store. He seems overjoyed to see me. Has he forgotten what I'm like? "Where's your kitty cat? I'm gonna kill her."

"Don't you dare say you're going to kill the cat, Greg," my mother says, appearing wraithlike in the doorway. "She won't know you're joking."

"Whatever, *femme*," my father says, releasing a low, loving toot in her direction. Unrestrained conversational tooting was considered a form of self-expression in his family. Ask my mother to sum them up, and she will suck a long breath through her teeth and say, "Ah, the Lockwoods. All the money in the world, and they couldn't keep their farts in."

IF MY FATHER is best described in terms of his nudity, my mother is best described in terms of her Danger Face, which is organized around the information that somewhere in America, a house is on fire. There are human Lassies among us, who are more alert to disaster, who feel a little *ding!* go off in their heads whenever a child falls into a well. She is one of them, and all humankind is her Timmy.

The only magazine she ever subscribed to was called *Prevention*, and it exclusively carried articles about which fruits could prevent cancer. The cover always featured a picture of a jogging young grandma in a sports bra pumping her fist in the air as she overcame any number of invisible diseases. My mother's expression, while reading it at the kitchen table over an antioxidant-rich meal of beets and steamed carrots, called to mind Edvard Munch's *The Scream*.

She gave birth to five children herself, and is now approaching eight grandchildren. She would tell you she was meant to be a mother, and it's true when she's in the presence of little children, she achieves her most concentrated essence. She stops speaking English at all and erupts into meaningless vocal improvisation, a sort of cautionary scatting. It sounds something like this:

"... honey ... no ... eeeeYAHHH ... uh uh uh ... STOP HER ... she's eating it ... no, sweetheart, that will kill you ... oh, look ... look look look ... she loves me ... all babies love me ... wuh uh, THE STAIRS ... get her ... SHE'S GOING TO FALL ... grab her before she breaks her neck ... ooooo AH-AH-AH-AH ..."

It is a miracle any of us learned to talk at all, but not so surprising that we had a strong sense of our mortality from an early age. It's all for the best that she was so watchful too. If it had been left up to my dad, we would have fallen off cliffs a long time ago.

MY FATHER DRAWS HIMSELF UP out of a loose, lazy pile of carnality and ambles off to introduce Jason to his latest terrier, a little black beast named Whimsy. She is, I regret to tell you, not the brightest dog. She knows one trick, and it is called Roll Over Three Times. Nevertheless, my father adores her, and talks to her in a baby voice he never used with us, singing a repeating chorus—PUP-py PUP-py PUPPity DOG—to her when no one is listening. She is his boon companion.

"Is she fixed?" Jason asks as she rolls in dark ecstasy at his feet. It's the only "dog conversation" he can think of in the moment.

"Naw, she's all woman, J," my father says, regarding her fondly. This is typical. My family has the most intact dogs on the planet. Do not even think one of our dogs does not have its balls, or is not capable of shooting out puppies at a moment's notice. When my brother Paul adopted a large Olde English Bulldogge he called Bacon, the first thing he did was send me an explicit picture of its equipment, as if to assure me the continuing existence of dogs was secure.

Bulldogs named after slabs of meat are too butch for my father, though. He goes in for trim and hysterical rat-chasers—rich, blue-blooded, and convinced of the need for a fence between the United States and Mexico. They're tiny enough to carry around in a purse, and he calls them by squeaky diminutives like Dicky and Tatty and Naugie. This must have something to do with the fact that his mother's people were from New England. When he is communing with his dog, he is suddenly a tall, overbred woman named Buffy, who plays mah-jongg on the weekends and eats only hors d'oeuvres.

Perhaps out of loyalty to the breed, he addresses my mother as *Cairn*. "Oh, yeah, he married me because I'm a human terrier," she told me once, with admirable equanimity. "I'm excitable, I'm hairy, I have a great sense of smell, and I'm a bitch."

THE DOG IS POINTING her head at the ceiling and trying to communicate something to us, probably about religion. "Hush up, Whimsy!" my mother commands.

My father is incensed. "What did you say? What did you say to my dog?"

"She's barking her head off, Greg! The neighbors are going to complain!"

"Oh, I guess you just wish that my *sweet little dog* was *dead*!" he yells, being somewhat given to dramatic overstatement. The dog is a bone of contention between them, because my mother is Highly Allergic. She is also Highly Allergic to the cat we're currently attempting to spirit upstairs before my father notices, but she never mentions that. My father despises cats. He believes them to be Democrats. He considers them to be little mean hillary clintons covered all over with feminist legfur. Cats would have abortions, if given half a chance. Cats would have abortions *for fun*. Consequently our own soft sinner, a soulful snowshoe named Alice, will stay shut in the bedroom upstairs, padding back and forth on cashmere paws, campaigning for equal pay, educating me about my reproductive options, and generally plotting the downfall of all men.

My mother hooks her arm through mine. "I'm not sure what reason he has to hate cats so much. If anyone should hate cats, it's me. When I was a girl, a cat snuck into my room and gave birth all over my bed." She smiles sentimentally, thinking of the carnage, and then sneezes. Then sneezes again, and sneezes again. She begins sneezing without interruption every night at midnight, like a werewolf that's allergic to its own fur.

On the other side of me, Jason squeezes my hand. From one Wonderland into another.

MY MOTHER LIGHTS like the first streetlamp when she looks at us— the coziest, homiest, most nostalgic one. She will have friends now, and new mouths to feed, and people to stay up into the nocturnal hours with her, talking and laughing. My father's move to the Kansas City diocese carried her away from all her children, who are mostly in Cincinnati and St. Louis, and she misses being close to her own mother and brother and sisters.

My father's sense of family is more theoretical. He likes having a lot of kids—the continuing existence of dogs is secure!—but I'm not even sure he knows where all of us live. He never socialized much with my mother's side of the family, either, so I doubt he's suffering from the distance between them. He feels a claustrophobia in crowds he never felt down on the submarine, and one of my uncles once gave him a copy of Carl Sagan's *Cosmos* for Christmas—to taunt him, he believed—and he has never forgotten it.

Even my mother was incredulous. "A book about the universe? Are you kidding me?" she said, as if *Cosmos* is generally found shelved somewhere between *The Satanic Bible* and the books about gay penguins.

"What's wrong with that?" I asked.

"Oh, Tricia." She clucked at my foolishness. "Even a book about the universe can have an agenda."

LET ME TAKE YOU ON A TOUR, my mother says, and guides us into the kitchen, where, she informs us with visible regret, a contractor recently lost part of his hand. The house is unfamiliar, yet somehow it contains all my childhood houses. There are the crucifixes I remember, the couches, the dishes. There is that same lingering odor of my father's cooking, which smells like ground beef being tortured in a pit of fire for its sins. There is, heaven help us, the art.

Pretty much all art in this house is of Jesus reaching out with two fingers and trying to milk things—the air, the clouds, the Cross, a cripple who wants to get blessed but who instead is going to get milked, by Jesus. Jesus stands against a celestial background. He reaches toward a plump, dangling ray of the sun. He is going to milk the hell out of it.

When the paintings aren't of Jesus, they're of ships and jungle cats, which fit better with the theme than you might expect. On one wall is a photo-realistic 1960s painting of a tiger, leaping at you so ferociously that you know he must have eaten Jesus, and that in fact Jesus, crouching inside him and full of a taste for human flesh, is the one who is hungry for you. Over the couch hangs a picture of a quail following a set of human footprints in the snow. Whose footprints is she following? I hardly need to tell you.

Above the fireplace hangs a painting of a full-rigged ship resting in the harbor at Nantucket. This is my father's most prized artistic possession. It is called simply "The Stobart," as other people might say "The van Gogh" or "The Banksy." The Stobart is perhaps the world's most literal ship painting—a setting sun, pearly blues and anemone pinks and oyster grays, puddles on planks, riggings painted with a single hair. Yet you cannot shake the feeling that Jesus is hiding out in there somewhere, as the weirdest, hottest cabin boy, or an incredibly ripped, tan parrot who repeats after no one and gives crackers to YOU. "I never get tired of looking at that masterpiece," my father remarks, gazing deeply at The Stobart, lusting for the cabin boy he cannot see.

"I hate all modern art, because it's mad at God," he likes to say. Most Catholics have never recovered from that painting of the Virgin Mary with elephant dung all over it. They are under the assumption there are entire museums in New York dedicated to anti-Catholic shit paintings, where all varieties of zoo scat are flung at pictures of the innocent Virgin.

"Did you see how ugly the church is?" he asks me now. I did. He suggests it's because it was built in the 1950s, when people were already starting to be Communists.

"I'll tell you what the problem is," he says, taking on the comfortable tone of instruction. "When people started forgetting about gender roles, they started building ugly churches. Architecture requires an equal balance of the male and the female in order to be beautiful." What? There's no way that can be right. According to those standards, the perfect cathedral would be a gigantic Prince symbol people could pray inside.

MOM HAS MADE her old sewing room ready to welcome us home. The walls are white as eggshells and the ceiling is low enough to touch. It's about ten feet by ten feet and there are two gable windows that add to the feeling of snugness. There are two big closets, the kind you would hide in with your notebook when you were a child, and there's a cut-glass lamp that throws pineapple-patterned light all over the ceiling. On top of the chest of drawers is my entire childhood collection of gnomes, accumulated during a time when I lusted after gnomes so strenuously I'm surprised I grew up to have sex with human beings as opposed to whimsical statues in people's gardens.

There is a painting of poppies above the bed that I gave my mother one Christmas, believing her taste in art to be immature. The poppies are red and pink watercolor splotches that look like spilled blood. A lot like spilled blood. A lot like spilled blood . . . on the panties of the snow. Oh my god, I realize, looking at it again, I gave my mother a menstrual painting.

"Mom, is that . . . are those . . ." I indicate the art.

She dismisses my astonishment with a wave of the hand. "I was wondering when you would figure it out. I figured maybe the painter had a trauma. Maybe she got her period one time in church."

I promise never to attempt to educate her again. It must have been very wrong of me. Jason enters with two suitcases and sees us staring. "Why is there blood all over the wall?"

FINALLY SHE CREAKS OPEN the door of the upstairs bathroom and shows Jason where the thousand-count bottle of aspirin is. "If you feel that shooting pain in your left arm, you bear down with all your might like you're sitting on the toilet and then you take two of these," she tells him tenderly. Peering past her, I notice an economy-sized bottle of Palmolive inside the shower.

"What's that doing in there?" I ask.

She is silent for a moment, as if debating whether to tell me. Then she sighs. "Your dad washes himself with dish soap."

AS I WALK BEHIND HER down the halls, it happens. I shrink inch by inch until I am no longer an adult, but a baby toddling along in a comically oversized business suit. I have been pretending to be a grown-up this whole time. My briefcase is full of milk; I have been found out.

This, then, is home. What is home? Is it a sort of lap of location, that exists only if certain conditions are in place? Is it the intersection of rigidity and comfort—a junction of familiarity that you curl into? Is it a feeling? I don't know, but I'm being hugged hard against it, and I can't tell when I'll be let go.

When we find ourselves alone for a minute, Jason and I hold each other tightly. I pat him on the back, and a helpless infant belch rumbles up from his underground. "You burped me!" he exclaims. So I'm not the only one.

WE FALL FAST into a routine. At night, we eat angel food cake with strawberries and whipped cream, and drink prosecco my mother chills in the freezer. It takes only two glasses before she's doubled over giggling and bellowing, "OHHHH YEAHHHHH." At some point during my childhood, she decided bellowing "OHHHH YEAHH-HHH" in a loud Kool-Aid Man voice was a catchphrase, and she has punctuated her speech with it ever since. When I inevitably begin hiccuping from the bubbles, she whacks me on the back and screams, "It's because you're gulping it! Drink it differently."

Starting at midnight, she opens up her laptop and begins reading the internet aloud. How long can it be? she reasons. Five hundred pages at MOST. She resisted the internet for so long, but has finally succumbed to its embrace: it is, after all, an excellent place to find stories about people who have died horribly. "Did you hear about this, Tricia?" she asks me, and then reads aloud the story of a young boy who smothered to death on his own teddy bear. "Who would have thought that a hug could be deadly," she muses. Or, "Did you see the story about the demonic rosaries? China has released demon rosaries into the market. They have pentagrams hidden on them and no INRI and a snake behind Jesus' head. My friend found one in her house and her husband had to take it out to the garage and destroy it. They say if you come across one you should lift it with a stick and then bury it in your backyard." Or abruptly, "There's a new kind of diarrhea, and it's killing senior citizens."

"Mom, Mom, Mom," I say, unable to hold my laughter.

She peers at me through her glasses. "What?"

"Nothing. Keep reading."

"WHAT ARE YOU FEMMES DOING," my father booms from the doorway. He always calls us femmes. It is, believe it or not, a term of affection. When he's angry, he calls you a feminazi. When he first encountered that epithet, on Rush Limbaugh's radio show in the early nineties, he hugged it to himself as wholeheartedly as a second wife. Nuns are feminazis, Democrats are feminazis, the secretary who asks him please not to call her "dollface" is a feminazi. It goes without saying that I am a feminazi. He finds uses for the word in all sorts of situations. If he were alone in the wilderness and a cougar charged him, he would yell, "FEMINAZI!" right in its tawny face, and I have no doubt the cougar would back down.

My mother ignores him. "Tricia, did you see this online quiz where you have to guess whether it's a Hot Dog or a Celebrity Leg?" I did, I tell her. Somehow or other, I did.

WHEN WE CLIMB the stairs to bed, we find sleep eludes us. Out in the darkness, yard to yard, dogs are answering no one. Whimsy is chief among them. All night long, she answers the questions no one has asked.

But there is, underneath that, a more disturbing sound. It is the sound of my mother creeping back and forth, patrolling the halls, sneaking on tiptoe past our door, pausing to check whether we're still breathing. Jason and I look at each other and realize, with sad certainty, that we will never have sex in this place. Just forget it. What if the crucifix over the door came to life? What if we were having sex and I caught Jesus' eye and saw that he was suddenly crying blood? What if the INRI above his head had rearranged itself somehow to read HORNI? Plus, I would probably get pregnant every time.

THERE ARE HOUSES people cannot seem to leave, even though the doors are wide open. You feel very slightly heavier in them, the way you would on Jupiter. This is one of those houses. There is more gravity in this room than there is anywhere else on the planet, so much that I can hardly step outside it. My hands weigh a hundred pounds each and I can barely lift my head off the pillow in the mornings. The bed fills the whole room, and I lie on it and float, thinking about what I should do. The world moves its scenery back and forth in front of the window; it has nothing to do with me; it is passing me by. I lie on the bed and feel myself gently going out of print.

I have always lived in these places, these places adjacent to the church and adjacent to its powers. There was holy water on the steps, which I sprinkled, and unblessed hosts in the closet, which I ate. The first rectory I remember was a mansion that stretched and stood up, and swallowed and rambled, and lazily ignored all laws of time and space. It was permanently three o'clock in the afternoon there, except when it was three o'clock in the morning. And it was so big I took it for granted that it regularly grew new rooms, and when I opened a door, I understood I might never see that room again. Once I turned a knob and found a room full of nuns sewing quietly on a quilt, with wire hair and support hose pooling around their ankles and glasses on gold chains and straight blue skirts. The nuns glanced up in unison and smiled at me, a sweet chorus of acknowledgment and acceptance, as if I were a baby in a basket they had found on their doorstep. I closed the door and tiptoed away and knew I would never find my way back. That is the way the house was. It was boxy and biological. It was now larger and now smaller, and there was a feeling at the end of each hallway that it was the tip of a twig, and when I wasn't looking it would leaf. This spell extended to the front lawn, where once I rolled an acorn down a hill and stared hard at the blue depression it made in the snow. Then I looked up and saw a great oak, which seemed to have shot up that minute, instant from my acorn. I could not recall it being there before and believed I had grown it, and feeling at the tips of fingers and toes the power of the twig I took it in my stride.

At the beginning of *The Princess and the Goblin*, a girl goes exploring her castle one rainy afternoon and is startled to find a white-haired ancestor where no ancestor was before, humming and spinning silk in a remote room that is sometimes there and sometimes not, collecting pigeon eggs from under the eaves for her breakfast. The ancestor is the past, of course, keeping elemental time in her rocking chair. She is the gathering of every gray and silver moment that has brought the girl to this point, to this present where she flourishes like a flower. Looking on her, the girl sees that she is beautiful, or at least that she can beautifully describe her.

A curious panting comes outside my door. It is my own ancestor crouched on all fours in the hallway, her hair gone mirror-colored at the crown, trying to guess whether I need to go to a restaurant or not. She believes if you don't visit at least four restaurants a day, you die.

"Mom, I'm working!" I call out.

A long pause.

"But do you need a hamburger," she whispers.

4

R ʒ R CIRCUS

When I last shared a roof with my parents, I walked around wearing a pair of protective shooting earmuffs all day. I removed them only to shower, and even slept in them sometimes. This was not an eccentricity. My father carries a personal armageddon around with him, made of the most violent and incomprehensible sounds, and no one within a square mile of him can escape it.

The majority of this armageddon consists of guitar music. Before I describe it, let me address an age-old philosophical question: is music always beautiful? Music is not always beautiful. In *The Screwtape Letters*, C. S. Lewis defines music as "a meaningless acceleration in the rhythm of celestial experience," but it can also be a sped-up inferno, complete with the cries of the damned.

When the biological urge comes upon him, he lifts his curvaceous red guitar out of its case with a hushed reverence and cradles it in his arms. Then he plugs it into the most powerful amp that's legal in the state of Missouri and begins rocking himself into a frenzy. It sounds like a whole band dying in a plane crash in the year 1972. He plays the guitar like he's trying to take off women's jeans, or like he's standing nude in the middle of a thunderstorm and calling down lightning to strike his pecs. It's not bad, exactly, it just makes you doubt your version of reality. He plays a lot of notes very fast and all in a row but they don't seem to have any relation to one another. I've never heard him play an actual song, not even by accident, and I've made something of a study of his style over the years. Some people are, through whatever mystifying means, able to make the guitar talk. My father can't do that, but he can do the following:

1. Make the guitar squeal
2. Make the guitar say no
3. Make the guitar falsely confess to murder
4. Make the guitar stage a filibuster where it reads
   The Hunt for Red October out loud

I can't figure it out, and I think for a living. He practices mainly in his bedroom, so it's possible he's having sex with the guitar? It's possible that somewhere out there I have a half brother who is a sweet lick from the waist down?

Alice, to everyone's surprise, cannot get enough. She rolls on her back and flashes her claws in the air when he plays. She is blown away by the concept of sustain; the longer a note lasts, the more she purrs; it seems to stretch her actual perception of time. She wriggles with pleasure; she twists and switches her tail; she forgets to close her mouth over her thirsty pink tongue. She is dropping her panties, catwise.

She is especially susceptible to The Riff. It is my father's custom to play a little riff of his own composition—it sounds like a Republican terrier howling the first three notes of "Smoke on the Water" to a blood-red moon—and bend the last note so hard it exits the sphere of music entirely, and then look at his audience with a sweet, expectant face, like, "Can you believe how good that was?" "It was so, so good," Alice answers him, writhing on the hood of his Corvette, purring in every cell of her, her whiskers vibrating as if they were recently strummed. Her body is a leotard, her fur is a perm. If I let her out, she'll wait under the star on his dressing room until he opens the door and carries her inside.

"Don't make fun," my mother says when she sees me standing in the hallway with a look of enormous concentration on my face, trying to make sense of one of these performances. "Your father is legit. Back in high school, he played in a very successful band called R & R Circus. They played a show for mentally retarded children in Kentucky once. Your father has always had such a big heart for the . . ."—she hesitates, then lowers her voice to a whisper—"for the mentally retarded."

"Did the children like it?"

"They were in absolute heaven. You know, it was a ten-piece band with trumpets and trombones. All the members wore crushed red velveteen suits, skintight on the leg. Nothing not to like."

5

MEN OF THE CLOTH

Did I mention there's a seminarian living in the rectory too? He's staying here on and off over the summer, and in the fall he'll return to Ohio for his last semester of seminary, after which he'll be ordained. All of this is unremarkable to me, who often saw these young men pass in and out of the house when I was growing up, but Jason is bewildered.

"I still don't understand what a seminarian is," he whispers in the privacy of our upstairs room. His understanding of my childhood religion hasn't deepened much since we first met. As far as I can tell, he considers a priest to be a sort of strict male witch, and he can't figure out why Catholics want to eat so much flesh all the time. "Please tell me before I mortally offend somebody."

"Okay. A seminarian is an unborn priest, who floats for nine years in the womb of education, and then is finally born between the bishop's legs into a set of exquisite robes."

"You can't say things like that anymore, Tricia," he warns me. "God will hear you."

"That's not God, that's Mom," I say, raising my voice and pointing at the closed door. Outraged silence. Then a soft rodent shuffling and footsteps retreating down the stairs.

I lower my voice again. I know it's only a matter of weeks before I fall back into the established family vocabulary, in which a wide variety of normal words are considered cusses, but for now I'm putting up a fight. "A seminarian is just someone who's going to school so he can learn how to be a priest."

"What kind of school is it? Is it wizard school?"

"No, it's not wizard school. It's regular school, but they study the powers of light and darkness all day."

"Wizard school," he says under his breath. "What happens when they graduate?"

"There's a ceremony at the cathedral where all the other priests kiss them on the head—I'm not totally sure why—and then they get to wear special clothes and do reenactments of Christ's death and resurrection."

"They seem to love all the same things you do," he says perceptively. "Cloaks and elixirs and singing elf songs."

"Yes, but women aren't allowed. Also, you never get to have sex ever, in your life, unless you're some earthy European priest who gets tempted by a peasant in an olive grove. For some reason, that seems to be more forgivable than any of the kinds of sex you can have in America."

He considers this information. "Are the seminarians allowed to look at porn?"

"They are NOT allowed to look at porn, and they don't even want to look at porn, because it has no respect for the holy nudeness of the bod, which was made in God's image."

"What do they do on the internet if they're not allowed to look at porn?"

"They look at pictures of jewels, and they read blog posts of bishops about how modern swimsuits are bad."

"Why do they do it? Why would anybody want to do it? Why?"

I shrug. Since the age of six, I have been a poet. "When you're called, you're called."

THE SEMINARIAN IS a crotchety young Italian man with a disapproving nose, a black boyish haircut, and eyes the precise shape of watermelon seeds. He was born, like many seminarians, at the age of sixty-five, with a pipe in his mouth and a glass of port in his hand. He is tall, but he hunches slightly under the weight of tradition, and whenever he emerges from the dark rectory into the sunshine, he blinks like an over-educated cave creature who is in the process of evolving away several of his most frivolous body parts. I expect his voice to be ponderous and dignified, to fit this overall picture, but when he opens his mouth he rolls out the broad and hilarious vowels of Chicago. I love him instantly and beyond all reason, in the way you love people you're going to be able to write about.

He is devoted to three things and three things only: God, Buicks, and Italy. He believes the ideal woman lives somewhere on the Boot, rolling down hillsides in a red-checked skirt with a bottle of wine in each fist, her boobs like perfectly twirled forkfuls of pasta. He will never meet her, but she is there. This allows him to feel content. "It would be very difficult to be celibate in Italy," he tells me, a muscle leaping in his jaw, probably one of the main ones you use when you eat lasagna. "Here in America, it's easy." I sit back and study him. Here is a man who heard a hot woman called a "tomato" once in his boyhood and took it so literally that the course of the rest of his life was set.

He knows he was meant to be a priest because once he had a girlfriend who wore an intoxicating perfume and then one day his mother bought it and started spritzing herself with it too. That is a sign if anything is. If my dad, at some point during the nineties, had come home on a skateboard, smoothing his butt cut and adjusting his wallet chain, I would have gone straight into the nunnery without a moment's hesitation. Such things belong to the realm of destiny.

WE READ TOGETHER in the cool, darkened living room in the afternoons, by the stripes of light that fall through the white plantation shutters. He reads a little leather book full of daily prayers, with ribbons to keep his place. He calls the book his wife, which is a sentiment I can respect, and moves his lips when he looks at her. These scenes are the very picture of peace, except for the fact that my father is often electrocuting a guitar in his bedroom, and my mother is often on the phone with my older sister in the kitchen, discussing various imperilments, catastrophes, and untimely deaths. Snatches of her conversation float through the hallways and make meditation of any kind impossible.

"Listen. Listen to me," we can hear her say. "When *Superman* first came out, there was a whole era where the kids thought they could fly, and they would get up on their roofs and jump, often to their death. Is that something you want to happen?"

The seminarian and I cover our mouths to stifle our laughter. Sometimes he even slaps his bare thigh. When he's off the clock, he strips down to a white oxford shirt, golf shorts, and socks pulled up to his actual knees. The sight of him in these clothes is rather magnificent. He looks like a cult dentist. Occasionally, as we listen, he makes a quacking gesture with his hand to affectionately indicate a woman is talking too much, but the fact is he talks more than anyone I've ever met. When he has to be quiet for any length of time, he grips both arms of his chair and trembles with suppression like a friendly teakettle. He doesn't mind our chatter at all, or the ongoing female background sound, and some human need will go unfilled when it is gone. "Where is your wife?" he asks Jason when I don't come downstairs. "Your wife is very fun."

Somehow we are perfectly comfortable with each other, in the way people who agree about absolutely nothing sometimes are. However, as the weeks pass, it becomes more and more apparent that I am a bad influence. In the course of a conversation about guitars, I accidentally introduce him to the word "wanking." "What's wanking?" he asks. "Do you mean, like, masturbating? Masturbating upon the guitar?" On cue, my father begins to play The Riff.

"What would you call that music?" the seminarian asks after a moment of speechless listening. He studied classical piano himself for a long time and knows there is something amiss here. "Is there a name for it?"

I weigh and reject the term "priestcore." "Technically speaking, I think it's just ass rock," I say.

"Ass rock!" he cries. It's clear he's never heard the phrase before. "That's very funny. Ass rock!"

I BEGIN TO SUSPECT I'm being fattened for eventual sacrifice on top of a mountain. My mother is cramming me with five or six meals a day, and slides cookies underneath my door when I don't answer her knocks. Not to be outdone, the seminarian tiptoes up to me one evening when

I'm napping on the downstairs couch and wakes me by dangling a slice of ham over my lips.

"NO!" I shout, because that's what they teach you in kindergarten: don't let anyone touch you with their ham unless you say yes.

"But it's such good ham," he pleads. "And you're really too skinny."

"Why, how much do you think I should weigh?"

"One hundred and ninety pounds," he answers instantaneously. Evidently this has been much on his mind.

I prop myself up on one elbow and stare at him. "Have you ever considered that you might be a feeder?"

"What's a feeder?"

If sex education has failed him, it's my job to fill in the gaps. "It's a sort of food daddy, who feeds a woman until she becomes plump enough for his erotic delectation. He gives her cookies and ice cream and second lunches and midnight snacks and eventually all her clothes rip off and both of them get excited."

His eyes widen. Voluptuous vistas are opening before him. "You can make her as big as you want?"

I picture a woman shooting up into the sky, bursting out of her dress, and raising her leg to crush St. Peter's Basilica. "As big as God will let her be," I promise.

He gives me a look of intrigue, second only to the look of intrigue once given to me by a surrealist poet when I told him some men desire above all else to watch truckers have sex with their wives.

"See, I need to know these things," he says, with the brisk attitude of a man filing information away for future use. "I just found out what a furry was. My friend told me and I was very surprised."

A wave of pleasure washes over me as I imagine this encounter: two young men, tall with theological purpose, discussing people who dress up as stuffed animals and scritch each other's bellies at conventions. "Why on earth do you need to know about furries?"

"Because people will confess to me about them. Someone will confess to me 'I am a furry,' and I need to know what that is."

It almost makes me want to turn Catholic again, just so I could go to confession sometime and lay a big, eloquent paw up against the screen right as he asked me what my sins were.

SOMEHOW OR OTHER, the seminarian has heard about milfs and he is haunted by the concept. He fears hordes of milfs are roaming the plains of dating, simultaneously breastfeeding and trying to trick young men into having sex with them. "Are milfs something that's popular in secular culture for guys in their twenties to go after?" he asks.

"Yes," I say gravely, signaling Jason across the room to write that quote down word for word. "Very, very popular. The most popular thing now."

His eyes widen and he crosses his legs, as if to protect his holy jewels from the very notion of a milf. I consider other possible lies to tell him.

In Britain they call them Nummy Mummies, and due to the gender imbalance left over from the Great War, there are two of them for every male.

There's no way of telling whether your own mother is a milf, but if she likes to play bingo, it's almost certain.

The wine of Italy is stomped out by milfs, so when you taste the wine, you are tasting their desire.

During the full moon a milf lactates a powerful sex milk that is instantly addictive to any man who tries it.

He interrupts my reverie to explore the subject further. "What's the difference between a milf and a cougar?"

"Cougars are . . . hornier," I say, thinking fast. "A milf doesn't have to be horny at all, it just has to be a Mom You'd Like to F, but a cougar is horny, and it prowls."

"So disordered," the seminarian breathes. Calling people "disordered" is practically his favorite thing to do, and a tawny animal woman who chases after tender cubs is about as disordered as it gets. "I hope I never meet one."

I get very close to his face and fix him with my most feline expression. "Too late, buddy. You already have."

I WANT TO TAKE the Gay Inkblot Test so bad I can taste it. According to my father, they administer an inkblot test to all the men who are studying to become priests in order to determine whether they're possessed by the handsome little demon of Same Sex Attraction. (He refers to it as SSA, both for jauntiness and to save time.) I'm not sure whether the inkblots themselves have been somehow designed to be gay—balls everywhere, kaleidoscopic bursts of abs, the words "I'M GAY" doing backflips in the ink, a dong on the classic Rorschach butterfly—or whether they just expect people to see gay things in them. Either way, the test cannot be categorized as either scientific or sane, but my father places great faith in it.

"It's foolproof," he tells me, with the self-satisfaction of a man who knows he would pass. If he took the test, he would see only Batmobiles, but these guys would see the naked body of Robin. His beliefs about homosexuality are in general keeping with those of the church, with a few small but distinctive flourishes of his own. Earlier this week, for instance, he informed me Elton John became gay because he was "raised by too many aunts."

When the seminarian took the inkblot test, he saw bunnies. "You saw . . . bunnies?" I ask. "Bunnies are fine," he says with authority.

"Bunnies are very wholesome. What you DON'T want to see is half-animal half-humans. That would show you were messed up." Regular bunnies are just evidence you love Easter, but woe to the one who looks into the ink and sees a rabbit with the luscious lower half of a man.

Important: do you understand how badly I would fail this test? I would get something worse than an F. But my father refuses to even let me look at the Gay Inkblots. He's afraid of what he might find. He knows he was saved from ever seeing me bring home a girl named Boots with screws in her ears for one reason and one reason only: because I got married when I was twenty-one to a man I met in cyberspace.

"We don't know if it works on women," they say cautiously, when I raise the subject amid the happy family clamor of the dinner table. "That's not . . . we haven't studied that yet."

"In fact"—the seminarian sighs—"no one knows how lesbians work."

"It's easy," I say. "You put one leg over her leg, and then she puts her other leg over your other leg, and then you brush each other's hair forever while not going to church."

He rolls his eyes. "You're not a lesbian, Tricia," he tells me patiently. "You wear dresses."

"If you're so determined to figure out who's gay and who's not," I say to my father, "then why don't you ask someone who has actually met some gay people, gay people who haven't had to pretend their whole lives not to be gay?"

Gaydar is not real, and I hope never to be in the business of perpetuating crude stereotypes, but the priest who owns his own harp and gets ten different brown-bagged magazines about the Royal Family delivered to him each month? Is possibly not a straight man. But Dad assures me the Gay Inkblot Test is quite sufficient for their needs. So a word to my queer brothers who are longing for a life in the Church: you are safer than houses, for the time being. Go with God.

THE SEMINARIAN TALKS FREQUENTLY about his "celibate powers," which mainly consist of being able to get up extremely early. No, it doesn't sound good to me either, though it's plausible my extreme deficiency of celibacy is the reason I often sleep till noon. To protect and strengthen these celibate powers, he has developed a move called the celibacy block, where he holds up both arms in front of himself in the shape of a cross to ward off the person who's trying to seduce him—mainly women, as he explains to me, who are "wearing volleyball shorts when there isn't even any volleyball going on." "You know what would be a better idea," I tell him. "To just point a gun at any girl who's cute and yell 'I DON'T THINK SO' at the top of your lungs."

The celibacy block is necessary, it seems, because the woods are full of women who lust after men of the cloth. "We call them chalice chippers," the seminarian explains one Sunday, piling his plate with the cold cuts and pickles my mother always sets out after the last Mass.

"They're everywhere," my father adds, vengefully forking a slice of roast beef, and goes on to tell us the story of a woman who once gave him "a teddy bear soaked with your mother's perfume, to try and tempt me."

How would that even *work*? Has any man who ever drew breath been seduced according to this method? Also, I would love to date a woman who soaks teddy bears in perfume and sexually gives them to priests, because she has got to be crazier in bed than any atheist ever dreamed of being. Maybe once you got back to her apartment you would see an even bigger teddy propped up against her pillow, soaked in holy water and waiting for you, with a Bible between its legs opened up to the Song of Songs. Maybe it's for the best, after all, that the seminarian knows what a furry is. If they ever come for him, he'll be ready.

I AM NOT SURE what the seminarian wants, exactly. He acts with admirable propriety at all times, despite the fact that all the chairs in this house are upholstered with velvet and leave perfect impressions of your hindquarters whenever you sit down on them. My mother obliterates the prints with the palm of her hand whenever she encounters them, but I sneak back in and sit on the chairs again when she's not looking. The seminarian is unaffected by this campaign, however. His sights are set on something higher. The firmest desire I ever hear him assert is that he would like to have a lady wash his clothes, *perhaps in a river.*

"Why a river, specifically?" I probe further, carrying two mugs of tea in from the kitchen to fortify us against the doldrums of four o'clock.

"I want to watch her rub my clothes on the stones," he responds.

I look down at him for a long moment, wondering if I should tip the tea out into his lap so he doesn't get too turned on by my gesture of servitude, and he shrugs. "I like domestic stuff," he tells me, his voice falling to a sudden romance-novel huskiness. So fuck a butler. Men, it bears repeating, are so weird. This is so far outside my area of sexual expertise it's not even funny. Tell me you want to role-play a butlerfuck while pretending to serve your penis on a big silver tray and I will nod with understanding, and perhaps even offer to film it. But you want a woman to wash your clothes in a river? What are you, some kind of pervert?

A PRIEST'S UNIFORM INCLUDES the following: a white collar, either cloth or celluloid. A black short-sleeved shirt, black slacks and black belt, black shoes. Black Gold Toe socks. No other kind of sock is even considered. Underwear, I *think*. They buy these items from a special Sacred Clothing catalog, which for some reason is illustrated with pictures of priests laughing insanely, raising crunk cups to Christ, and posing in close embraces. No one knows what they're doing, but they appear to be having just as good a time as the Victoria's Secret models. Pillowfights do not seem far away. When my father started saying the Latin Mass, he gave up the short-sleeved shirts and slacks and took to wearing a cassock, which is just a long black dress for a man that everyone refuses to call a dress. ("It is a dress," I have reiterated many times, trying to open people's eyes to the truth. "And the pope wears what a baby would wear to the prom.") The seminarian wears a cassock too, because he's traditional, and he asked for thirty-three buttons on his: *one for each year of Jesus' life*. On formal occasions, both of them affect a pompom hat, which has no utility as far as I can tell and which no one has ever been able to explain to my satisfaction.

"Really, a pompom hat?" I ask one day, when the seminarian and my dad are both sitting across the table from me decked out in their full regalia, looking like two dark Muppets from the realms of hell.

"It's not a pompom, it's a tuft," the seminarian tells me. "A pompom would be silly."

"We don't call it a hat, we call it a *biretta,*" my father adds, his tuft going absolutely wild.

Ah. Why wear a regular hat, when you can wear a hat that sounds like a firearm. I begin flipping through the latest Sacred Clothing catalog and pause at a picture of a hundred-year-old priest and a twenty-five-year-old priest spooning each other in front of a stained-glass window. "Look at these incredible fantasy scenarios," I say, turning the picture sideways. "I'm taking this upstairs with me. This is my *Playboy* now." A few pages on, a photo of a female minister wearing vestments in all colors of the rainbow catches my attention. "Wait a minute, there are women in this?"

My father screws his eyes up very tinily, as if to cause the female minister and all others like her to disappear. "Those goofy Anglicans," he says, and then makes the distressing moo-cow noise he always makes when imitating the communications of feminists, who lurk in his imagination in rabid, milk-spurting, man-stampeding herds. "MooOOooo, we all gotta be equal, don't we?" he mocks, with such perfect assurance of my agreement that I wonder if he has ever really looked at me, or heard a single word I've ever said. Perhaps, when all is said and done, I am more like a son to him than a daughter.

THERE IS A LOVE for structure in them that I recognize, and a desire to worship correctness that I know I share. When I look at them, I think: to prize traditionalism above all else in a church that began in revolution is to do a great violence to it. But I feel that same ache for the past in myself: to uphold the columns of literature, grammar, the Western tradition. The English language began as an upheaval; I am not protecting it when I try to guard it against change. The Jesus Christ of it, Chaucer, walked across the water telling dirty jokes, made twenty stories stretch to feed a million people, spelled the word "cunt" five ways, performed miracles. Any innovation I put down on paper is an attempt to remind myself of this. I am not modern. I was not born to blaze new paths or bring down walls. I break form against my nature to tell myself that revolution, too, is a tradition that must be upheld.

. . .

"THE SATANISTS ARE AT IT AGAIN," the seminarian declares, bursting into the calm of the living room and waving a piece of paper urgently. "The Italian Satanists are at it again!"

Understand that hard-core Catholics get their news from different places than the rest of us. I look at the telltale paper in his hand. It's probably a newsletter called *Satanists: What Are They Doing Now?* that he reads to keep abreast of their activities. The more people believe in a religion, the more they trust smudgy, paranoid newsletters printed off in a church basement by a woman named Debbie. I swear that for a while in the nineties, my father got a newsletter that listed every celebrity who had AIDS. He would pass through the room while we were watching *The Brady Bunch*, announce, "Big-time AIDS. Big-time," or, "Guess what: America's favorite dad had a secret," and then continue on his way, leaving a couch full of distressed children in his wake.

"Did you say *Italian Satanists*?"

"Satanism is on the rise, especially in Italy," the seminarian informs me, collapsing tragically into his favorite chair. "They roam the city in packs, and they throw rocks at priests as they walk down the street."

That sounds kind of fun. I try to imagine these Italian Satanists, with their black-and-white checked tablecloths and their straw-covered bottles of blood and their accordions full of screams and their salamis made of Christian babies, hunting down priests for pure sport. Secretly the priests must enjoy it. Since the days of lions, there is nothing a Christian likes so much as to feel that he is in danger, simply for believing God was put on this earth in the form of a man with eighteen abs and a virgin mother.

"It's not always the people you think," he continues. "It's not the goths. It might be . . . a businessman, with a family, and secrets in his basement."

The scent of wrinkly black peppercorns and Old Bay floats in from the kitchen, along with the sounds of my mother's out-of-tune humming. Every Friday we eat fish, as if we lived a hundred years ago. We used to abstain from meat on Fridays only during Lent, but now my parents do it all year round, rotating weekly through shrimp and cod and langoustines squeezed with lemon. Sometimes my father even contributes a dish of his own devising that I call Pasta Being Barely Touched by Clams.

We wait for the customary crashing avalanche of pans that comes halfway through her preparation of any meal, followed by a faint "It's okay, I'm okay," and when we hear it, the seminarian smiles. He loves those sounds of women in the kitchen. I am not a Satanist, I cannot lie, I love them too. She brings us each a glass of wine, her color high and happy, and he smiles again and says thank you. In a minute he will get up and slice cucumbers and tomatoes for the salad, or set the table with five neat places, or find some other way of helping her, but not just yet.

"What are we talking about in here?" she asks, in her wide, expectant way.

"Satanism in Italy," we answer together.

Instantly her face empties itself of all contentment. "You know, it's on the rise."

I TRACE MY MODE of interaction with all men back to early encounters with seminarians. Somewhere along the line I got the idea that the most fun you could have with intelligent, studious men was teasing them. It was as easy as eating the apple. They were eternally deep in the writing of some paper. They adjusted their glasses and sat with one leg crossed over the other and made finicking movements with their fingers, as if they were playing small pianos. "Actually," they told me, "actually . . ." What else could I do but tease them? I had no real power; it was men like these who were in charge of my life. If they decided tomorrow I had to cover my hair or wear skirts or pray separately, or be barred from reading certain books, or take certain pills and not take others, or be silent in the presence of men, I would have to do it. To have that bald dynamic of power on display in your home every day, pretending to arch over and protect you—it does something to a person. The seminarian calls women the "tabernacle of life." The tabernacle, if you do not know, is an ornamental box that is largely important for what it holds. It is shut up and locked when the men go away, so the consecrated elements inside cannot be stolen.

I must still place some automatic trust in the office, though, because I find myself telling him all about what brought us here. While I talk, the phenomenon happens; I watch it happen. The bread is changed. The personality absents itself and he becomes a pure receptacle of listening. "You're a good wife," he tells me when I am finished, and I suffer vertigo for a minute, because there is no one in my waking life who would ever think to call me that. Yet there the designation sits between us, archaic and human as an old Greek head, still meaning something to someone.

IT ASTONISHES ME again and again how we know all the same people, though I've been gone from the Church's country for years. There was a priest I was particularly close to in high school, who used to come to our theater rehearsals, perhaps out of loneliness. He was pink and oily and had flat black pebbles for eyes, and he combed six strands of black hair over the top of his head, and he was funny, and he seemed to especially love the citric humor of high school girls—which is eternal, but which tasted new to us at the time. My friends and I were four full oranges of it, with a resilient shine on our leaves.

The Cathedral Basilica of St. Louis rose up across the street from the school. It was a Romanesque dome covered with greeny scales like a sea monster, full of wonders and mosaics and marble folds of robes, and it had an atmosphere of solemnity so dense that even high school girls couldn't cut through it. In the middle of its darkness, I felt like a scintilla; I didn't need to speak. If you melted down all the gold in that place, it would be the size of one of God's fillings, enormous. It loomed in the background of everything we did, so that all our small dramas seemed to happen in relation to it. In spring and fall, we read our lines long into the night. The darkness that fell between my school and the cathedral had an enclosing quality, like the part of the blanket that's tucked right underneath your chin.

Rehearsals were held in the school gym, which had a large, incompetent mural of a purple "Kougar" mascot on one wall, and a black empty stage opening up the other. Our dances were also held there, and I suspect that under the hungry gaze of the Kougar, the boys at our dances got fewer boners than usual. No matter how much we attempted to infuse the atmosphere of this gym with the fire-breathing intelligence of The Theater, it remained full of the ghosts of volleyball games, which gave the Holocaust play we were rehearsing a sportiness it shouldn't have had. Whenever I raised my arm in a fine gesture, it looked like I was about to serve. I have no idea why an all-girls Catholic school was putting on a Holocaust play in the first place. It was about an orchestra in a concentration camp, and I was required to pretend to play a trumpet and later to feed pieces of raw potato to my lesbian lover in a cattle car. It was called *Playing for Time*, a pun that seems gruesome in light of the fact that nearly all the musicians died at the end.

These were my friends: there was Mary, tall and brassy, who once stared at her desk ferociously as the teacher read aloud a sentence she had written about Emerson's transparent eyeball; and there was Jamie, a showoff and a dancer, who had a streak of daffodil hair among coarse dark curls, she was born with it; and there was Elizabeth, with her witty bugged-out eyes and her deep-sea-crustacean privacy. She was the one the priest liked best. She knew absolutely everything about television, which at the time made her seem worldly and wise, rather than simply a person who watched a lot of television. We stayed after school and pretended to play our instruments, and the priest stayed too, for the entertainment. Picture that pageant of smooth-faced teenagers, practicing the rictus of real suffering while pretending to tootle on little flutes.

During school hours, the priest functioned as our sex-ed teacher, even though we knew everything about sex already. He used to waggle his head back and forth and say, "No beejays, girls! No handjobs!" There were three main things, in the nineties, that sophisticated people knew you could do besides have biblical intercourse. The third thing could not be spoken out loud, not in this room of the convent made almost completely of windows. The desks were arranged in a circle, which signaled it was an unconventional class where you could speak freely and ask the questions that really mattered, like could you get pregnant in a hot tub. Occasionally one of the mad downtown masturbators would appear at the windows to flash us, which was an education in itself, but by the time we called the police, they had always disappeared.

I ignored the priest as he told us what we could not do, and tapped my pen and thought about poetry. I never met any boys anyway. Only a few seminarians, from time to time. Only a few of my father's students. I stared down at my notebook that had the word "MORALITY" written on it in black block letters—that's what the class was officially called—and tried to dream up great last lines, ones that hit like a sock in the gut. As the priest lectured, the expression in his eyes was unchanging and his glasses flashed opaquely. His skin was so carnation-colored a blush would never have shown. You could not tell what he was thinking, which meant that later, people would say they knew it all along.

You see it coming a mile off, but I didn't, none of us did: the priest was arrested for having sex with a fourteen-year-old boy, and he went to jail soon after I was let out of high school for good. Everyone was shocked, everyone is always shocked. I was shocked—not because I had never witnessed it before, but because it had never been my priest. One of my classmates said, "All I can think about is the people he must have helped," but that didn't enter my mind. I was thinking about the cathedral, and its buttressed stone walkways in the middle of the air, where you saw black figures hurrying back and forth to their hidden business. I was thinking when a priest shone his spotlight of attention on you, it was always considered an honor, a sign you had been chosen. The boy had stood in that place too, and felt like the gleam off gold. I was conjuring the room where it must have happened, the sort of room I had been in a hundred times, with a desk and wood paneling and a stark brassy cross on the wall, where even the paperweights were religious and the potted plants kept their palms pressed together. And the ceiling was so low and the walls so close that you felt more inside than you ever felt elsewhere. And a priest was in it, and a boy.

"Oh, I knew him," the seminarian says. "I met him at a retreat when

I was twelve years old." My heart twists horribly inside me—other stories had come to light later, stories almost too black to write down. The priest had a habit of seeking out boys who thought they might have a religious calling, the serious-minded ones with bright auras, ones who wanted to stay up late into the night talking about what it might mean to give themselves to God. One of his victims drank antifreeze after an early teenage encounter with him—the pain and the shame, he said, were too much—and then was told he couldn't enter the priesthood because of this attempt on his life. He tried annihilation again when he was twenty-one, and this time he succeeded.

"Tell me you escaped," I say silently, as the seminarian describes how the priest shone that spotlight of attention on him. He gave him a relic—a piece of the One True Cross, of which there were no fewer than four thousand chunks floating around the greater St. Louis area, orbiting each other but never touching, burning holes in the khaki pockets of Christian teenagers. That was all that ever happened between them, but that was strange enough.

6

DINNER WITH THE BISHOP

There is always someone in a writer's family who is funnier and more original than she is—someone for her to quote and observe, someone to dazzle and dumbfound her, someone to confuse her so much she has to look things up in the dictionary. That would be my sister Mary, whom I worship as people used to worship the sun.

Every time I try to capture her and force her into my private zoo of description, I fail. I have, on different occasions and in different moods, described her as "a tricked-out club Chewbacca," a "highly literate female Tarzan," and "a jaguar who went through a human puberty." One thing is certain: she is straight out of Nature. She speaks a made-up language largely consisting of the words "ayyyy" and "baybay" in various combinations, interspersed with nuanced and meaningful growls. She's always wearing a tiny fur vest of some kind. If I tracked her through the woods on a snowy night, I am sure she would leave paw prints.

The first time she ever saw a *T. rex* skeleton in a museum, she stared at it with passionate attraction. I'm surprised she didn't try to climb up into its rib cage and hang there as its heart. "Ayyyy," she whispered in a voice full of emotion, "it's just a little baybay."

Unsurprisingly, she's the only one of us who ever made it all the way through college and got a real job. "I saw what happened to you and Christina, and I knew I had to do it myself, I had to figure it all out for myself," she has told me, and that is what she did. She chased the scholarships, she submitted the paperwork, she kept after my mother to file our taxes on time so she could apply for financial aid. She graduated from pharmacy school in 2012, and soon after married a fellow pharmacist, a soft-spoken man named Jon who seems to have drunk more milk in his life than other people. At their wedding, while attempting to fulfill the duties of a bridesmaid, I fell down the marble steps in front of the whole church, causing everyone except my father and my husband to burst into joyous laughter. Then, at the reception, I gave a sentimental toast where I pretended I had carried the bride and groom as twins in my womb. Later, I learned quite a few of the groom's guests believed I had extemporized the whole speech while on mushrooms. God bless them. If that's what mushrooms did, I would take them all the time.

Under the influence of tequila, she once wrenched a toilet paper dispenser off a bathroom wall and threw it in the Ohio River. Also under the influence of tequila, she once strode down the streets of historic Newport, Kentucky, grabbing fistfuls of leaves off the decorative trees while screaming, "I hate plants, bitch!" and daring unseen cops to arrest her. "COME AND GET ME!" she yelled, throwing her arms wide, slapping her chest, and ripping off a jacket that looked freshly killed. The pleasure is in never knowing what she's going to do next. I think when I threw that firecracker directly at her face, so long ago when we were children, it might have granted her the superpower of unpredictability.

. . .

A BREAK IN THE CLOUDS: Mary and Jon are driving in for the weekend so we can all go to dinner with the bishop. "It would mean a lot to your dad if you came," my mother hinted gently on the phone last time they talked, and my mother's gentle hints are law. "This is a big night for him—it's the seventy-fifth anniversary of his church, and the bishop is going to give a speech." Jason and I have promised to attend as well. My father wants the smaller congregation of his family to surround him again. He persists in considering us a credit to him, despite the fact that Mary is from the jungle, I am from the devil, and neither of our husbands has ever held a gun.

In the sideways light of late Friday afternoon, they pull into the shade of the spreading oak tree, and Mary leaps from the passenger seat of the car and runs to hug Mom. "Baby, how are you?" she cries, cupping her face in her hands, petting her red hair. "You look a little tired."

"I was up till four in the morning shredding documents," Mom informs her, the light of vigilance shining in her eyes. My mother shreds documents with the ruthlessness of a person who believes a French con artist named The Mustache is trying to steal her identity. Woe to The Mustache if he succeeded. As soon as he realized what living her life entails, he would very quickly give it back.

They go arm in arm through the yard, remarking on the disrespectfulness of the local squirrels, who, as my mother has observed, are "just a bunch of nasty little, horny little teenagers." "Oooo, how pretty!" Mary says, indicating the ornamental shrubs along the walkway. We are not at all fooled by this pleasantry. We know as soon as she gets a few drinks into her, the garden will be in real danger.

Mom points a dreadful finger at a clump of shiny leaves. "I've been after the handyman to burn this entire area, because I think that's poison sumac," she says. "I have told him many times that if I breathe poison sumac into my lungs, there will be serious consequences."

"Okay, Mom needs a glass of wine!" Mary hollers as she enters the house, and claps her hands to get the party started. She is, after all, a pharmacist. She knows what people need. The floor, I notice, is covered with hundreds of tiny slivers of evidence, the only kind of confetti my mother can enjoy.

"Wassup Tee," Mary says, hurling herself on me and stroking my ear. "Little beebee. Babygee."

"Hay booboo," I answer as an involuntary reflex, then cover my mouth with my hand.

"Jay! Burd!" she calls to my husband. "Ay JayJay!"

"Mur," he responds. "MurMur."

"Gurl," my mother says graciously, as Mary gives her a glass of wine.

"How's it going, J-money," Jon asks Jason in a businessman's no-nonsense tone.

"Dawg," Jason says, shaking his hand as a show of respect.

My father comes in through the side door, cooing to his puppy as he goes. "Ay baybay," Mary greets him, in the same vein in which she began.

A silence as he lifts his black dress over his head and hangs it on the back of the basement door. Then, "Hey bay-bee," he replies.

I turn to Jason, much struck. "The random nicknames . . . the bizarre ejaculations and fake catchphrases . . . the mispronunciations of the word 'baby'? It's Dad. *It's all Dad.*"

"Hahaha," Mary says, overhearing. "Tricia. T-rish. Ya big dino. Ya old *bitch*."

. . .

"WHAT ARE YOU GOING to wear tonight?" she asks me, perching on the edge of the guest-room bed and looking at my current outfit with great pity. I can't blame her. Ever since we came, I've taken to dressing like a nun who is extremely cold—mostly out of respect for the seminarian, who has "gone up to the lake" with the other seminarians this weekend and won't be able to join us. She refrains from mentioning my head at all, understanding certain things cannot be helped. As I lack the money for a proper cut, my once-chic short hair has recently reached a stage I can only refer to as Fashion Hitler.

"Don't worry, I have the perfect thing," Mary purrs, slapping me on the butt. She rummages in her suitcase for a minute and then presents me with something the size of a panty, composed largely of spandex and black mesh.

"Go try it on, baby!" she calls, throwing one arm up to the ceiling, as if she's expecting an angel to hand her down a mimosa. I take it to the bathroom, strip down, and somehow rearrange my atoms to fit inside it. Could it even be called a dress? I ask the mirror, philosophically. It ends fourteen inches above my knee. The mesh is so see-through it opens a window onto my soul. Wearing this in front of the bishop would be tantamount to going to confession again.

I exit the bathroom and they study me. My mother gasps like she's been stabbed in the park. Jon averts his eyes, as if at the terrible passing of an eclipse. My sister hollers something that can be transcribed only as "GIT IT GYOORL!" and then performs a brief indecent dance against the arm of the couch.

"YOU'RE NOT WEARING THAT!" my father yells, appearing out of nowhere to loom large in the doorway. For a man who only ever wants to be naked and spread-eagled in front of other people, he sure has a lot of provincial ideas about clothing. I turn around and shut myself in the bathroom again.

THE DINNER STARTS in just an hour. In the end, I dive deep into my single garbage bag of clothes and decide on a silky blue dress with lounging cats printed all over it, to show my allegiance. It has a round schoolgirl collar, to remind me to behave myself. I look decent, but Mary, once she finishes getting ready, is even more glorious than usual. Her hair looks like a lion explosion. Her outfit is almost impossible to deconstruct. Is it a dress . . . over another dress . . . over a pair of pants? Is she wearing three shoes? Atop all of it, she is sporting a businesslike white coat, to remind us she is in charge of the drugs.

"Are you ready for me bishop," she says in a low, threatening voice, holding up her paws.

Noticing that we seem jittery, Jason proposes we all take a shot to strengthen ourselves—well, all except Mom, who believes shots are a sin. Then we take another, just to be safe, and set out in high spirits for the church. The shots take quick effect. Halfway across the parking lot, we break into a spontaneous tribute to Biggie's "Hypnotize":

"Bishie bishie bishie, can't you see
Sometimes your Mass just hypnotize me
And I just love your flashy ways—"

"Guess that's why tha pope says you're so saved," Jason finishes in a rich baritone.

"Oh, *nooooooo*," Jon says softly, as he always does when something's funny. "Oh, nooooooo!"

WE ENTER THE CHURCH and take the elevator downstairs, where the doors open on a cross-stitched portrait of the Virgin Mary, holding a malformed fiber-art Jesus against her chest and rolling her eyes back in her head with suffering. I know just how she feels. The light of the basement throbs and fluoresces, and shines down on all our defects. My mother guides me over to the bishop to introduce me. "He's a saint," my mother, my father, and the seminarian have all assured me with the utmost sincerity. "He can tell anything about a person just by looking at them." Anything? I think back to my first confession, when I simply sat in the booth across from the priest and streamed tears, because I had once lied to the school principal about a winter hat.

"This is our second-oldest daughter, Tricia," my mother tells the bishop, and a sweet, unprejudiced smile spreads across his face. Ha! The man doesn't know who he's dealing with. I lie about hats every day. To anyone. *And I never cry about it anymore.*

"And what do you do?" he asks.

"She's a poet," my mother says, knowing instinctively that this is one of the few jobs bishops have to respect. King David, after all, was a poet. He was also a man who liked to krump down the street and bang the clean wives of soldiers whom he would later have murdered, but somehow the poetry is never counted among these more questionable peccadilloes.

Behind me, exactly in tandem, I can hear a member of the congregation asking my husband what *he* does.

"I work in newspapers."

"Oh, a member of the media," comes the sorrowful response.

We check our seating cards and discover the whole family has been assigned a place of honor on a dais at the front of the room. A hundred kind faces are turned toward us with respect and admiration; it's a living nightmare. I close my eyes and visualize a stretch of empty white beach, far away from it all. No, that's no good. Any minute now a missionary is going to land on shore and whack me with a Bible for being naked. Next to me, I can feel Jason slump into a corpselike position. I can tell he's practicing Progressive Relaxation, where you relax your body parts one by one until you feel so calm you're almost dead. He finds it works for him in stressful situations.

A row of priests, with the bishop at the center, is sitting just parallel to us, so that I'm making eye contact with at least one man of God wherever I turn. Mary and I play a frightened footsie underneath the table, lacking any other outlet for communication. "Our salvation has arrived," Jon tells us on the way back from a trip to the bathroom. *"The alcohol is free."* He is carrying an armful of Mountain Vodka Dews, a sophisticated yellow cocktail he invented two minutes ago, and he distributes them with the efficiency of a nurse passing out pills in paper cups. "Keep them coming," we instruct him, and he nods. There is also champagne in the middle of the table, which we drink in the panicked moments when we find ourselves between Mountain Vodka Dews. Never in my life have I needed so much liquid reinforcement.

One of the men of God is pacing back and forth behind the banquet table, addressing the crowd, telling the sorts of jokes you only ever hear at church functions. Often these jokes involve sporting events that are being broadcast that day, and then all the men groan, because they love sports very much and would rather be watching them, but just kidding, because

Jesus is a football that all of us can carry down the field for the win. Other times they involve pop culture figures the priests perceive to be current, such as the Power Rangers and Cher. After a beat, I recognize the man who's talking—he's the priest who's always coming over at odd hours of the day to confess his sins to my father. When that happens, we all have to vanish instantly. Once Jason got trapped in the basement for three hours because my dad forgot to tell him he could come back up. "He must have been extra bad this time," he said when we finally let him out.

When the priest is finished, the bishop himself takes the microphone and begins to speak. He is a sweeping black figure accented with fuchsia, and appears to have been dressed in the morning by spiritual birds, fresh off the outstretched fingers of St. Francis of Assisi.

He has the look of someone whom a great deal of reverent attention has been poured into for a long time. He begins to list my father's accomplishments, his years of service, his dedication, and my father's face flushes. The bishop makes the predestined joke about football, and my father laughs, long and loud enough to reveal the gap on one side of his mouth where a molar was removed a while back. When I see that black space I feel the same tenderness that wells up when I look at pictures of the Sacred Heart, that tenderness just where the thorn touches the meat—an empathy for his body I could not possibly feel for his mind. "This guy seems nice," Jason whispers, raising his Mountain Vodka Dew toward the bishop. "It's hard to believe he drinks human blood."

Suspecting these speeches are going to continue for a while, I address myself to my catered meal, which is chunks of the lord crucified on a tall Golgotha of green beans. I eat with gusto. Jason passes me his plate and I polish his off too. I look fondly at my sister across the table as I chew, and think how much we have in common. We both make this little snort in the back of our throats while we eat, a sort of airy hog sound that comes and goes at will. I'm sure it's the result of some inner deformity. Absorbed in thoughts of my heritage, I forget myself for a moment and shove an entire medallion of christ into my mouth at the exact moment I hear the words "We're very lucky to have Father Greg's daughters with us tonight. Stand up, girls!" I gulp, and the medallion lodges halfway down my gullet. I shake my Fashion Hitler playfully at the bishop, as if to say that modesty does not permit me to make such an exhibition of myself. "Go ahead, let the people get a look at you!" I stand with all the grace I can summon, and Mary, her keen medical eye alerting her to the fact that I am choking, whacks me on the back as if to congratulate me. Tears begin to trickle down my right cheek. I raise my arm and wave to the congregation, which murmurs with approval and appreciation. I press my hand to my lips, as if overcome with emotion, and spit a whole wet mouthful of meat into it.

A teenage quartet erupts into jazz, signaling the end of the speeches and the beginning of the party. The teens are dressed as Bible salesmen, in black slacks and black ties and white shirts, and the jazz they're playing sounds suspiciously Christian—there's no heroin or adultery in it at all. What are they doing here on a Saturday night? We should all be out drag racing, having knife fights, and getting arrested. We should be playing chicken on a deserted road up by the old quarry, then dying intoxicated in the arms of our busty, pink-sweatered girlfriends. Instead, we're trapped together here. I walk past them and hurl a dollar into their midst, hoping it will persuade them to let loose and play something a girl can get pregnant to.

"Jazzon," Jason says, standing up and executing a vigorous male pirouette. "What if I spelled it *Jazzon*." He used to play the horn himself when he was younger—perhaps that was his first step down the path of immorality. Jazz presents many temptations. The stand-up bass is shaped exactly like a woman, and the saxophone is just a trumpet that's trying to blow itself. No wonder the seminarian had to give it up.

The room, I regret to report, is drunk. Very irresponsible of it. It's whirling around, and it keeps flinging parishioners at me. "I could feel your intelligence shining at me all the way across the basement," one woman tells me, leaning close to deliver her message, smelling of baby powder and church flowers and her smile a wide watermelon slice. I forgot that to members of the congregation, my sister and I are Celebs. They are indifferent to the existence of actual Celebs, with their side-boobs and their gay divorces, but at the approach of anything belonging to the priesthood, their faces lift and bloom. They touch you shyly, with a hint of timid ownership. They tell you things about yourself that you've always suspected to be true, such as "You wear an aura of holiness wherever you go," and "You look like that one girl on TV." My intelligence DOES shine, I flatter myself. My aura of holiness is so bright even bats can see it. I DO look like that one girl on TV! Our voices change when we talk to them, they fold themselves up into white linen napkins. We sound as polite and well-bred as our mother. "Thank you," we say, "thank you so much!"

I suddenly feel a claustrophobia I haven't felt since I was a teenager and still a believer. There is the clamor of so many human lives in one room. There is the panic that always rises in church places, that I've been shut up in a dark stall, herded into a stable with my kind. When you are born, you walk on the ark. The ark is the earth. From there, the elephants go with the elephants, and the little gold mites with the little gold mites. It makes me long to see a different animal, from a different story. I wish Grendel would burst into the hall and eat us.

Another parishioner toddles up to us. His name is George and he has been in a war. He points an accusing finger at me. "She's cute," he pronounces in a sly, sepulchral voice, then toddles away again, having unburdened both his heart and his loins.

The compliment from George recalls me to my lighter self. I throw a wink at one of the female caterers, but the wink is unfortunately intercepted by the bishop. He smiles with encouragement, as if I just expressed interest in entering the convent. I wonder what would happen if I sent a Mountain Vodka Dew over to him with my regards. We haven't gotten to chat as much as I would like! I have a few things I want to say to him about condoms.

I glance at Mary and notice her pumping her pelvis subtly in her chair. She's trying to hide her true nature from the bishop, but this is difficult when a teenage jazz quartet is releasing such smooth and carnal music into the atmosphere. My dollar worked! We both feel it is important to express ourselves through dance, and begin to edge our way to the center of the floor. We are interrupted, however, by the approach of a slow-stepping but determined George, who is back and eager to resume our conversation. He points at me. "She's cute," he repeats, and then toddles away again, just as before.

The room is finally so wasted it's barfing all the people inside it into the night. Time to go home. The bishop bids us good-bye. "I will look up your poems," he tells me, and I physically restrain myself from saying, "Please don't do that." Mary makes a gentlemanly move to kiss his ring, but I grab her by the hand and drag her behind me. She has passed the point of no return, and if I don't get her out of here soon, who knows what will happen.

Outside, the moon is casting a powdery round halo, the kind that draws you up toward it like the silhouette of a wolf. Mary, responding to its call, regresses to full bestiality. She wiggles out of my grasp and is gone like a flash across the parking lot. Despite all her clothes, she gives the impression of streaking. When we catch up to her, we find her engaged in gleeful and wholesale destruction of the front yard. "Fuck the police!" she shrieks, kicking crazily at the poison sumac. "Ahahaha!" She wrenches one of the decorative stones out of the landscaping and hurls it at the rectory. With a warlike cry, she leaps three feet in the air and high-fives the American flag that hangs above the door. Jon wrestles her down with one neat motion and carries her bodily into the house.

My father is spreading his legs wide on the couch and my mother has two bottles of champagne in her fists and is attempting to drink out of both of them at once, punctuating her refreshment with unlawful whoops. She raises one of the bottles to The Stobart, as if to christen its prow. She had only one glass at dinner, but she has the exquisitely low alcohol tolerance of all Flamm women, the tolerance that is currently causing my sister to crawl seductively across the floor on all fours, mouthing come-ons at the tiger painting. Not that I'm any better. I found a crayon and a scrap of paper somewhere, and I'm writing it all down.

"I think that went well," my father says, showering the great big blessing of a smile all over us. He has known us since the minute we were born. We are bone of his bone, flesh of his flesh, and just bad enough to keep him in business. God made us; we are little green apples.

THE NEXT MORNING, to the accompaniment of a mental marching band, I decide to look up the bishop, since waking up with a hangover is the closest I ever get to feeling like a detective. I sit cross-legged on the bed in the middle of wild white sheets and read newspaper clipping after newspaper clipping, several from *The Kansas City Star*, which my father has accused of having a particular vendetta against the Church. (The only newspaper he doesn't consider unforgivably liberal is *The Cincinnati Enquirer*, which I think endorsed a crucifix in the 2004 election.) The clippings are not under the impression that the bishop is a living saint.

In 2012, Robert Finn was the first American bishop to be criminally charged for failing to report suspected child abuse. After a Kansas City priest named Father Shawn Ratigan tried to commit suicide by running his motorcycle in a closed garage, Finn and his diocese learned Ratigan had hundreds of pictures of children on his computer, including a photo of a toddler with her diaper pulled away to expose her genitals. This wasn't their first warning: the principal of the Catholic school next to the parish where Ratigan served had previously sent a memorandum to the diocese, saying of the priest: "Parents, staff members, and parishioners are discussing his actions and whether or not he may be a child molester." After the suicide attempt, Finn and the diocese waited five months before informing police. Instead of turning in Ratigan, Finn ordered him to undergo a psychological evaluation and then sent him away to a convent, with orders to have no more contact with children. During that time, Ratigan took more pictures of kids he met through the church. He was eventually sentenced to fifty years in prison after pleading guilty to five counts of producing child pornography. Finn was sentenced to two years of probation for shielding him.

I CONNECT THE NAME RATIGAN with a bizarre snippet I heard floating around the house: "They took his computer, and they found panties hidden in his planter." "Panties in a planter?" I thought at the time, not knowing what they were talking about. What was he trying to do, grow more? I drill down into those details: panties in a planter, a motorcycle in a garage, a computer in a convent. Beloved daughters and trusting parents. If you live with the details, even briefly, the newsprint vanishes and the real scene appears, impossible to dismiss or forget.

Bishop Finn is the man I met last night, who asked if I wanted a picture with him. He really thought I might; many of the people he meets do. Here is the smile, here is the hand that signs the documents, here is the measured voice that tells the priests they must go away until everything dies down. Nothing permanent, of course, nothing ever permanent. Here is the little hat, which confers total power. Here are the glasses through which the eyes scan the numbers, how much it is worth, how much must be paid out. Here is the compassion in the face, that flowed toward the sinner and never the sinned-against, that forgave before justice had even been meted out.

How am I still held by the code of silence? Why do I feel it's a betrayal to even write this down, these facts that float freely in the public domain? "Oh, a member of the media," as if the collection, arrangement, and publication of the facts is the real crime.

Renata Adler wrote: "'He has suffered enough' meant if we investigate this matter any further, it will turn out our friends are in it, too." To the best of my knowledge, no bishop or archbishop my father ever served under was innocent of participating in cover-ups, shuffling papers, hushing up victims, sending offenders away for rest and rehabilitation. When I looked up Bishop Finn, I held my breath until I came to the sentence that laid it bare. I held my breath because I knew it would come.

. . .

THOSE SNIPPETS ALWAYS FLOATED through the house. We knew things the way you know about that one high school teacher or that one babysitter or that one coach or that one scout leader, except our neighborhood spanned the whole country. The topic of which priests had been removed from their parishes, which priests had been ordered not to interact with children, which priests had been sent off for counseling, and who had been arrested was discussed over the dinner table. When the first wave of scandals broke, in 2002, I felt briefly confused. Didn't everyone know? Or was it just that no one had access to that accumulation of information, that stack of maybe and possibly and definitely, that constellation of things we knew and things we guessed and things we suspected?

At my father's current parish, he took the place of a priest who was under suspicion, and I don't think that was the first time he was ever sent somewhere to restore a congregation's faith. People place more trust in him—he's married, he has children. He wouldn't want you to draw a lesson from that, but I don't see how you could help it. At his last assignment, the previous priest had covered his walls with pictures of boys torn out of Norman Rockwell books, their peachy faces scrawled over with crazed capitalized words about "temptation" and "the youth." "When we first moved in," my mother told me, "every surface of the house was covered with collages and writing, even the mirrors." She cleaned the house from top to bottom until it was livable again. Somehow, that had always been part of her duties.

I REMEMBER THE CLAUSTROPHOBIA of last night, the feeling that I was too much with my kind, that I had been shut up with people who had as many spots as I did. When I left the church originally, was it because suddenly those spots seemed of a different nature? Did I leave in protest? That would have been foolish, any priest would tell you. That would have meant I had lost my perspective, had misplaced the blame, was ultimately only punishing myself. But religion, above all, must recognize the power of the symbol. It must recognize the power of standing up and sitting down. If the church teaches anything, it's that sometimes we have to answer for what other people have done. Let me do it by standing up and walking out of the countinghouse, and saving my number for the smaller side.

All my life I have overheard, all my life I have listened to what people will let slip when they think you are part of their we. A we is so powerful. It is the most corrupt and formidable institution on earth. Its hands are full of the crispest and most persuasive currency. Its mouth is full of received, repeating language. The we closes its ranks to protect the space inside it, where the air is different. It does not protect people. It protects its own shape.

You have belonged to many of them. So have I. The church was one of mine—it was my family. The story of a family is always a story of complicity. It's about not being able to choose the secrets you've been let in on. The question, for someone who was raised in a closed circle and then leaves it, is what is the *us*, and what is the *them*, and how do you ever move from one to the other?

IN THE NOT-SO-FAR FUTURE, Bishop Finn will be forced to resign by Pope Francis, who is proving to be a figure worthy of some study. My father will publish a letter of staunch support in the church bulletin, suggesting that the bishop was being persecuted for his conservative beliefs, that in fact he had committed no crime at all, and that the prosecutor in his case was a mercenary with "strong ties to the abortion industry." I will be so disheartened by this that I can barely speak to him or meet his eyes for weeks. Though later he will tell my mother, with perhaps the first stirrings of doubt, "I'm beginning to think any one of them would have done it. That the position is more powerful than the man."

7

PUT IT IN PRINT

A t the end of July, when the air outside is sweltering and the air inside is the approximate temperature of a glacier, the online magazine *The Awl* publishes a long poem of mine called "Rape Joke." I wrote it in a strong fluent flood down in Savannah, sitting in a white towel on the edge of the bed while afternoon sunlight lavished over my shoulders and my coffee left a cold ring in its cup. Poetry is a companion: you sit with it mostly in silence, and look up from your reading every once in a while and nod to it, and sometimes there are great rushes of like-minded, sentence-finishing conversation. It came all at once, the lines racing off the edges of the pages as if to jump back into the stream of present time: all of it happened again, red and fresh, but I could move my body through the narration as I could not move it through that night. Beads along a razor blade, but this time I controlled the cut. I didn't know if I ought to publish it, because I never wrote about the things that really happened to me, the real things. But after enough time passes, you can publish a poem like that without feeling your own palpitating heart is doing the New Year's drop in Times Square, watched by a million people, reflecting back a face to every one.

Usually publishing a poem is like puking in space, or growing an adolescent mustache—no one really notices, and it might be better that way. Something about this one catches, though, and in the space of a day it is everywhere. Thousands of replies, messages, and emails pour into my various inboxes. A dozen girls send me their own versions of the poem, filled in with their own details. One friend writes, "The same thing happened to me, except a week later he gave me a book about the Beatles with the words 'I'm sorry' written in it."

Finally I come downstairs, wrung out from responding to this avalanche, and see my mother sitting in the dimness of a soft, bruised dusk, her face illuminated by her laptop screen. There are tracks down her cheeks.

"I just read it," she says, quiet, below the sound of my father's voice in the next room. He and the seminarian are discussing the case of a priest in St. Louis who was recently caught forcing a fourteen-year-old girl into his car and kissing her—in the parking lot of the cathedral, no less, because the scene would be incomplete without that one grotesque detail that makes everything rouse to life. "She shouldn't have put him in that position," I hear a male voice say, and an old familiar wildness flutters up my chest and into my throat, sending feathers and flames into my voice box until I cannot speak, that same phoenix heat that still rises up in me no matter how many times I force it down.

"I just read it," my mother repeats in her lowest and most doom-filled tone. "THE RAPE JOKE."

This would be the wrong moment to laugh, but I almost do, remembering the time we drove past a bridge in Cincinnati that was famous for being painted purple, and my mother turned to me with enormous, electrified eyes and said, "Someone got raped, Tricia. *Someone got raped on the Purple People Bridge.*"

She stands and embraces me, more to give herself comfort than to impart it, and her hands describe small circles all over my back. I do not melt into it—the memory of the original pain, and the night I snuck into my parents' room to tell them, and their reaction, is still too vivid. It prickles over the skin like a sweat, or a flush. My mind fixes on the indelible image of kneeling next to my mother's side of the bed, in that bedroom filled with decorative gold balls, and telling her what had happened, and her asking with a sob, "But you didn't sleep with him beforehand, did you?" And when I told her I had, of my father rising, holding me against his great patriarchal stomach, and making the sign of the cross over me to absolve me of my sins. It moves next to the image of sitting in the cold, clinical office of the pro-life gynecologist my mother had designated for all her daughters, and telling him what had happened and hearing him say, "Well, now you've learned that you can't trust everyone, can you," in a voice wiped entirely of human sympathy, as he squared my file with two brisk taps against his desk and stood to leave. It must have been then I began to suspect, something is not right with the way these people have arranged the world, no matter what their intentions.

"You're still here. You're still standing," my mother says now, and then I do relax. It is sweet, sometimes, to hear clichés after long days of trying to say something new. And to be fair, since we can never really see into people's minds or motives, the actual reason she chose that gynecologist might have been because the other doctors in his practice were named Dr. WeeWee and Dr. Bosom, which was a symmetry she would have been powerless to resist.

"I hope your father doesn't read it," she adds, but to my knowledge, my father has never read anything I've written, for one simple reason: no submarines.

"Did you see some of those comments, though?" she asks, dabbing her eyes and sinking back into her chair. "One of them said drinking alcohol around men was like smearing yourself with salmon oil and blackberry juice and walking into a forest full of bears. No it isn't! It's not like that at all!"

Now it is my turn to soothe. "No, no, no, no, no, no, Mom," I tell her. "You must never look at the comments."

Back in bed, watching shadows slash across the ceiling, I draw the comforter up to my chin and try to keep my teeth from chattering. I have almost never felt so bare—something even beyond bare, as if some interior room had been turned inside out and I found it was large enough to contain the whole world. *What have I done?* I ask myself, wishing suddenly to return to yesterday, when no one knew and I was no one's confessor, but then I call up the perfect rhythm of that afternoon in Savannah and am calmed. A trick I often use, when I feel overwhelming shame or regret, or brokenness beyond repair, is to think of a line I especially love, or a poem that arrived like lightning, and remember that it wouldn't have come to me if anything in my life had happened differently. Not that way. Not in those words.

TWO DAYS LATER, I wake from a dream of God creating the pig for the first time. I have these dreams at least once a week now, and they always mean my father is in the kitchen cooking a whole pound of bacon. I yawn, begin to sip the milky tea that Jason has left for me on the bedside table, and open my email.

There is a note from the editor of the Penguin Poets Series, who had asked to see my manuscript about six months earlier. He apologizes for not responding to me sooner, but says he read my collection again the other night, and found it to be so *blank* and so *blank*, two words that look like fireworks, and he would like to publish it next year if I am willing.

I spill hot tea on my naked boob, but I don't even notice. There is something about an acceptance. It makes the blood and the brain effervesce; it climbs the ladder of the happiness you felt in the heat of the work. There is no jolt like it, except the one you would experience in grade school, when just after lunchtime your English teacher would say, "Today in class we will be writing a story." And your fingertips would turn to glad ice, and the bottoms of your feet would thrill, and the bologna sandwich in your stomach would flip over, because she was speaking directly to you. If I am ever medically dead, try whispering that in my ear and see if I don't sit up again gasping, ready all over as the tip of a pen. *Today we will be writing a story.*

My first book had been published in 2012 by an indie press that paid in copies: a hundred for every thousand printed, so that after a while, you found yourself with a definite surplus. Before that, I remember only a decade of desperate unconnectedness and of knowing no one, which towered like a pile of unread papers. If reading was the highest form of seeing, how would I become visible? I had no professors to guide me, no fellow students to accompany me on my way. The few times I snuck into a university library, hungry to dip into the books I could not find elsewhere, I felt I was about to be tackled any moment by the police. Once I crept into the stacks at Washington University, where my sister Christina had so hoped to study music, and I can still feel the sharp stamp of bricks against my back as I crouched in a shadowy corner with my paper, scratching out the line "teeth infinite white and infinite many" with the wild lawlessness and curtailed breath of someone who lives in a country where poetry is illegal.

I wrote and Jason licked envelopes and we sent out; I slept with pencils under my pillow and scribbled images on the backs of my diner order pads; we scraped together twenty-dollar entrance fees for contests I did not win. Every poem of mine that was ever accepted was picked out of the slush pile. It went on that way for ten years. I stood strangely by myself, a shifting, shimmering, mutable manuscript in my hand, new poems roosting in it and other poems departing, first poems about Jesus, now poems about murder, now poems about lizard people for some reason—and came no closer to being acknowledged by that great, scanning eye which didn't know I existed. What reached out of me then must have been ambition, but it felt like longing.

Still, remembering the raw crackle of that poem racing to the four corners, I think, "This was the price? This was the purchase of entry, into that closed and impregnable world?"

If it had been a letter, Jason would have snatched it out of my hand and clasped it to his heaving breast. Instead, he makes me read the email to him over and over, until my voice begins to sing in its familiar course. "You did it," he says, bursting into tears. "This is just like when an animal succeeds in a movie."

"There's nothing in this rulebook that says a dog can't play basketball!"

"There's nothing in the Constitution that says a lizard person can't be president!"

We high-five and race each other downstairs, toward the ever-present scent of bacon.

My father, sipping hazelnut coffee out of an oversized mug that reads I LOVE MY "WHITE-COLLAR" JOB! is really delighted. He chuckles, the way he does when the rogue cop gets the better of the by-the-book police chief. "I told them you could make it on your own," he says, almost to himself. "Hoo-hoo, bay-bee. I told them you didn't need to go to school." He has always revised history to larger and smaller degrees, but lately the revisions are so complete as to be disquieting. Within a year's time, he will have progressed to the story that I stood in that room and told him college couldn't teach me anything anyway, because writers didn't need it.

"Congratulations!" the seminarian cries when we tell him. Then, taking into account my roosterish hair, my cutoffs, and the striped Ernie shirt I threw on in my haste, "Wow, you really DO look like a monster in the morning."

That night, stretched out across the bed with the cat in a chinchilla curve on the small of his back, Jason asks me to read the email again. "You'll get a thousand dollars when you sign the contract, and then another thousand when the book comes out," he says, his eyes so wide that I see the bionic flash of his lenses, the one that always reminds me that I am outside of him and his most fundamental perceptions, that we have brought different pasts to our place of overlap. "Maybe we'll be able to move out sooner than we thought." A little candle lights in him. It is hope, and it is necessary, because I know he is starting to feel it: the craziness of the house, closing in on him too.

THE SORT OF DIARY that fixes my body in time and space, that records the weather and my moods and what my rosebushes are doing, has always been impossible for me. As soon as I begin to set down the facts, the old childhood chorus of *Is that true? Is that really true?* starts up, and I hesitate, and then I scratch out the sentences until they're solid black.

Here, though, I find myself carrying around a slim cardboard notebook and a felt-tip pen and jotting down everything everyone says, as fast and free as it comes out of their mouths, feathering the fresh ink as I go. Sometimes I just sit in the dining room with my cheek propped on my fist and transcribe my father's running commentary while he's watching sports. ("I like Chunky Soup . . . *oh yeahhh* . . . I'd like to have a whole room full of that stuff. Make it Sirloin Burger," he said last week as he and his dog watched commercials. The mental image this conjured may never leave me.) There is something pleasant about this, almost like having a real job again. It forces me to participate in the household, in the regular course of human days, which I have so long ignored. Occasionally it even forces me to attend breakfast, with its pointless toast and stupid eggs, for fear of missing one of my mother's literary eruptions. I haven't fully formulated what I'm doing yet, but I carry a notebook and listen, and Jason listens for me when I am not there. "Oh my god, you will never *believe*," he tells me, breathless from running up the stairs, his tummy bulging with whatever my mother most recently fed him. "Don't worry. I wrote it all down for you on a napkin." I smooth out the napkin and read:

"Did you know rats in big cities are getting aggressive from eating too many cigarette butts? They're addicted to nicotine and they want more." —Karen Lockwood, *nearly screaming, while eating an omelet at a breakfast restaurant in the year of our Lord 2013*

I copy it conscientiously into the notebook. Ever since I confessed I might be writing about her, my mother has risen to heights of quotability exceeded only by Confucius, Muhammad Ali, and that guy who was always saying things like "You have hissed all my mystery lectures. You have tasted a whole worm." She claps her hands joyously at me and commands, "Quote it!" She has been shy since she was a young girl, in knee-socks and prim pointed collars. She blushed whenever anyone looked at her, so fully and furiously up to the hairline that classmates called her Red. She is one of those fabled survey respondents who would rather die than stand up in a spotlight or give a speech, but still she wants the same thing I did: to meet the ideal reader. To be visible, at last, in words she has chosen.

"I can see right through you," my father used to tell me when I was little, and the cringe of that feeling, of being transparent to God and everyone, was so strong that I swore off all forms of autobiography for a long time. How could I be sure I was telling the truth about myself when he claimed to know me better than I did? How could I state anything with absolute certainty—whether I liked a particular song, or wanted to get up and go for a walk, or even whether I was hungry or thirsty? The only time I didn't feel like a liar was when people asked me what I did and I told them that *I wrote*, and then I became a great ivy-wrapped I, just as I would have been in the illuminated manuscript. Of course that is what I would grow up to do. Of course I would find a way to live inside that sure, swift, unassailable answer. My heart fluttered and faltered within me; it was not strong and I knew it; I would replace it with that sweet pang of purpose that came chasing after *Today we will be writing a story.*

That was the bargain, and I shook my own hand on it. I would write forever, but not about myself and not about what happened, and never about my most profound and deforming secrets—that I had been raised in an alternate reality, that my childhood sky was green. There were many, many other things to occupy me, I reasoned: Dialogues Between the Pines and lewd copy for dildo catalogs, for starters. But how long can you outrun your subject, when your subject is your own life? Dialogues Between Pines and lewd dildo copy are necessary contributions in their way, but it seems more necessary, back in this house and back under this roof, to simply record what I can see from where I am. Everyone gets a window. This is what mine looks out on: that same stunning, disorienting view; that square of deep green sky.

8

TOUCH OF GENIUS

didn't kill him," comes a spectral voice over the phone. "At least, not all the way."

Groggy, I reach for the alarm clock and squint at the blood-red numbers. It appears to be fourteen in the morning, but that's not a real time. "Who is this?"

"It's your mother." She sounds offended. "Who gave birth to you without anesthesia. Anyway, I've had a little accident."

"Where are you?" It occurs to me that I haven't seen her in a while. I've been completely absorbed in writing a poem called "Genie Penis," about the little tip of the genie that goes down into the lamp, and I haven't left my room much for the past week. Her answer could be as various as either "downstairs," "at the grocery store," "in Canada," or "playing chess with a chimp in a rocket ship." I brace myself for the unexpected.

"I'm in Cincinnati, visiting your brothers and sisters. I snuck out of the rectory two nights ago, under cover of darkness." She's always sneaking out of the rectory under cover of darkness so my father doesn't catch her and trap her under a vast pile of his laundry. The fact that her children live in three different cities means she long ago mastered the art of trilocation, much like the godhead himself. "I peeked into your room before I left and asked if you wanted to come with me, but you sat up in bed and gave me the finger and said you needed to stay home to get ideas for your writing."

Yeah, that sounds like me. "Wait a minute, go back. You had an accident? What happened?"

She takes a deep, shuddering breath. *"A pedestrian ran into thegrindup .com."*

That is not an English sentence, I recognize. Let me explain. thegrindup.com is a rap entourage van my sister Christina purchased for the express purpose of conveying her six children from one place to another. Modern vehicles are no longer built with Irish procreative capabilities in mind, so when you get to the point where you have six children and are pregnant with your seventh, your only options for transportation are church buses and rap entourage vans. My sister has a sense of style, so she picked the second, and found it a perfect match for her needs. It's a van of transcendent beauty, black as a stallion and glossy, with the magnificent website address WWW.THEGRINDUP.COM stenciled hugely across one side. Its size cannot be overstated. All the clowns in the world could fit inside.

According to legend, The Grindup was an up-and-coming St. Louis rapper who spread the word about his work by driving thegrindup.com up and down the city streets while his friends partied in the back. One day they must have partied too hard, because the van ended up at a police auction, where my sister acquired it. She plastered the back with Catholic radio bumper stickers, which was the final insult, because if you've ever listened to Catholic radio then you know the flow is awful and the beats are not remotely tasty. Not only can you not dance to it, but it makes you want to lie down on the ground and never move again. It's just a bunch of call-in shows where people talk about whether something is a sin or not, and they almost always decide that it is, in fact, a sin. If the sad transmissions of Catholic radio ever reach the aliens, they will never even try to conquer us, figuring that some other overlord has already taken care of it.

She continues her tragic tale. "I was driving past a bus stop when a man wearing earbuds suddenly raced out into the middle of the street. He was listening to *music*," she says, aggrieved. "You can't listen to music all the time or else you get hit by a car. By my car," she amends.

"He just ran smack into the front corner of the van and bounced off. You should see the dent he made. He was quite a large man; I'd say he weighed at least two hundred and eighty pounds. People say it isn't good to be big, but sometimes if you're not big . . . you're dead."

I'm aware I'm making the low continuous moaning noise of a fearful cow, but I can't seem to stop. This is the worst story I've ever heard. This is worse than *Ethan Frome*.

"Luckily I was only going about thirty miles an hour. Oh, Tricia, you should have heard the meaty sound. It was so frightening. I slammed on the brakes, and your sister jumped out of the front seat and began to yell at his body."

"She *what*?"

"Tricia, she's pregnant. You have to be alert when you're pregnant or else you become vulnerable to predators. It's a biological adaptation."

"Ah. Well, I can't argue with that," I say, silently adding . . . *without making myself crazy for the rest of my life*. "I guess we're just lucky she didn't experience a sudden craving and try to eat him."

"The worst part is that all of your sister's kids were riding in the backseat, and they saw everything. They were so upset, but they knew what to do. After they stopped crying, they started reciting Hail Marys in perfect unison."

Well, at least someone is getting influenced by the incantatory power of the rap van. According to my mother, the only one who didn't pray was the second-oldest child, Aria, who heard the sirens speeding toward them and calmly decided they were all going to jail, where perhaps they would meet The Grindup for the first time.

"What happened to the poor pedestrian?" I ask.

"He broke his arm, and he'll be afraid of vans for the rest of his life. But he's alive."

I can't believe I missed this. "Stay home to get ideas for my writing," indeed. The reality is, I wouldn't know a good idea if it ran over me while driving a two-ton black van called thegrindup.com. Then again, it's probably better I wasn't there. If I had been riding along, I have no doubt my mother would have killed the man completely.

After I hang up, I come downstairs and find my father subjecting the seminarian to an actual fashion show, sashaying back and forth in the new crimson robe he just bought from a dying nonagenarian priest who was selling off all of his clothes in preparation for his entrance into heaven.

"The embroidery!" the seminarian swoons, on the point of losing consciousness. "Do you see the detail on those lambs?"

"Dad, did you hear—"

He cuts me off. "I heard that your mother has creamed a man." He shakes his head, as if he always saw it coming. "A dangerous woman," he says with a hint of awe in his voice, smoothing the loose gold threads of his symbols. "An unbelievably dangerous woman."

. . .

THE MACHINERY of book publication soon whirs into motion. When I am asked for a bio, I write a lighthearted one harking back to my trailer origins; when asked for a description of my poetry, Jason offers, *"Electrifying . . . like if a bumblebee stang you right on the clit."* When an author photo is requested, Jason takes me into the front yard, leans me and my Fashion Hitler swooningly against the oak tree, and submits the resulting picture under the name Grep Hoax. We have always run a mad two-person operation, held together with rubber bands, paper clips, and near-rhyme, but I sense with some wistfulness that it will not be mad for much longer. I am about to become legitimate.

At the height of these absorbing activities, it arises that I need to travel back down to Savannah to get a few of our boxes out of storage. Mom volunteers to take me before I even ask the question, headlights of anticipation shining out of her face. Someone needs to be driven somewhere? This is the moment she was born for. Jason has a job interview scheduled for the next week, and Dad would sooner die than submit himself to ten hours in the car with a woman who prefers to stop at actual physical locations to go to the bathroom, instead of peeing in a bag of beef jerky or whatever it is men do, so it's just me and my redheaded author.

We drive southeast toward Tennessee. The highways of Missouri cut through round-shouldered limestone cliffs, buff and cream and foam and gray, dove and scum and chalk, but as we get farther down the interstate, rustic woods start to thicken and picturesque valleys dip down. The landscape suggests gaps and hollers and falls. The water gets lazier, the glitter goes slower, and here and there the air multiplies itself into fog.

"This scenery really is . . . GORGE-eous," my mother says slyly. She's ingesting caffeine at a suicidal rate, and her puns are beginning to overtake her.

Just at that moment a man in a truck cuts her off. She rolls down her window and calls him, quote, "A Piss!" I slide down as far as I can in my seat; this interchange is all too familiar. My mom's inability to cuss like a human, as opposed to a prudish extraterrestrial attempting to approximate human behavior, is legendary. In a fit of road rage, she once called a man Mr. Silver Dildo. "Mom, WHY," I said, aghast. "That silver car is his dildo, Tricia," she explained. "He's compensating with that car." She regularly accuses men of jacking off in their vehicles, despite the fact that she doesn't know what the act of jacking off physically entails. She just thinks it's an extra-bad kind of wasting time, of the sort practiced in prison yards, public schools, and Washington, D.C.

"Don't mess with me, bud!" she yells now at the man in the truck, who is refusing to take her homicidal hints. "Cops compliment me on my driving every day! I will run you off this road!" Sensing the white-hot force of her disapproval, the truck turns off at the next exit, and she nods with satisfaction while reciting his license plate number out loud in order to commit it to memory. She never forgets a bad driver, and she never forgives one either. I wouldn't be surprised to learn she prowled through parking lots at night, castrating the Truck Nutz off of vehicles that had crossed her.

I turn the radio to the only hip-hop station I can find, and my mom experiences "being in the mix" for the first time ever. It is no exaggeration to say that The Mix blows her mind beyond repair. Every time the song switches out before it's finished, every time someone blows an air horn, she gasps. She looks like she's been reading Borges. When the DJ asks if we're ready to party, she unconsciously nods her head. As we drive deeper into the valleys, though, that radio station fizzes and goes out, and all we can find is a classic rock station playing "Imagine," which is my mother's enemy in song form. "Imagine there's no heaven?" I don't think so. "Imagine there's no countries?" Then we would be France. Sure enough, one verse in and she becomes enraged. She shifts gears so murderously my organs all relocate one inch to the left.

"I can't stand it how every Sunday the radio plays this and that's the religion for the day!"

I check my phone. "Mom, it's actually Monday."

"Oh." She is placated and takes a long magnanimous pull of iced tea. "Well, that's all right, then. John Lennon was truly a wonderful lyricist before he was murdered."

We are intrigued by the Tennessee natives, who sit idle in rocking chairs on their porches. They look like they do stuff to logs in their spare time. I think about those cartoons where someone swings an axe in thick woods and all the timber falls down into a cabin with a tinkling xylophone noise. The landscape is dotted with pristine lakes where feral eighties Jet Skis run loose, and gas stations begin to sell fresh crickets. Staring contemplatively out the window, I bite into an extra-long beef stick called The Sasquatch.

I can feel the country turning into the South—a slight shift in the air, in accents, faces, birdsong. She must feel it too, because she asks, "Do you miss Savannah?" I do, with an intensity that surprises me. I miss the walking and the sherbet-bright azaleas and the ghost tours outside my window just at dusk, and I miss working in that lusciously monastic room with five windows. Above all I miss the food: split biscuits with honey, coarse ribbed greens cooked with pork, ornate gold fried chicken, sweet potato casserole and brisket sliced against the grain, oysters so creamy they tasted like the absolute center of the sea. And the ocean so close, and the sun buttering the blankness of my mind, and my hands unknotting knots in the warm, uncomplicating water.

She pats my arm. The South is devoted above all else to iced tea, so she understands. "Still, it's good you moved away from the South when you did," she comforts me. "According to a website I was reading about gators who kill, more and more gators are becoming killers. One gator, they opened him up, and they found twenty-two dog collars inside."

A pause.

"Mom, that doesn't sound . . ."

"No, it doesn't sound real at all, now that I say it out loud."

"Is your head just full of things like . . . *gator killers . . . we swallow seven spiders every night . . . rainbow parties and jenkem . . . money is covered with cocaine . . . a dangerous new game called 'chubby bunny' . . . men hide under cars in mall parking lots and slash your ankles with a razor when you walk by . . . Satanists have a new plan to eat the pope . . .*"

"Promise me one thing, Tricia," she begs me. "Promise me you will never play that deadly game called Chubby Bunny."

We pull into a rest stop nestled against blue, hazed hills, and Mom leaps from the car and speed-walks past the picnicking families while yelping, "Emergency!" Sometimes it strikes me that when my mother is gone, I will remember her most vividly in rest-stop bathrooms, rubbing her hands under the keening dryer, smiling at me adventurously in the warp of the mirror and fluffing her hair with her fingertips; I will think of her cross-country, still in the middle of a trip we are taking together. Turning to me and speaking, repeating beautifully and always like a villanelle.

MY MOTHER'S FEMINISM goes on four wheels. Don't get me wrong, she would never actually describe herself as a feminist. Sometimes, after consuming large bars of chocolate, she comes dangerously close to advancing the opinion that women should not be allowed to vote. Here in the rarefied space of the car, though, it's different. The song of the summer comes on, a particularly disgusting selection that pretty much goes, *"Girl, I am going to freak you to death, whether you like it or not."* She hesitates. She tries something out. She says, "I think this song is sexist."

"It is sexist!" I cry. "I think it's sexist too!"

"Why doesn't he just go stick it in a HOLE in the ground," she says, stabbing the air with one finger for emphasis. That escalated quickly, probably because we've had so much caffeine that we're on the verge of escaping our bodies. Our hearts have sped up to pass. We've had so much caffeine at this point that we've become geniuses.

The sky has gone pink and white at the very rim, like watermelon rind. I regard it with a certain watchfulness, just as I regard The Stobart. Perhaps if I had been born in more secular circumstances, I would not think sunsets look so Christian. It's so spectacular it can mean only one thing: my mother is about to ask me how I "give birth to a poem."

She really does want to know. She doesn't consider herself creative. She follows recipes down to the last half teaspoon and cuts patterns millimeter by millimeter and reads the directions before she begins, but during the meditative phase of a drive, she always wants to talk about it. We first tackled the subject when I was eight and still figuring out how to rhyme decent couplets. We were on a woodsy weekend camping trip, and I had just written a long poem about Narcissus, influenced equally by a glimpse of still white water through the trees and the consumption of a rare soda from the vending machine. I showed it to my mother, and after she finished reading, I burst out, "I feel so pure and so clean—I feel all emptied out," just those words, without any embarrassment at all, and she said eagerly, "Oh no, I would think you would feel all filled up," and I laughed, and didn't volunteer information of that kind again, because after all it wasn't necessary to tell your mother everything. A kind of stinginess, it seems to me now.

"Is it ADD?" she asks me. "Your father gave you all ADD, you know." Sensing that this is not entirely fair, she adds graciously, "And then I gave you ADD as well."

"Maybe," I say, laughing again. It was true I always had trouble listening and remembering, trouble hearing people when they explained simple facts to me. When I read, my head seemed to go diagonal, and I swore I saw things in the sentences—not what I was supposed to see. When I read the words "moonlit swim," I saw the moonlight slicked all over the bare skin. The word "sunshine" had a washed look, with the sweep of a rag in the middle of it. The word "violinist" was a fig cut in half. "String quartet" was a cat's cradle held between two hands. "Penniless" was an empty copper outline and "prettiness" seemed to glitter. "Calamity" was alarm bells, and in "aristocrat" there was the sharp triangle of a cravat, and in "sea serpent" one loop of the green muscle. It was as if I could read the surfaces of words, and their real hearts, but not their information. Even "word" had a picture—I saw a blond hostess in a spangled dress turning black and white letters over one by one. When I read, the meaning swam and the images leaped out and the words gave up their doubles. When I wrote, the same thing happened with the paper.

"You start by thinking sideways," I tell her. "First you sit in a sunlit room, and you look at the wall but really look through it, and you read your book but really read past it."

"Sounds like a *recipe for insanity*," she interrupts, tipping back her head and pouring a barrage of chocolate-covered blueberries down her throat, all the while holding the wheel steady with one wrist.

"Then pretend you're washing your hair under warm water, and unfocus your vision like you're trying to see a Magic Eye, and loosen up your hearing like you're trying to understand Donald Duck."

"All at the same time?"

"Yes."

"Better not let Jason see you that way," she says, alarmed, laying on her horn at a slow Cadillac driven by a ninety-five-year-old man in suspenders. "Hesitation causes accidents!" she calls out as she passes him.

"And after a while, if something wants to happen, it will happen," I say, tossing a chocolate-covered blueberry into the air and completely failing to catch it in my mouth, after which I eat it directly off the floor. "When it does, it's just like getting struck by Pun Lightning."

Her brow smooths with recognition. She understands Pun Lightning, that jolt of connection when the language turns itself inside out, when two words suddenly profess they're related to each other, or wish to be married, or were in league all along. "When it hits you, you know just what to say," she nods.

"Right." I find myself slurping her tea against my conscious will, and note with interest that my voice is operating at nearly three times its usual speed and volume, always a sure sign my metaphors are about to become ludicrous. Rolling faster and faster, the wheels urge me on, saying *What is it like, what is it like*. "It's like when the Rain Man looks at the spilled matches and knows without counting how many there are."

"The Savants Have Much to Teach Us," she agrees, shoving a hand violently into her purse and eating a fistful of B vitamins just before gliding smoothly across four lanes. "You know, your dad thinks he's the reason . . . he doesn't think I could ever . . ." she says, and doesn't finish. The scenery blurs by in a great green flash of coherence, the power lines swoop by in their continuous ink, all as if to demonstrate what I'm talking about.

"No," I say after a while, "it's you. Remember the time you said, *Fluent is in the ear of the beholder*? You could do it, easy."

We see the first sign for Nashville. Currents of music begin to run alongside the car; I could reach out the window and dip my hand in them. The lights of the city cluster and grow dense, neon is traveling in every direction, and the night curves over us dark and sparkling, the perpetual entrance to a cave of wonders. We lapse into silence at the same time, the caffeine at last sending our heads diagonal, calmed by the color and clamor outside. Inside the car we feel a very fine companionship, set side by side like two words.

Of course she could do it, I think. She could write the whole next chapter.

9

THE CUM QUEENS OF HYATT PLACE

All year long I have found myself as ubiquitously in hotel rooms as the Gideon Bible. I have stood in the light of hotel lamps and switched myself on and observed. I know all the soaps. I know all the shower-heads. I know that the most popular hotel paintings are: beach after everyone is dead, beige interpretation of the rage of a cat, squares going wild, a rose's period. One by one I have pocketed the complimentary pens, and one by one I have memorized the mottoes on the stationery. LEAVE A TRAIL OF GENIUS, the Marriott notepaper tells me, which is so optimistic it's actually touching. All year I have sat in hotel rooms and nothing has happened to write home about, which is the beauty of hotel rooms, really. Tonight, however, is different. Tonight is different, because:

My mom believes there is cum on the hotel bed. We are in Nashville and it is midnight and my mom believes there is cum on the hotel bed. We were looking forward to an innocent Christian visit in the city of rhinestones and cowboy boots and blond hair and wholesomeness, and have instead found ourselves in the cum capital of America.

It happens this way: after driving all day, after getting lost on our way into town, after a steak dinner at a local roadhouse staffed entirely with aspiring country singers, we feel we have earned our rest. We check into our room at the Hyatt Place, and we wash our similar faces and change into our respective pajamas and yawn identical yawns and then, and then, as it sometimes does, the whole world stops spinning on a single second. My mother turns back the blanket and gasps. From the look on her face I can tell she has seen cum.

She throws back her head and howls, and the sound chills me to the bone. It is the consciousness of a thousand cums crying out for a body. This is a Catholic's worst nightmare: souls all over the bed.

"Touch it!" she commands. "Touch it and tell me what that is!"

I silently beg the fourth commandment to release me, just this once, from its power. Is this how God wants me to honor my mother—by touching half of a stranger's baby on a hotel mattress? When Moses came down from the mountaintop, did he make the people touch it? I pause so long I get something pregnant.

"Mom, I'm not going to touch cum."

"Just touch the cum and tell me if it's cum."

"Please don't make me touch the cum."

"If I hadn't touched the cum . . . then you would never have been born."

One look at her tells me I have no choice. I reach out a trembling hand and suddenly she changes her mind.

"No no no, wait! Before you touch it, get on your internet and google *How long does cum stay alive?*"

"Mom, you're a Catholic! Isn't that one of the main things you're supposed to know? Haven't you guys written entire books about how long cum lives?"

"I can't remember! Look it up, we need to know!"

According to the internet, there are two possibilities. Sperm either die shortly after they leave the body, or else they live eternally, first on earth and then in heaven, banging themselves adoringly against the great gold egg of God's face. No one can decide.

I can't handle this on my own, so I head over to Twitter and start sending out bulletins about my current situation as fast as I can type them. I start at the beginning and waste no words. "MY MOM BE-LIEVES THERE IS CUM ON THE HOTEL BED AND SHE'S TRYING TO MAKE ME TOUCH IT, TO VERIFY THAT IT IS CUM. NO, MOM, I WILL NOT." Immediately one of my friends re-sponds, "Touch the cum. Touch the cum with your mom."

Pathetic fallacy is real, so just at that moment a storm begins to beat itself against the window. Thunder bares its crack to us and raindrops wiggle their long tails down the glass. Lightning shoots down the sky and illuminates us, and I see that my mother has undergone a change. Her eyes are open so wide it is impossible to imagine them ever closing. Her hair runs in wild locks away from her forehead. She looks like Edgar Allan Poe, haunted by cum, chased through the slick streets at night by cum. She shivers, as if someone just came on her grave. An unmistakable look begins to tiptoe across her face. I know that look—all of her children know it. We saw it bending over us tenderly when we were babies in our beds.

"Mom, no. We're not calling the police."

"Can't we call the police . . . just a little bit?"

"Absolutely not. There is no Special Cum Division."

She sizes up the distance between herself and the phone and then somersaults across the bed. It's a nimble move, the move of a burglar on her way to steal a Pollock from MoMA. If the police won't help her, she's going to take matters into her own hands. She rises out of the somersault with catlike grace, snatches up the phone, and starts to dial the front desk, but I see where this is going and wrestle it bodily away from her. I was once forced to switch hotel rooms at midnight because she saw a pube on the bathroom floor, and I swore to myself I would never let that happen again. ("Pubes aren't *contagious*," I told her. "Then why do we all have them?" she retorted.) I slam the phone back down and we stand staring at each other, panting.

Craftily, she decides to switch tactics. "Do you think I am over-reacting?"

I consider my answer carefully. My mother's reactions are very often indistinguishable from demonic possession, but it isn't always wise to say so.

She presses on. "I guess a 'fun mother' wouldn't care about all the cum?"

"I think a . . . fun mother . . . would care the most about it."

Bingo. "That's right. Because you can't have fun if you know that somewhere in the world, someone is being disgusting."

"Mom, it's late. Let's just sleep on the cum beds. Let's just sleep on these cummy, cummy beds."

"Tricia," she says, "beds are supposed to be comfy, not cummy." Oh my god, she really is my mother. There were times in the past when I had my doubts, but no longer. I have gazed into a puddle of genetic matter and seen my own DNA. We are more related than we've ever been; we are the Cum Queens of Hyatt Place. All opposition between us dissolves and we find ourselves in perfect cooperation. We hide the spot with a fresh hotel towel and then lie awake for the next hour making puns to each other. How did we end up here? There was a moment, when she first turned back that blanket, when we looked into each other's eyes and a blue current crackled between us and our bodies made a sudden decision: we were going to say the word "cum" to each other. It had to be done; the story had given us no choice; there was no turning back.

"Who did it?" we wonder. She thinks it must have been a pervert who "gets off on voyeurism of porno," but I think it was probably a businessman with a hotel fetish who shouted the word "amenities!" as he came.

"A jizzness man, you mean," she says, and I feel like I just taught a baby how to read.

The art on the walls has become more abstract. The squares are creaming themselves, and the roses are practically giving birth. I close my eyes and see bright splotches. After a while I start to drift off, but I can feel my mother's eyes burning a hole into my left cheek. She is awake. She will be awake forever. "Tricia," she whispers, "I can't fall asleep. I'm afraid to turn around and face the cum."

The next morning she stomps down to the front desk and registers a complaint about the amount of semen in our room—the ideal amount of semen in a hotel room being none, the amount in our room qualifying as an actual wad. She has never felt more alive, you can tell. She is enjoying herself with all the immensity of a recently inseminated elephant. She inserts the phrase "COME on" into the conversation wherever possible, and when the concierge attempts to make excuses, she tells her not to give her that load. The concierge's face is serene—so serene that I become suspicious. Perhaps she is the cummer. A concierge SOUNDS like a person who cums on beds. Maybe she got to be the concierge because she was able to cum on more beds in one night than any other employee. I believe it, actually. I have never had a real job in my life, so this scenario seems plausible to me. In my secret heart I believe this is how the president is elected.

My mother continues to talk, sounding more persuasive with every word. If Daisy's voice was full of money, my mother's voice is full of coupons for free appetizers. She once sent back a piece of Weight Watchers cake because it was too small, and the waitress ended up giving her three additional pieces of Weight Watchers cake to take home. If you think that defeats the whole purpose of Weight Watchers, you're missing the point. The point is that my mom wasn't even trying to lose weight.

"Let me get the manager," the concierge says at last.

I'm not capable of listening to the story one more time, so I slip outside and watch the interaction through a window, concealing myself behind a large potted palm. The manager looks to be an ordinary woman, but not for long. The scene begins to unfold, and it's more dramatic than even I expected. My mother is starring in a one-woman play called *Biohazard* and the critics are loving it. Unable to capture the full feeling of the experience with words, she resorts to interpretive dance, throwing back her head, making jackoff gestures, leaping back in horror, and finally shaking both fists at God. At one point she appears to yelp, like a guard dog who has been trained to bark whenever cum gets near it. The manager watches in a trance. She's completely caught up in the drama. She needs to know what happened next. What happened next is that your hotel ejaculated on my mother—at least as far as she's concerned. An open mouth, a shuffling of papers, a tapping of keys! Hotel managers are geniuses at accommodating my mother without ever admitting that her wild-eyed pubic speculations might be true. Now the manager is taking my mother's hand and my mother is squeezing back gratefully, as if to say that she might recover someday with the help of the purest, most asexual angels, but that day will be a long time coming. She crushes a Kleenex against her face, as if to say that she can never wipe away what she saw.

My mother walks through the sliding doors triumphant, and informs me that we have been awarded a staggering ten thousand Hyatt points. If you're not familiar with the Hyatt point system, that's like . . . the most you can get. She believes this is in recognition of our trauma, but I think it probably has more to do with the fact that she was flashing the manager her Let's Call the Police Look the whole time. Either way it means we get to stay in the hotel again the next night, except *this* time it's free. Success. We join hands and set forth into the morning, united by that human glue which cannot be dissolved.

10

SWIMMING HOLE

After two glorious nights in the old city, which I spend replenishing my dangerously low lard levels and remembering what it's like to wear ho clothes, we return to the welcome news that Jason has been offered a job at the local paper in Shawnee, a barren suburb just across the state line. The news in Shawnee is a bit sideways, as it is in all the rest of Kansas. During his first few weeks, he writes a story about a patricide in a cornfield, interviews the owner of a "gun store for women," and profiles a man who keeps nine thousand pounds of bees as a memoriam to his dead father. He takes it all in stride. "At this point," he tells me, "I would be happy taking minutes at a cow meeting, as long as the cows didn't talk about religion."

The seminarian, meanwhile, has disappeared to help out at another local parish, where the goddesses of the congregation grow their hair to their waists and invite him over for hearty, home-cooked dinners on a weekly basis. One woman, he tells me in an awestruck, passionate voice, even has a fig tree in her backyard, and as far as I can tell this is not a euphemism whatsoever.

Now that he is gone and Jason is at the paper all day, I am left alone to write for the first time in months. I ought to be rejoicing, living on nothing but coffee and oranges, reveling like a madwoman in my new-found freedom and writing whole stream-of-consciousness novels on rolls of toilet paper while my hair grows progressively more deranged, but instead I find myself in a lull. Somehow I feel more alone here with my family than I ever did in our long succession of isolated apartments. Back then, it was just me with a cat on my lap, but at least the cat was like-minded. Here, I have fallen away from the world. I cannot bring myself to call or write my friends; my situation is too strange, and conversation in this house travels right down the vents. The solitude presses in on all sides. As T. S. Eliot put it:

> I should have been a big crab
> pinching loneliness on its ass
> under the water

I sink back against the pillows, turn on the TV, and watch an Esther Williams marathon, culminating in that film where she dresses up as a mermaid and breaks her back doing a hundred-foot dive. Nostalgia washes over me in warm, sequined waves. As a teenager, whenever I found myself alone in the house for a miraculous afternoon, I raced to the television and flipped through the channels until I found an old movie. It hardly mattered what it was—I watched the Nicholas Brothers tap-dancing up and down stairs, Marilyn Monroe stretching her bright lipsticked mouth as if she were speaking two languages at the same time, Bing Crosby with the voice that glided in lazy swooping figure eights and the barely concealed fatherly rage just underneath the blue of his eyes. I watched everything, swimming with the sensation of learning what I liked.

Then, usually just before the movie ended, my dad would come through the door, strip to his underwear, take the remote from me, and without ceremony switch the TV to something like *Bag of Guts: How Much Blood Is in a Human Body?* or *Boom! A Toot from the Bum of the Apocalypse* or *Ragged Claws: Hideous Mutant Poem from the Deep.*

Esther Williams hits the water, and I wince. Then, as if to distract me, a savage burst of sound comes cannonballing across the hall from the direction of my parents' room. In the summertime, my father watches action movies, one after another, pumping his fist, hooting with overflows of masculine feeling. Above all else, he loves trilogies. There has never been a trilogy he didn't like, and if you don't understand why, I have three words for you: father, son, and Holy Spirit. Foremost among his favorites is the original *Star Wars* trilogy, which he fervently believes is about priests in space, and the first three *Alien* films, which he believes are about how all women are destined to be mothers. Currently he is obsessed with the *Transformers* movies, because the greatest Transformer of all . . . is Jesus Christ. He even sat me down one day to have a serious discussion about "moral choices the Transformers are forced to make." At no point did I interrupt him to say, "But Dad, they're cars." This means I am becoming an adult. Because truly, the Transformers are more than cars. Some of them are trucks.

I brought a box back with me from the storage locker, stacked with half a dozen filled-up notebooks. I haul it up beside me on the bed and begin flipping through them until I find an old scratched draft, the pencil gone soft and ghostly. Alice walks over to sniff it, touching her eraser-pink nose to the page. It is calling her back home, but she doesn't understand how. I wrote it tipsily the night before we packed up and left—I remember almost nothing about it except the title.

I GUESS THE PLOTS OF MY FATHER'S FAVORITE MOVIES BASED ON THE SOUNDS COMING THROUGH THE WALLS

Two guns are in love, and they CANNOT stop shooting fucks at each other all day long.

A rapping kangaroo witnesses the brutal murder of his wife. Ever after he wanders the earth, searching for her killers and rapping brokenly about his grief.

A remake of *The Ten Commandments* where the lead actor is just an AK-47 wearing Moses robes. He parts the Red Sea by shooting it.

Some of the lambs are being silent . . . and some of the lambs are being so loud they are breaking the sound barrier.

Someone is trying to give Dirty Harry a bath, but he does not want it. "I SHALL . . . NOT . . . BE . . . WASHED!" bellows Dirty Harry at the top of his lungs.

Sherlock Holmes keeps having insights, in the form of huge cannonballs blowing themselves out of his face.

A lightsaber has figured out how to masturbate, and every man in the world is cheering.

Indiana Jones flips through his dad's diary and finds a map to the clitoris. "IT'S MINE," he yells, but will the Nazis get there first?

God is a cop with a monkey sidekick, and the monkey sidekick is mankind.

I examine the handwriting. The lines slant sharply downward, the way our floorboards used to, toward the river. I've always held that you get your best thinking done on the top floor, because the roof forces your head up—it's the reason all those historical geniuses did their finest writing in towers. Still, it might have done them some good to breathe fresh air once in a while.

"SEE YOU IN HELL!" some cinematic voice screams, and a murderous splash blasts through the wall. I add another plot to the list, "Jaws has learned to crave the flesh of Jesus, and now he'll stop at nothing for another taste," and slam the notebook shut. "All right, I need to get outside."

SUMMER, LIKE A GOVERNMENT, has instituted a permanent noon. The curfew calls everyone out of the house. It's a cicada year, so when I walk through the door to get a sense of the temperature, green missiles bomb tunelessly into my face. The scream of them is shrill and fuzzed at the edges, and fills the sky with the signal of an ancient technology. It sounds like the Old Testament is yelling at me.

I turn on my heel and walk back inside. When this spell comes over the Midwest, there is only one thing to do. "Is there anyplace to go swimming around here?" I ask my mother. She's standing at the kitchen sink rinsing a colander of blueberries, so thoroughly that the front of her shirt is soaking wet. According to her philosophy, if you do not rinse blueberries thoroughly, then you end up eating chemicals, and if you end up eating chemicals, you die twelve minutes sooner than you otherwise would have.

The outlines of a getaway begin to sketch themselves above her head. "Have you ever been to the Shut-Ins?" she asks.

Excuse me? "How rude. I very certainly have not. I have many friends, and am well-loved across America."

"No no no," she says, losing control of the sprayer and shooting it across the room. "Johnson's Shut-Ins. It's a state park, a couple hours southeast of here."

"It sounds like a hospital. It sounds like Nature's mental hospital."

The sound of two ambulances having sex whirls down from the upstairs room, followed by the sound of my father's passionate appreciation. "YEAH, BAY-BEE!" we hear him call out.

My mother looks at me with silent laughter and shrugs. "Maybe it will cure you."

IT IS SETTLED. We make plans to spend a day at the Shut-Ins with my sister Christina, her husband, Paul, and their six children: Wolfgang, Aria, Seraphina, John Paul, Gigi, and Gabe. The babies are homeschooled, and when times were trying, they all lived with my parents too, piled together on two futons in the basement of a bygone rectory. Ever since they left, they've been homesick for my mother, and probably also for the stained-glass window of a hunter raising his rifle to shoot a deer in the face that featured so prominently in one of the rectory's walls.

Certain signs set them apart. In the course of regular conversation, they sometimes burst into Latin. In regular children, this would indicate a need to call the exorcist, but in them it is just the opposite. The boys wear the sort of navy uniform pants my brothers used to wear to school, and the girls wear long skirts and veils on Sunday. This is hard to reconcile with the daisy-patterned short shorts Christina used to wear as a teenager, or the T-shirt she once smuggled home from the mall that was printed with the words PLEASE BLOW ME (on the front) and A KISS (on the back). I still have trouble parsing this. Are people blowing girls, or was that shirt meant for a dude, or what? The question was settled for good when my mother found it wadded up in a laundry basket and cut it into a hundred pieces.

The kids call my father Big and Scary. Not your typical Pop-Pop or Pappy or Gramps, but it suits him. When he enters the room, they regard him with a row of pale, solemn faces, and then he drops his jaw at them like a tall shaggy wolf and a suppressed communal giggle runs through them faster than a flick through a whip. They cannot laugh until he gives them this signal. When the patriarch of your family is a priest, it can be difficult to tell what is church and what is not. As they perform this ritual, I almost have to turn away, thinking again what a boomeranging, out-of-body experience it is to watch a religious childhood from the outside, when before I was in the very marrow of it. After five minutes—I clock it—he heads upstairs again. He likes them to be there, but five minutes is his limit.

. . .

WE DRIVE UP in a caravan one Saturday morning, with my mother leading the way. The highway carries us by tame scenery for a long stretch, but after a while the vegetation ceases to comb its hair, and we find ourselves out of reach of all cell and internet service. There are no gas stations, and houses turn to prefabs and then to trailers and become fewer and farther between. When we do pass them, the yards are full of heaps of rusted parts that come to look increasingly foreign and strange, as if they were once components of dismantled time machines. At one point we pass a little dirt path called DeCuntry Road.

"Can you still see the rap van?" my mother asks, peering into the rearview. My sister and her family are supposed to be close behind, but my mother is nearly impossible to follow, so they vanish from the road every once in a while.

Jason and I twist around in our seats and keep watch through the back window. After a minute, thegrindup.com crests a hill in all its majesty, and we note the crumpled dent in the front hood where the man's shoulder must have made contact. "Did you ever hear anything more about that guy?" I ask. The collision of the rap van with the desperate, unheeding pedestrian has been haunting me.

"I did, I talked to the policeman who was at the scene. He told me that if anyone else had hit that man, he would be dead." She lowers her eyelids modestly. "So actually, in a way, I saved his life."

WE PULL INTO THE ENTRANCE of the park a little after lunchtime. The afternoon is as fresh as a fish. The white quartz light falls everywhere, and the trees billow toward the clouds. The trees of the Midwest have not been sufficiently praised. There is a subtle, continuous movement among their leaves that looks like communication. When they huddle together, they seem to surround a shadowy swimming hole, hung all around with rope swings, a hidden launching point only the locals know about.

This is the Black River, which flowed peacefully through wide valleys for ages until it reached this spot. Here it became trapped by boulders and thrashed in its stone cell like a wedding veil, all pearls and lace and foamy netting. It continued in this furious loop until it began to carve a deconstructed palace out of the pink granite and sparkling blue rhyolite.

The welcome center exhorts us to:

Take a dip in the famous shut-ins surrounded by billion-year-old rocks.

Marvel at the forces of nature responsible for creating this shut-in.

Yes, it takes a great deal of Nature's energy to produce a single shut-in. I ought to know.

The welcome center posts on prominent signs that people swim in the shut-ins at their own risk, but I don't pay much attention to these. There are no lifeguards, and only a single park ranger—how dangerous can it be? But I have underestimated the recklessness of the local population. When I see the park laid out below me, I am stunned. It is wall-to-wall rocks. It looks like the gnashing ruins of a giant's mouth. The stones still carry with them the sound of geological groaning, grinding, cleaving, shifts. "Oh my god, it's the devil's obstacle course," I exclaim.

"It's not the devil's obstacle course, it's a *naturally occurring water park*," my mother informs me loftily. "Over millions of years, erosion carved the rocks into natural chutes and water slides for people to enjoy." A nearby child dashes his small rump against a stone and begins to howl.

"How many people die here every year?" I ask, appalled, but for once in her life my mother hasn't looked it up.

Landlocked people everywhere have one thing in common: a mad lust for water parks. I still remember the commercial for the St. Louis water park that used to play on television in the summer. This park went by the sad name of The Beach, and the jingle was sung by a man pretending to be Jamaican. "Come to da beach! C-come to da beach!" the jingle coaxed, while the camera flashed on images of a surprised grandpa nearly being carried away by an artificial wave. It was the sort of place where a ride was always being closed down because someone had sustained a grievous injury on a flume. But no one can ever close down Nature, no matter how many patrons it kills.

BETWEEN THE MASSIVE BOULDERS, the water boils or is still. Missourians lie beached and belly-up everywhere, lounging in the pools with the physical frankness of people drinking beer in hot tubs, their elbows hoisted up on either side of them. The water is a trouty brown in the shallows, but becomes a startling YMCA aqua where it carves itself deeper. This must be the most hazardous place in the world to take six children who cannot swim. "I know I need to teach them," my sister says as we pick our way down the shuddering wooden steps toward the river, "but do you remember how traumatic it was?"

She and my mother climb over a glittering granite upheaval to a smoother area of the shore. I have noticed that at a certain point women in my family stop going in the water. I guess after we have our first children we become afraid a fish is going to swim up us and we'll have to carry it to term. I step into the nearest shallows with the two youngest toddlers, holding their chubby, resilient wrists in my hands, and immediately my every sense is locked into the ancient, timeless female effort of Preventing the Next Generation from Dying.

At the bottom of the pools are thousands of pebbles sparkling with velvety druzy—infinitesimal crystals that resemble pollen, or butterfly feathers, or book gilt. I instruct the children to look for lucky ones. That way, I reason, they'll keep their heads down and move inch by inch, instead of rushing headlong to their doom. The oldest kid, Wolfgang, approaches me in private, adult to adult. His voice has that sandpapery sound that means it's about to plunge down. He inclines his buzzed blond head toward me and says, "Mom says we shouldn't have anything to do with luck, because it's like saying that you don't need God."

"Oh, I wouldn't worry about that," I hazard. It can get tricky, being the heathen aunt. I am sometimes called upon to tell my nieces and nephews that I go to "mental church," or to explain why my friends are not named after saints. "I really just mean that they should try to pick a favorite, or one that looks like it means something." Favorites are all right. Even God had them. And meaning, after all, is a kind of luck—some things just shine with it, and no one knows why.

Meanwhile Jason, who has forgotten to bring water shoes and is uttering chihuahua yips of pain with every step, is ready to embark on the equally timeless male pursuit of Introducing the Next Generation to Danger. He points out the forbidding cliff that rises up over the most spectacular and fathomless swimming hole, and he and Wolfgang set off together to explore the possibility of hurling their bodies off it.

When darkness falls, the welcome center warns us, teens sneak into the park and party in this hole. It is implied that many of them drown this way. It is implied that many of them climb to the highest point and dive their way into eternity—or something worse. The bottoms of my feet thrill as I call up the height, the tensed muscle, the poise to jump. Just as I am about to make that free, wild leap in my imagination, a man flings a baby off the edge of the cliff with visible exhilaration. Presumably there is someone to catch the baby at the bottom, but who knows.

My sister's sentence continues in my ears. Of course our aquatic education was traumatic. How could it be otherwise? Greg Lockwood was our teacher.

MY FATHER TAUGHT, in one form or another, all throughout our childhoods—mostly at all-boys high schools. He was renowned for his methods, which included throwing pieces of chalk and keys directly at the heads of his students, so expertly that he only ever hit them by accident. Nowadays this would not be allowed, but back then parents would actually call him up and thank him for being tough on their awful sons, whom they hated.

When it came to our own education, my father declared himself in charge of only two subjects: religion and swimming. He was, on the one hand, an elevated man; he was, on the other hand, a subterranean man. His lectures on religion were endlessly absorbing, and centered largely around a scene where a virgin woke up one morning and found herself pregnant with a piece of fire, and then gave birth to it nine months later surrounded by a bunch of donkeys. This meant you should never have sex before marriage. Christina and I listened, and then looked at each other and shrugged. It was as plausible as anything else.

When it came to teaching us to swim, though, my father dismissed my mother's suggested strategy: first we would dip our faces in the pool every day for one year. Then we would submerge our bodies in the water every day for two years. Then we would meditate on the beauty of the dolphin every day for three years, and at the end of a decade we might be ready to learn how to swim. "BULLSHIT," he told her. "My kids only need one kind of swimming lesson. The kind where I throw them into the damn pool."

The first weekend after school let out, he drove Christina and me to the YMCA and dropped us into the deep end with huge zest. Christina, who lacked buoyancy, sank instantly and silently to the bottom like treasure. I thrashed my powerful midwestern legs and squealed, swallowing half the pool in the process. After a long minute of watching us struggle, he leaped into the water with the grace of a hefty ballerino and dragged us to safety, one daughter on each arm. "That's your first lesson," he told us, as I struggled to hold back a forceful cascade of aqua puke. Neither of us died, so we passed.

So began the summer of our training. We were forbidden to dog-paddle; we were forbidden to hold our noses. Flotation devices were not allowed. Water wings were a sign that a child needed to be picked off by predators in order to strengthen the herd. Rules about waiting a half hour after lunch to go swimming were to be as strenuously disobeyed as the laws of Bill Clinton. Above all, we were never allowed to "ease into the pool." He believed that if a child was plopped into the water without ceremony, some bone-deep mammalian reflex would take over and its arms and legs would spontaneously erupt into textbook swimming strokes. If a baby drowned, it was because it wasn't listening to its body.

Somehow or other, this strategy worked. It had to. The alternative was a grave with the words HERE LIES A CHILD WHO HAD NO INSTINCTS written on the headstone. My mother's face, as she witnessed these lessons, belonged to one of the hellscapes of Hieronymus Bosch—the figure being crucified on a harp, perhaps, or the man giving birth rectally to a glass egg. Still, she never interfered, and my sister and I became brilliant swimmers, speeding through the water as if our lives depended on it, as if our own mortality were chasing us.

"WATCH YOUR FORM!" my father shouted from the sidelines, and then buried himself again in a thick Tom Clancy novel about men being nervous on a submarine. He adjusted his sunglasses and smacked his lips with satisfaction. The men were SO nervous.

Despite these beginnings, I soon came to adore the pool, because the pool meant teens. By the time I was seven or eight, I was a devoted student of the teens and their ways. I observed them from every angle, and marveled at the way they had somehow come into possession of beach bodies. Beach bodies had a stillness, a turning, a restless luxuriation—an introduction of every part of the body to the sun. They stretched on their white plastic chairs. They stretched and stretched. Legs and arms, columns of backbones, necks. Even their long tan lineage stretched, back to some previous life as a basking animal. Their hair grew half an inch; their fingernails; the future.

The teenage boys were fed on hot dogs, and turned the color of hot dogs in summer. They glistened like wiener advertisements from a golden age. If you had thrown an ice cube, you would have hit a boy named Brad, which even sounds like a hot dog's name. All of the girls were named Danielle or Stephanie and qualified as actual bikini babes, with sunglasses and raunchy perms. I, on the other hand, was named after a repressed Irish nun, and I had recently gone to my mother's salon for the first time and been given a haircut that was called "the nest." No one else in my class had "the nest," and subsequent research has failed to prove it even existed. I raised a hand to my neck and touched the fringe of it self-consciously. I would be a teen too someday, I would attain beach bodiness, but for now I waited. I held my breath the way I had been taught, and I watched.

THE SWIMMING POOL posed three dangers. The first was that you would drown. The second was that your little brother would do a number two in the kiddie pool, which happened so frequently it was hard to believe it wasn't part of a malicious campaign. The third was that you would be struck by lightning. Moms were very concerned about lightning at this point in history—I don't know if it was part of the satanic panic or what. The way they talked about it, you'd think whenever it stormed, the sky turned into black leather and Satan started ripping open his shirt, and if the lightning touched you, it was with the devil's finger on a genital you didn't know you had. Lightning was sunlight played backwards, and moms hated it. The rule was that whenever the lifeguard heard even a rumor of thunder, we all had to get out of the pool for fifteen minutes so we wouldn't be electrified. I considered this to be a great pity, as well as a blatant attempt to hamstring my genius.

Dads didn't care about lightning, because lightning was on the cover of all their favorite albums. Sometimes it was painted on their trucks as well. You could tell that if their kids were killed by lightning, they would be sad, but they would also feel superior about it for the rest of their lives, because it was without question the most hard-ass way for a child to die. "My son Rondy . . ." they would say, their voices trailing, "taken from us by pure electricity in the year Nineteen Hundred and Ninety . . ."

Still, we took pleasure in prolonging that space after the lifeguard blew her whistle. We stayed for as long as we could, the water suddenly blood temperature, the sky a witching green. The best was when the rain came up so fast that it happened while you were under, and then you could feel the dimples all over the water as if it were your own skin.

IT LOOKED LIKE RAIN on this particular Saturday, as my father made the turn off FeeFee Road and parked the van on the blacktop, which was just beginning to ooze. "Now don't forget," he said, handing me my COWABUNGA! towel. "You go off the high dive first, and then you get to swim."

That long-ago trick of flinging us into the pool had worked so well that my father decided to re-create this triumph every time he took us to the Y. Before we were allowed the freedom to enjoy ourselves, we first had to jump off the twenty-two-foot high dive, whether we wanted to or not. This is the sort of rule only a father would institute. A mother would far prefer to tell you a story about a high school football star who once jumped off a high dive the wrong way and became so paralyzed that ever afterwards he could only move his left pinkie finger in order to signify that he was thirsty. Why had he done it? Because he had had beers. But dads had reckless, cliff-jumping pasts. Dads had drunk beers in their youths and done backflips into lakes and saw those backflips replaying whenever they closed their eyes in the sun.

The diving board was a terror. It bellied, gulped, and shuddered. The sound of it was wrenched straight off a pirate ship, and one after another they walked the plank in front of you. This is where kids sometimes lost their minds, and where I first saw the word "rictus" applied to human faces. One boy got all the way up to the edge and then sank straight down on his butt as if all life force had been removed from him, suddenly realizing this jump was a rehearsal for his own death. He hid his freckled face in his hands and refused to budge until a lifeguard came up to carry him off. Most likely he never recovered, and became an emo with a paperback Nietzsche in his back pocket later on. The high dive was a test, and when it came to the crucial moment, many of us failed.

This afternoon was like any other; this jump was like any other. I set my footprints on the hot concrete one by one, as permanent as if the concrete were wet. I stepped on the bottom rung, which hurt my insteps because I was tenderfooted. I held my lucky pebble in my hand, my portable piece of meaning, the coherent shape of a kidney bean and beige. I squeezed it and surveyed the landscape. The pool was surrounded on all sides by a diamond-patterned fence that was always sending up a ringing kennel sound where someone had shaken it. I could see my father, wearing a submarine hat with the logo of the USS *Flying Fish* embroidered in yellow across the front. He was damply thumbing through his Tom Clancy novel and wearing a pair of shorts that appeared to be trying to enter his lower intestine. Every time he shifted position on the chair his shorts got one inch closer to his pancreas.

Most people who went off the high dive were in love. The teen boys, especially, stared moodily out at some indistinct point in the crowd and then cannonballed down as if to obliterate themselves. The ones who were the most in love were the ones who yelled things like "HEY, KEVIN, YOU GAYWAD!" across the pool. They closed their eyes and thought of some untouchable classmate and plunged right into the center of the earth, which was molten. I was not in love; I had no business going off the high dive.

"Brad, you butthole," a boy above me shrieked, with a look of inexpressible longing.

At last I stood at the top. It was a little stage and a little spotlight. Time slowed down, and stretched, and exposed every part of itself to the sun. The high dive meant leaping off the edge of a moment and trusting the next one would catch you. The plunge down, like all plunges down, was a short segment of infinity. Your heart flew up out of the top of your head and the red silk of it caught and billowed out and you hung from it for a second in the middle of the sky.

There was a sea sound in the leaves, a rolling and a breaking, a surf. The sun and my brain were directly overhead; both beat down. My shadow walked alongside me down the board, straight and black and doomed.

"DO THE RIGHT THING!" my dad called up to me, sensing my hesitation. "DO THE RIGHT THING!" was a phrase he hurled like a thunderbolt whenever someone wasn't doing what he wanted or wasn't doing it fast enough, and I was trained to respond to it instantly. I heard him and obeyed.

There is a trick to entering the water gracefully. In that split second, I forgot what it was. I forgot the cardinal rule of the high dive, which was to enter the water with as little splash as possible. I splashed into the water spectacularly, and the water splashed spectacularly into me.

A sharp pain, a shock in the loins, a sudden feeling of worldliness. I bobbed up to the surface, treaded water for a minute, acknowledged the pulse between my legs, and looked around me in a panic. "Oh god, it's my herman," I thought, forgetting the correct word in the heat of the moment. I had heard about girls who busted their hermans riding horses, but since I had never mounted a horse, I thought I was safe. I had heard about girls who busted them doing gymnastics, but since I was incapable of standing on one foot without falling over, I had assumed I would remain intact forever. The pulse said otherwise. A slight scarf of blood in the water confirmed my suspicion. I had lost my virginity to the swimming pool.

"NICE!" my dad shouted, giving me a poolside thumbs-up. Little did he know that his daughter's dowry had just gone down by at least ten cows. What man would marry me now? "REMEMBER TO KEEP AN EYE ON YOUR FORM, THOUGH," he continued. "YOU WERE A LITTLE BIT SLOPPY GOING IN."

Suddenly I felt romantic toward the aqua-blue water. I scissored through it in languid strokes and pictured the baby we might make together. From the waist down, it would be a manatee who flopped its tail in my tender arms, and from the waist up it would be a hot woman with good boobs and a nest haircut, which would be popular in exactly fifteen years, when the product of my unusual intercourse had finally matured.

I hauled myself dripping up the ladder and wrapped myself in the COWABUNGA! towel. The beds of my nails were blue and my teeth were chattering, and the little piece of meaning was still closed in my hand. I had not lost it. The lifeguard whistled and ordered everyone out of the pool; someone had seen lightning. My father smiled at us and continued to read. He was just getting to the best part, where everything was moving as liquidly as a movie. The men in the submarine were freaking out—they were about to blow up the sea.

11

HART AND HIND

By the end of the summer, we have saved four thousand dollars, not a round number but a nice rectangular one, the shape of a cozy living space. It pleases us to dwell on it, and make plans, and talk about where we will hang our pictures and stack our dishes and set our favorite lamp with the red cardinal perched on it. We will, as Jason remarks with some awe, have our own bathroom again, with no Rag in the sink (more on this later) and no dishwashing liquid in the shower. "There won't be any more Mr. Horni, either," he says, pointing to the crucifix and raising his voice. "NO MORE MR. HORNI, WHO CAN'T KEEP HIS EYES TO HIMSELF." Perhaps our rejoicing is a temptation to fate, because we are just beginning to search apartment listings when with one terrific bang our ten-year-old car breaks down in the driveway, sputters out, and refuses to be resurrected.

We pass one afternoon in despair, drinking local Missouri wine out of goblets, burying our faces in the cat's sympathetic stomach, and pacing the perimeter of the upstairs room.

"It's too Catholic!" Jason bursts out, gesturing to the walls, the books about Marian apparitions on the chest of drawers, the flamboyantly injured Mr. Horni hanging above the door. "How can it be so Catholic! The Council of Trent wasn't this Catholic! Wait, which one is the Council of Trent again?"

"The one where they decided that everyone had to wear a baby hat," I say, splashing more Jazz Berry into his glass. He is losing it, and I am the one who must engineer our escape. "It's all right. We'll spend the money on a car, and I'll figure something out."

He takes a gulp of wine and his face contorts. "This wine is *disgusting*."

"Yeah. The winery literally recommends that you pour this one over ice cream."

We begin shopping right away. Jason is looking for "a car of the future, large enough to hold only one half of an American person, that runs on trash." But my father, who got a mad glint in his glasses as soon as he heard that someone in the household would be making a major machine purchase, is trying to convince him to buy a sports car. He makes racy, curving motions in the air as he tries to persuade him.

"They build 'em like a shark, J," he says wistfully. "Nature's perfect shape."

"Well, I was thinking of getting a Smart car," Jason tells him.

My father almost cries. A car that is smart, as opposed to a car that failed out of tenth grade, wears black leather jackets, and gets bicycles pregnant on its days off? He turns to me. "Can't you influence him?" he begs.

"I *need* an intelligent car," I say. "Mom taught me to drive, remember? The majority of her instruction consisted of telling me to double-check my rearview so that I would not one day run over my own child."

"Of course he wants us to buy a sports car," I tell Jason later in private, over the remainder of the Jazz Berry. "My dad has never even owned a car with more than two doors."

"Oh my god," Jason says. "Do you remember the time one of his parishioners gave him a sensible Buick, and it had so many doors that it made him insane, and within six months he had given it to one of you . . ."

". . . and leased a Jaguar for himself," I finish, closing my eyes, as the familiar head-to-toe blush begins to overtake me.

He tips his glass back to the dregs. *"This wine,"* he repeats, his awe increasing. "It tastes like a grape's hormone. It tastes like going down on a jar of jam."

People do give us things. They always have. They give us buttery homemade caramels and free haircuts. They send over plates of gnocchi at the local Italian restaurant, where the owner nurtures a fervent love for the Virgin. Once someone gave us half a cow—first when it was living, and then when it was dead. The steaks of this cow tasted like they had been stockpiled for the end of the world, but what else could we do? We ate them. It is steaks like these that have sustained me throughout my life, no matter what I believed.

THEY GIVE US OTHER THINGS TOO. One inauspicious morning, someone leaves a Piggly Wiggly bag full of human crap on the rectory doorstep. We assume the crap is human, at any rate. Jason lifts it in one objective hand and says it is "definitely heavy enough to be a man's." We set it on the scale and it weighs four pounds, which ought to tell you something about my husband.

We don't like to admit it, but the bag of crap unsettles us. It forces us to imagine a furious churchgoer, squatting in righteous indignation over

the Piggly Wiggly logo. My mother has a guess as to who it might be—
"She would be capable of it. She would be VERY capable of giving this
poop to us"—but she won't tell us anything more. My father has had
enemies in the parish from the very beginning. After he closed the
school due to low attendance, these enemies multiplied and grew louder,
especially when my father turned the building and its supplies over to
the homeschoolers.

The seminarian and I had explored the echoing school one summer
day in darkness: cases of trophies and water fountains, chipped plaster
statues at the turns of the stairwells, ghosts of information still on the
whiteboards. As soon as I stepped inside, I could feel myself getting a
C in history. My education in these places was dry, strict, and limited,
but I am grateful for it now—now that my father has taken to wishing
that my mother had homeschooled all five of us. "Now," he tells her,
"kids go away to college and then they're not Catholic anymore. Except,
sometimes, the homeschooled ones." Tiptoeing up the stairs, I gave a
sort of shuddering laugh. On the one hand, being homeschooled by my
mother would never have been boring; on the other hand, I would have
come out of it knowing only lists of diseases, and not in a doctor way.

Scattered through the hallways were piles of books. I recognized
nearly all of them—literate spiders and magic wardrobes, tubby Hob-
bits fighting over jewelry, children escaping suburbia to camp out at art
museums and children escaping cramped city apartments to hide out in
hollow trees. Those were the most domestic books of all, the ones where
a boy made his way in the forest with nothing but a knife, his wits, and
a crudely fashioned diaper made of deerskin. By the end, he was never
just surviving but living like a lord—the woods a great estate broken
free from its walls, doors gone feral and refusing to close, escaped gar-

dens and fountains and featherbeds and fireplaces, banquet halls laid with drumsticks and fresh fruit.

The seminarian's skirts swept the linoleum. He went through one of the doors, lifted off his dress in one bat-winged black motion, and began to play the baby grand piano that my father had purchased on a whim during one of his lunatic moons, for a sum I cannot even set down. The money could have been a college degree for one of us, it could have been the down payment on a retirement house, it could have been that feeling of green security that none of us have ever had—but instead it was this music, tumbling like a loose class through the school, sounding like an entire education, sounding like the reason why.

I stretched out on a sofa, propping my bare legs on one arm of it while I listened. The seminarian assiduously avoided the sight of them and plunked away at his classical compositions. When he finished, he pulled his dress over his head again and straightened its long lines with decorous hands. "That would be a misunderstanding, if anyone saw me taking off my clothes in here," he said, buttoning thirty-three buttons with limbered fingers. We went back through the door together, and I contemplated taking a book from each stack on the way out, as much to save them as anything else. My father had told me that one of the home-schoolers had called to ask if she could throw away "the sinful books." I thought, "Yes, but I will write another, and then another one after that, and another and another."

THEN THE AIR TURNS crisp and appleish, and it's time to burn the leaves like *Animal Farm*, like *Lolita*, like *Are You There God? It's Me, Margaret*. I have lived for the last eight years in seasonless places, where things do not die, but revolve in a constant tropic sun. I had forgotten how the fall sharpens pencils, gray and colored ones. I had forgotten that when you pay attention to the seasons, you are returned to school and all its feelings, the freedom of three o'clock and the nameless dread of Sunday night, when the sky looms over you like the deadline of some paper you haven't even started. I want to drink cocoa out of a thermos; I want to go to a high school football game. I want to watch my father strolling up and down the sidelines the way he did when he was an assistant coach, hurling his hat to the ground and stomping it with one bengal-striped leg, shouting at the cornerbacks, doing a general impersonation of a man in the grip of a fatal coronary. He looked then, as he looks now, like a man who lived his whole life on meat.

In the middle of November, a parishioner surprises him with a large, reeking venison sausage from a deer he shot himself. Jason loses his head when he sees it and runs upstairs, terrified that my dad might offer him a slice of it to bond them together as men. "I just remembered that I have to . . . put different pants on," he says, and then vanishes, leaving a comet trail of cowardice in his wake.

As it turns out, my father can't manage more than two inches of it himself. He would like to be the sort of man who loves venison, but the reality simply doesn't match up with his romantic conception of it. I sympathize. I once bought a pound of salt pork, believing the taste of it would transport me back to pioneer times, only to find that one of the slices had a distinct, tweakable nipple on it. The sausage rests in the refrigerator, an accusing tube. Every time he opens the door, the foot-long appendage taunts him.

"What is this piece of SHIT," my mother says when she first encounters it in the vegetable drawer, but with my father she is more circumspect. "Do you want me to throw it away, Greg?" she asks every so often, with tact, but he keeps insisting he'll eat it. "Are you kidding? That's great stuff. GREAT stuff," he says, much louder than necessary, smacking his lips with the fake gusto of a child actor. "That's the stuff, bay-bee," he finishes weakly, in a voice that fails to convince even himself, then walks straight into his room and closes the door. Finally we smuggle it to the dumpster when he's over at church, and the dogs of the neighborhood are a little wilder the next day.

"Can't believe your mother threw away that wonderful sausage," he says when he notices, unable to hide his relief, and his shoulders straighten as if a huge buck has been lifted off them. "I'd love to get out in the woods and snag some of that meat myself," he adds, but that isn't true either. He and venison have a long and troubled history reaching all the way back to my adolescence. It betrayed him once, and he cannot forget.

BECAUSE MY FATHER WASN'T allowed to hunt hippies, he decided to settle for hunting deer instead. It was a good compromise, all things considered. Deer were the pacifists of the animal kingdom. They sat around doing weeds all day and didn't even try to get jobs. The males of the species pranced and ate salad and had a hundred kids they didn't know about. In November, a long line of them marched to the polls, leaves held delicately in their mouths, each marked with the name of the Green Party candidate. A deer, in short, was a peace sign made out of meat, and the only way to fight it was with bullets.

"PROPAGANDA!" he once burst out suddenly, when he caught Mary and me watching *Bambi* in the living room, curled up together on the couch. If there was any fictional character my father hated, it was Bambi. "Acting all innocent. Oh yeah, the hunter's always bad, isn't he!

He has red eyes and he kills your mommy!" Flames began to gulp up the screen. "Booooooo-hooooooo, the precious forest is on fire!" he continued, in the same tone he used when he openly mocked Earth Day. "Sack up and be a man, Bambi. I'm coming for you."

He wanted to feel that if the whole world ended, he could still live in it, and inhabit the sphere like his own backyard, roasting its megafauna on spits and drinking its lakes when he was thirsty. In reality, if my father were ever called upon to survive on his own in the wilderness, he would very quickly die of treat deficiency, or of tripping over a big rock while bellowing, "WHO PUT THAT THERE," or of trying to use a snake as toilet paper. I doubt he could build a fire, unless it's possible to start a fire by yelling at logs. And what about clothes—in the wintertime, when it got too cold to go nude? I pictured him trying to shove his feet through the back legs of a moose to make pants. No, the rugged life was not for him, but he didn't know it. The belief that he was a born outdoorsman could not be stripped from him—being stripped of his beliefs was the one kind of nakedness my father didn't go for. He continued in his fantasies of fringed buckskins and rifles painted with moonlight, cold notes whistled solo under the stars, and excerpts of a fictional deer smoking over hickory logs.

He read instructional books with the ugliest covers I had ever seen— uglier even than the classics of theology. He studied thorny pictures of men posing with fourteen-pointers. He shopped for reflective vests, overalls, and various scraps of oiled and gleaming gear. He visited websites with tasteful patterns of targets and crosshairs in the background, called things like *Doug's Killing Corner*. After worshipful, hyperfocused research, the same kind he lavished on guitars and other engines of beauty, he chose the correct guns. He was giddy with that high altitude he sometimes climbed to in his mind, that giddiness that made him buy things, things he needed for the journey. You could not grudge him this, really. It was still a height, it was still exhilarating to behold. These moments were still, on the map of my childhood, elevations.

Then it happened. A friend of his owned some land outside of Cape Girardeau, near the fringe of the St. Francois Mountains, and when my father mentioned that he was interested in taking a hunting trip, he granted us full use of it for the weekend. "Oh god, stop giving us things," I said to that friend in my mind. "Please stop giving us things."

My dad was overjoyed. "I tell you what, the kids are gonna love this," he exclaimed, but after much wheedling, the only children who could be persuaded to accompany him on the hunt were Paul and Christina. Paul was a hunter from birth. He was feral and patriotic, like a boy who had been raised by coonskin caps, and my father had high hopes that he would join the military as soon as he was of age. Christina, however, had only ever been to the shooting range once, and when *she* had expressed a desire to join the Navy, my father sat her down and told her that if she did, she would most likely be assaulted on a large boat when she was least expecting it. She would have to follow in his footsteps some other way—by playing the guitar, or by climbing up a tree in a hideous outfit and taking dead aim at woodland creatures. If only there were some sort of guitar that shot notes instead of bullets, they could indulge in both forms of bonding at the same time.

The rest of the family had no interest in killing deer, but that didn't deter him. He dragged us all along and booked us into a forest motel that was favored by out-of-town hunters. I had always thought the words "hotel" and "motel" were synonyms, but as soon as I stepped across the threshold, I understood that a motel was grosser. It looked like the place where Smokey the Bear went to cheat on his wife. My mother hefted our bags inside and almost fainted. She was a good Republican woman, but this was really too much. She nudged open the bathroom door and stared in horror—no doubt she saw a bear pube—but my father looked around him and sighed with contentment. Among his other vocal talents, he was capable of issuing the most expansive sounds of physical satisfaction, like the Ghost of Christmas Present or Caligula. "Nice," he said. "Very nice."

There was an erotic painting of ducks bursting breastily out of a bush hanging over the bed, which he took a long moment to appreciate. The bedspread was patterned with a melancholy design of bare branches and puddles of despondent mud, to remind us of how much everything was going to die someday. "Especially deer," my father whispered to himself with visible anticipation. He felt this was where he belonged, on an icy brown afternoon when the sky looked like rain, or snow, or doom. He was participating in an age-old ritual, where a boy becomes a man and a man becomes a psycho.

He was wearing a camouflage hat, as if inconspicuousness were even possible for him. Like a deer would see that hat and think, "That is a tree with a lot of religious opinions." Though it did give me pleasure to call up an image of my father tiptoeing cartoonishly through the underbrush, autumn leaves crunching under his feet like snacks. My father is a large, swaggering, legally blind man. Autumn leaves had no chance against him. Deer, on the other hand, were almost certainly going to be fine.

Mary and I were feisty after a long car ride through the skeletal woods. We felt persecuted worse than the early Christians. "Why would you want to kill deer?" we argued. "A deer is the last thing that needs to be killed."

"There are too many of them," my father said forcefully, as if any day now the deer would realize their advantage and stage an uprising, herding all of us into empty prisons and gently licking the salt off us. "Too many of them," he repeated. "Also, they eat people's gardens." I promise you that my father had never even looked at a garden. Flowers registered to him as very small bitches, far off in the distance.

"Well, I think it's murder," I reiterated.

"I don't give a dog's butt what you think," he said. He made no sense but he didn't have to, he was my father. He turned his back on our effeminate protest and nodded at my youngest brother. "In a few years, it'll be time for Daniel to get up there in one of those trees, eh, Daniel?"

Daniel rolled his inscrutable head toward my father and raised one silky black eyebrow. Like me, he was suffused with a physical laziness that verged on the spiritual. Normal human movement was impossible for him—he tripped, fell, stumbled, and rolled to his destinations. It seemed likely that at some point he would be killed by a baseball. Whenever he wanted to shock us, he would take off his shoe with great ceremony and reveal a toe that had been hammered absolutely flat by some misfortune. It didn't bend at all, but stuck out at such a pure angle that Euclid would have cried in its presence. He would force us to admire it for a moment, and then tuck it back into his sock with quiet pride.

"No," he said in the startling baritone he had had even as a baby. Back then, women regularly screamed when my mother brought him into the ladies' room, believing a fully grown businessman had burst through the door and was requesting a diaper change. He subtly extended the deformed toe toward my father. No, he would not be getting up in any tree, unless perhaps a hound chased him up there, recognizing him as some new and pinker form of prey.

"Jeez Dan," Paul said, bristling at this display of inertia. His hair was rumpled up all over his head like a dead squirrel. He couldn't wait to get out there and didn't understand why the rest of us were passing up this

opportunity. He bounced up and down with that ricocheting energy our houses and streets and suburbs could never quite hold. He looked like what he was: a boy who would eventually grow up to pronounce the name of our country *Murica*, exclusively date women with patriotic eagle noses, and get a huge gun tattooed on his beefy side.

Dad lowered the thermostat to sixty-two degrees, told my mother not to even think about touching it, and set the alarm clock on the bedside table for five a.m. Next he unzipped his bag and took out a bottle of sumptuous gold liquid, holding it up to the light with the same reverence that flowed out of him during the consecration. It was, I regret to inform you, doe urine. It had been harvested from does when they were at the peak of their estrus cycle, and it claimed to "drive the big bucks wild." Horniness and death, as usual, went hand in hand. I wasn't sure how you were supposed to use it, but I guessed the hunters splashed it over themselves luxuriously like fine cologne and waited for the big wild bucks to trot toward them with unconcealed erections.

Finally he opened our green alligator overnight case and removed a bar of special soap that hunters used to strip themselves of all human odor. He had forced Paul and Christina to shower with it for weeks before the trip, so the deer wouldn't be able to catch a whiff of their original sin. Successful hunting, according to my father, had everything to do with the deer not smelling you. Apparently the deer's nose is an omnipotent organ, like God's eye. He wanted the rest of us to shower with it too, so we wouldn't rub off on them, but we refused.

"The deer are going to smell my candy ass . . . and they're going to love it," I said, rubbing a raspberry lotion all over my calves that smelled like the pure essence of womanhood to me at the time. I was going through a rebellious period, which meant that sometimes I said the ass-word kind of loudly, and sometimes I didn't feel religious at all. I took a defiant note in my notebook about "trees rising antlered between the ears of the land" and closed it with a satisfied bang. Nothing escaped my artist's eye.

My father ignored me. "I can't wait to get my mouth on that Bambi meat," he said, which sounded more suggestive than perhaps he intended. In fact, in the past two weeks he had lapsed into a vocabulary that was almost wholly suggestive, invoking phrases about "sniffing the tang of the woods" and "turning boys into men" at every opportunity.

"All right, idiots, lights out!" he commanded, as soon as he was finished with his ritual tasks. It was only eight o'clock, but they needed lots of rest. My mother was so disgusted with the motel that she stomped outside to sleep in the van, wrapping a towel around her shoulders and yelling "NASTY!" as she went. The rest of us girls squeezed ourselves into the single double bed, underneath the bedspread whose camouflage was so effective that we couldn't see any of the body juices it must have been stained with. The men settled into their cots, shifting and restless, and we drifted off to the soothing sounds of my dad and brother discussing what protocol they should follow if one of them accidentally shot the other.

The hunters woke at the red sound of the alarm and crept out of the motel room with their guns slung over their shoulders, dabbed at all pulse points with doe urine. My sister and I sat up when the door slammed, blinked, and then fell back asleep under the influence of the erotic duck painting. It affected Mary so strongly that she threw one solid thigh over me and locked me in a forceful hump, all the while still unconscious. This always happened when we shared a bed. It was a spontaneous, lewd, and uncontrolled habit. If she had lived in the Victorian era, she would probably have been put in a Home for it. God only knows what she dreamed about—rocking horses and pony rides and endless turns on carousels. Perhaps, as she slept that night, she dreamed of galloping on the back of a deer, urging it faster and faster away from the pursuers in camouflage.

A black gap of sleep, where I seemed to be sitting cold and motionless in the burly crotch of a tree, and then hours later, we heard the door creak open again. The party had returned from the hunt! I opened my eyes, expecting to see them with expertly disemboweled carcasses slung over their shoulders—where would we put them? in the bathtub?—but no. Christina stumbled jerkily inside and then fell to the floor with a paralyzed thud, unable to walk. My father had strapped her with a belt to a tree trunk, handed her an SKS and told her not to move, and then left her there for three hours. By the time he came back, she couldn't feel her legs and had, as she described it, "accidentally hypnotized herself" by scanning back and forth for deer the entire time he was gone. "I never saw a single one," she mumbled from somewhere down on the carpet. "Nobody ever saw any deer."

My father stepped forward to elaborate, his arm around Paul's shoulder. He cleared his throat, embarrassed, and then explained that not only had they not killed any deer, but my brother had crapped himself in a tree stand because he got too excited. "Poor little dude," my father said, shaking his head sympathetically, "he got so worked up, he crapped himself." He said it like that was just something people did, just one way young men reacted to the overwhelming stimulus of their first hunting trip. My brother nodded, as if to confirm both the crap and the excitement. There are two kinds of people in the world: people who care if they crap themselves and people who don't. My brother manifestly did not. Probably the crap was keeping him warm.

If I were writing this chapter about one of my other brothers or sisters, I would have to call it "Mary's Secret Shame" or "Everyone Is Disappointed in Daniel" or "Christina Couldn't Wait." Disgrace didn't stick to Paul, though. He stood there with a look of self-congratulation on his face, as if he had just graduated from a VERY private college. His affectionate nickname P.J. now stood for something else: Poop Jentleman. I could be wrong, but I don't even remember him changing his pants, I just remember us bundling up our things sheepishly and checking out of the motel, Daniel rumbling out a vengeful man's laugh the whole while. It was Sunday, though, so before we could leave, my father led a small group into the woods and said Mass for them among the pagan columns of the trees—not because he wanted to, but because that was the only church available. I imagine the only prayer in his heart the whole time was the one that went WHY LORD WHY.

The ride home had the feeling of a funeral procession, but where was the body? Every other car on the highway had a dead deer strapped to it, but not ours. Whenever we pulled into a gas station, we were surrounded by vehicles flaunting their corpses. I ventured the opinion that perhaps we should have strapped my brother's tiny crap to the top of the car instead, to save our pride. "If you stuck two tiny sticks in it, it would look like antlers." But my helpful suggestion was met with silence. My father's seat belt hung free; he could not buckle it over the gut of his sadness. He was a broken dad.

Later we found out that the whole time Paul was forced to shower with the special hunting soap, he was also ordered to eat only apples and bagels so the deer wouldn't be able to smell his meals. My brother was vindicated, but the rest of us were never quite able to shake the suspicion that he had done it on purpose, for fun or pleasure or out of sheer scatological whimsy. Poop Jentleman worked in mysterious ways.

After this notable failure, the whole family gave up hunting for the next ten years. We never even spoke of it, except to laugh at my brother's youthful incontinence, until one moonless night when we were all vacationing on a little island off the coast of South Carolina. My mother and I were driving on a winding road that ran from the heart of the island toward the beach, where the ocean made a fine continuous flushing sound. Light pollution laws meant that streetlights were dusky and spaced far apart, and we rode under a canopy of live oaks so shaggy with Spanish moss that we were cut off from the disclosing glow of the sky. Out in the darkness, life stirred everywhere. Through our rolled-down windows we could hear the round rattle of the palms, crickets applauding, bullfrogs belching out their personal ads. "Don't you just love Nature?" my mother remarked, and then: *thump.* A fawn darted in front of us and her black van of death struck him with all the force that a non-grindup vehicle could muster. I got a glimpse of his gooseberry-green eye just as it took the full impact of the headlight. With that single thud and a cry of WHOOOPS, she became a more successful hunter than my father ever dreamed of being.

When he heard about it, my dad asked wistfully if she had left all that good meat lying on the side of the road, but from the look on his face, you could tell he already knew the answer. It was all right, he wouldn't have eaten it anyway. Who knew where it had come from, who knew where it had been. Who knew who had given it to us.

12

MEN OF THE CLOTH II: THE CLOTHENING

"The Rag," Jason whispers to me one night in late autumn, as he's cocooning himself in the multiple blankets necessary to protect his dainty body against my father's thermostat. He snuggles down inside them and shudders. *"It's following me again."*

We first noticed the Rag shortly after we moved in, when it appeared one morning without seeming rhyme or reason in the sink of the upstairs bathroom that we share with my parents. Since then it has attained almost the status of a cryptozoological myth. It is a simple unadorned washcloth, but it has a sinister significance. It might be alive. It is always wet. We never, ever feel at liberty to move it.

"Where am I supposed to spit my toothpaste?" Jason asks, the whites of his eyes showing all the way round. "I just swallowed so much that I seriously considered calling Poison Control. If it happens again, I will. The number is on the back of the tube."

"And how am I supposed to wash my face?" I wonder in my turn. "If I bend too low, the Rag brushes my cheek . . ."

"Like the little finger of a drowned child," Jason finishes, his voice rising into a sort of wail. A thought occurs to him. "Do you think it's trying to get revenge on me for drinking all of the bourbon your mother bought for the bishop? Because that was a mistake. A wonderful, delicious mistake."

Sometimes the Rag even migrates to the shower, where it lurks in a malevolent wad. This means that it can walk . . . or *crawl*. From the corner, the wad follows our naked movements with invisible eyes. If it could speak, it would call us dirty.

"If Stephen King knew about this Rag, he could write such a scary book," Jason says. "Where the Rag follows innocent people around and scrubs them against their will."

"Instead of dressing as ghosts for Halloween, kids would dress as the Rag."

"The sound of blood dripping would be less frightening than the sound of the dripping Rag."

"Rip the Rag into a hundred pieces and it throbs under your floorboards like the telltale heart."

One pavement-gray, sleeting afternoon, we go grocery shopping with my mother. As the year winds down toward the fireside holidays, daily errands with her become almost unspeakably soothing. I avoided accompanying her on them during spring and summer, but I am irresistibly drawn to them now—being with her feels like existing in the overflow of a cornucopia. We go to three different stores looking for the best pomegranates. We have to pick up a copy of *Pat the Bunny* for my sister's baby so she "can learn about softness, and not have a deprived childhood." Cornish hens are on sale at the market across town, and "you know how crispy their little bodies get." And always, throughout, we must tend to my father's long and clamoring grocery list.

We are making our way down the breakfast aisle when my mother picks up a box of granola, reads the product description, yells, "Don't TELL me it's all-natural. So is CRAP from a CAT," and shoves the box back into the stack as if she's administering a punch to breakfast itself. That duty to truth dispensed with, she maneuvers the cart into the next aisle and picks up a spotless bundle of fresh new Rags. Jason gives me an agonized look and tugs the sleeve of my coat. If we don't ask now, we might never find out. We might go to our graves without knowing.

"Mom . . . the Rag," I begin.

The squealing of the cart's wheels stops abruptly. She has been expecting this moment, and bows her head as if waiting for the stroke of the executioner's sword.

"Why is it there?" I ask. "What is it for?"

"I can't take it anymore!" Jason shrieks, unable to control himself. "What's on it? It smells like a crime."

With alarming speed and force, she yanks us both into the freezer section where no one will overhear our secrets. She slams the door behind her and exhales a cold cloud, gazing past us with war-torn eyes at a point in the middle distance. "Ooooo, what a deal on chicken breasts," she says, momentarily distracted. Then she turns to me, grips my forearm, and gives me the same haunted look she gave us when she told us about the economy-sized bottle of Palmolive. "Oh, Tricia. Do not post this on the internet, but . . . your father washes his legs with that Rag."

13

BLOW, GABRIEL, BLOW

The only Christmas present I ever really wanted, besides various large marbles carved of semiprecious stone and purchased from the gift shop at the Natural History Museum, was a radio . . . inside a stuffed cat. A stuffed-cat radio. It was called the Pettable Portable Fluffy Kitty, and it had a functioning AM-FM radio inside it. "You've done it, Radio Shack," I thought when I picked up the box and saw it staring out at me with eyes as gold and seductive as a saxophone solo. "You've finally made me care about technology."

"Please, Mom," I said, turning to her in desperation, unable to fully articulate my need. What could I say? That the cat's face was as symmetrical as only the mathematics of immortal composition could make it? That it had the Fancy Feast of music in its stomach? That it was a longhair, like Beethoven, and I wanted it? I resorted, as I always did, to reading. "Please. The box says it's HUGGABLE, and a PERFECT COMPANION FOR CHILDREN."

When Christmas came, I tore through the pyramid of my presents in a frenzy. Nothing. No stuffed cat radio anywhere. In despair I picked up the final package, which seemed too light to accommodate something as momentous as a pettable portable perfect companion that contained actual radio music. Yet when I ripped the wrapping off, there it was, one of its eyes set crooked in its socket so it looked like it had gone daft with pleasure, waiting for me to turn it on and unleash its Top 40 meow.

I had never been happier in my life. I still remember the look of bewilderment my father directed at me as I whispered "thank you" to my parents and then buried my face in the cat's fur. "What the hell," he said under his breath, and then set about installing batteries in that empty part of its belly where the uterus had been scooped out.

It was an unusual Christmas, because he was there. Priests have better things to do on December 25. They must rise early, put on their vestments, and bring Jesus into the world through the legs of Mother Church. Picture a priest's Christmas. He says two or three Masses in the morning, then walks through the old snow to an empty rectory, cutting a hard black shadow on all that whiteness. He enters a kitchen that was last remodeled in the 1970s, one with marigolds printed on the linoleum, and reheats a dinner the housekeeper prepared for him the day before. Today she has gone to visit her family. Her sister, maybe, in Michigan. The priest is alone among old *Life* magazines. He is tired. All that lifting of the arms; all that dry singing, rattling with the seeds of Latin; all that blessing and handshaking and smiling. He turns on a small fizzing television and adjusts the antenna. The black cat of the house, with a solid patch of white on her throat, comes and rubs up against his legs. When he falls asleep on the couch, with the light of the television still pulsing on the ceiling, she licks him, hoping that he's dead and that she'll finally get to take his body and eat. No wonder my father distrusts them.

KEEP THE CHRIST IN CHRISTMAS or else my mother will leave the planet. The day after Thanksgiving, I noticed an unfamiliar magnet had materialized on the refrigerator: a black square showing the silhouette of Mary kneeling over a swaddled bundle in the manger while the various elected representatives of livestock looked on. KEEP THE CHRIST IN CHRISTMAS, its slogan begged me.

Now that December is under way, the situation has become urgent. The spies of Kwanzaa surround the house. Assassins hide in our hedges, holding machine guns in the shape of menorahs. "Get the Christ out of it!" the enemy orders his troops, red and green lasers shooting out of his eyes. My mother isn't having it. She would slit the throat of Baby New Year himself if he tried to say "Happy Holidays" to her. She has heard distressing rumors that young people now just "put a pole in their house for their tree" and "donate goats to each other" for their presents. Surely this is the mark of a degenerate age.

She engages in strategic maneuvers while the rest of us are sleeping. She hangs fir wreaths and clusters of holly, winds garlands up the banister, and arranges and rearranges the components of her Dickens village. Dishes of nuts appear in odd places, and the number of gold balls in the house increases exponentially. Late one night we creep downstairs in search of cookies and find her gazing at her preferred erotica on the internet: authentic German Christmas handcrafts, carved from the finest wood.

"Mom, what on earth is this website?" I ask. I have no idea where she finds these places. I am willing to posit the existence of a Dark Internet only mothers can access, as much a threat to American law and order as those shady networks where hackers in fedoras buy synthetic drugs called, like, Dust and Aligatür.

"You're telling me you've never been to *Erzgebirge-Palace*?" she asks, incredulous. "Dot Com? It's famous!"

I admit that I haven't. I lean over her shoulder to get a better look and see that the sidebar shows a smiling Aryan woman calling their twenty-four-hour customer support line—not to complain, but to express the pleasure that Erzgebirge-Palace's products have given her over the years, perhaps accompanied by some tasteful heavy breathing.

"See, sometimes I teach *you* something," she says smugly. "This web-site has everything. Look, there's Nutcracker Forest Man with Squirrel; Large Egghead . . . Only Legit with the Red Nose; Natural Santa; Cinnamon Dwarf; Snowboy with Violin; Mini Gnome with Package (6 Inches); and something called Music Box: The Birth."

"The craftsmanship . . ." Jason breathes, his glasses reflecting the ro-tating pageant of items. Despite ourselves, we are succumbing to the lure of Erzgebirge-Palace. Perhaps it was inevitable. After all, I am a person who once had an extensive gnome collection, and he is a person who wore a pair of knee-high silver boots to school every day until he was eight, like a sugarplum fairy.

"Get a load of these NUTCRACKERS," my mother says, overawed, and then reads aloud: "'Often the Nutcracker is the image of authori-ties from the past. Especially kings, soldiers and gendarmes are often used as a model. At that time the population was dependent on the benevolence of the authorities and tried to express some protest by giv-ing the Nutcrackers a grim look. His energetic face makes him look very powerful.'"

I venture to suggest to Germany that making its nutcrackers in the shape of "authority figures of the past" is not the best idea? A small figurine in the likeness of Charlie Chaplin also seems misguided. But my mother is not listening. She has returned to perusing the nativity scenes, settling at last on the largest and most expensive. Her lust for nativity scenes is a hole that cannot be filled. She is convinced that some-day she will find one that falls just short of the scene itself: the camels humped within a hair of real life; Joseph a patient shadow, cucked by God; the baby with its skull shaped like a lightbulb, like an idea the world is about to get.

This is not that good, but it is good. "That's a cute little Christ," Jason says sincerely.

"Damn, and Mary's not so bad either," Mom says, appreciating the generous curves of her halo. She pauses and gives us a sly pregnant look. "You know, before Jesus was born, Mary got an ass ride."

MOM SEES THE NOTEBOOK sitting next to me on the table and asks where I'm at now, as if a book is a kind of verbal America that can be driven across in a car: one week you're in Connecticut, the next in Cali-fornia. "I'm writing about all your babies," I say, and read from my latest paragraph.

How many kids should a priest have? One? Two? Three, if he's Irish? Not even close. How about five. How else will anybody know he's balls-deep in his hot wife all the time?

I glance up from the page. "Am I allowed to say that last part?"

"Well . . ." She weighs the pros and cons. "'Balls-deep' is very bad, but I like the part where you say 'hot wife.'"

She is excited I have found my subject, even though my subject happens to include her. If I am writing about her, I am *with* her, talking and laughing and listening to every word, and not locked up in my room waiting for the summons to come. Between books, a writer feels like an angel in that idle time between missions—you are all atrophy and dimpled elbows; you are simply decorative; you are good for nothing. But when the fresh scroll is handed to you, and speed is put back into your heels, and your body re-remembers the straight line, the happiness cannot be described—not in the new book or any other. The feeling is arrowness, nothing else. Hit the apple or split the head, you are happy, you are straight ahead, you are flying.

While we were growing up, there was another painting in our house: Fra Angelico's *Annunciation*. It was one of those paintings that seem to continue outside their own borders and reach into real life; this, I thought, is what "good art" must mean. Two hands stretched out of the sun and shot a streaming gilt tassel into Mary, who bent over the place where she was struck. The angel, with feathers like a fractal quail, delivered his message directly into her eyes. Mary's face was an unripe peach, not ready, not ready; a little book slid off her right thigh like a pat of butter. Stars in the ceiling pierced down. Far to the left, those two green grinches of sin, Adam and Eve, began their grumbling nude walk offstage.

When I left home, I hardly ever saw pictures of the *Annunciation* anymore. I was not expecting this somehow—I thought I would still encounter the messenger angel everywhere. It was the messenger angel who captured my attention, and not the angel with the flaming sword and not the dark-hooded angel of death and certainly not the angel with the regrettable name of Phanuel. By instinct I understood that the most interesting one is the information angel, who carries the newspaper that is meant for you over your doorstep and into your life.

And how does the good news arrive? It does not arrive in your ears, exactly; it arrives in your face as a great gush of light. It is carried to you, not like a rose but like the symbol of a rose, straight into your understanding. There is no sound. It happens in your bedroom, or in your cave in the middle of the desert, with a lion's head spreading on your lap, or on top of the pillar where you've sat for a hot century. It happens in your study, wherever that happens to be.

"I should probably tell him I'm doing this," I say, and pop into his bedroom across the hallway, where he's spread out on the bed like an outsize pinup model. "Dad? I'm writing . . . well, I'm writing a book about you."

"Hahahaha!" he says, throwing back his half-cherubic, half-satyric head. His angel and his demon aren't even posted on opposite shoulders. They're standing on top of his neck, making out. "Hahahaha. I'll murder you."

"Don't say you're going to murder her!" my mother calls out. "Not nurturing."

"*Ho*

Re-

Lax," he calls back to her.

"The working title is *Priestdaddy*," I say, determined to make a totally clean breast of it.

Not that my father believes a breast can ever be clean. "Wait till *The New York Times* gets a load of that," he says evilly. Then, turning his attention back to the football game, he bellows, "C'MON, ANDY!" and kicks a meaty leg in the air. He refers to all athletes by their first names, as if they are his sons.

Jason, editing a story about corn on his laptop, has overheard this entire exchange. "Why are people always having to Get Loads of things in your house?" he asks, exasperated. "Why do Lockwoods have such a rhetorical fondness for the concept of Loads?"

"It's how there got to be so many of us," I say, squinting at the shape of my father on the bed. "He doesn't seem bothered at all. If my daughter told me she was writing a book about me, first I would scream, and then I would physically suck her back into my body so that she no longer existed, and then I would uninvent sex so that no one could ever have a child again."

"That's because you don't like to be *watched*," Jason says, following my gaze with his own greener, wiser one. "You would wear an invisibility cloak if you could. Whereas your dad . . ."

"CATCH THE FOOTBALL!" the man in question shouts, and rolls from one decadent haunch to the other.

"Would wear an extravisibility onesie," I finish.

"Exactly. I think your dad has been waiting for someone to write a book about him his whole life. One with submarines in it."

"Just don't tell any secrets," my mother says. "Like about the time he shot the German shepherd that bit his bare legs in their little jogging shorts, or the time I got so mad at that priest who insulted my interior decorating that I told him I was going to *come down so hard on his dick*."

"It's all secrets, top to bottom," I say, with despair at the magnitude of the task before me. "Everything that ever happened in our household should probably be a secret. Whenever I call Mary, she asks if I'm going to talk about the time Dad almost killed her because she accidentally turned off his computer with her foot. Whenever I call Paul, he asks me if I'm going to talk about how Dad used to take him into the backyard and throw baseballs at him."

"What?" Mom exclaims. "Why did he do that?"

"To cure him of his fear of baseballs."

The sky has turned as black and bracing as coffee and the air is taking on the scent of a feast, so we go into the kitchen and I begin to stir a lemon and rosemary sauce for the pork tenderloins we're roasting. I whisk in little pats of butter to silken it, while Jason rustles through the refrigerator for a vegetable that might be acceptable to my father.

"Asparagus?" he asks, holding out a bunch with purple-tipped stems.

"Oh no. Your father refuses to eat asparagus, because it causes impotence," my mother informs us.

"Too late," Jason says solemnly, gesturing with the asparagus to a portrait of the five Lockwood children posing in front of an immaculate Christmas tree, with its feathery boughs cradling dozens—maybe hundreds—of gold and silver balls.

She looks at the picture and laughs, partly at the joke and partly at the absurdity of what happened to her: married at eighteen, no degree, no job, no fixed address, and five children scattered across North America. "I chose it," she says with great stateliness, the way she sometimes does. "If I hadn't, you'd still be out there." Still out there, somewhere in the night—an idea that just missed her, an undelivered piece of mail.

An angel appears to announce: a child will be born. "Mom, let's be real about this," I say, squinting at her. "Was it weird when I came out of your vagina?"

"No," she says, her voice turning suddenly wonderful. "No, it wasn't *at all*."

SHE LEAVES A FEW DAYS before Christmas to race around the Midwest visiting all of her far-flung descendants. She invites us to come along with her, but we decline, recalling one notorious Christmas Eve when we got stranded on an iced-over highway with her for six hours.

Jason had to excuse himself from the car and pee his name into a snow-bank, and I had to crawl like a snake through the backseat and force one of the seat backs down so I could retrieve a bottle of wine from the trunk, and my mother meanwhile was raising all the questions about art, philosophy, and ethics that humankind had found no answer for yet. This was her established practice. If we refused to discuss the issues with her, she simply called my sister Christina and talked to her on speakerphone for forty-five minutes about euthanasia in Canada. The day flashed almost unbearably outside the windows. Every twig and blade of grass was coated in ice, and icicles hung from the shelves of rock by the roadside, so that everywhere we looked were penknives, daggers, letter openers. Tinsel.

"Please water the tree," she tells us before she departs, "or else it will die, and this is how fires on Christmas get started. People go to sleep thinking everything is fine, and then melt in their beds like pieces of candy."

Soon after she's gone, the seminarian returns for a visit, accompanied by his black overnight bag and the book of prayers he calls his wife. We congregate in the living room again, listening to the coziest and crackli-est old Christmas records we can find. He has taken to wearing Grey Flannel as his signature scent—the closer he gets to being a priest, the more poisonous he is trying to smell, in order to create a wide radius around him where women will not wish to enter. "A priest should smell nasty," he tells me. "A priest should smell SO nasty. You know what I really want to get, though. This scent that Pope Pius IX used to wear. Very subtle, very nice. They formulated it from his secret recipe."

"What does it smell like?"

"Orange blossoms. It's VERY chaste."

"And what's that called?" I ask. I can guess what the answer will be, but I want to hear him say it.

"The Pope's Cologne."

"Ah," I exhale with reverence. He has not disappointed me. "You know, Jason wears a really nice fragrance. It smells like a sweating lumberjack chopping down a cedar tree while simultaneously smoking a pipe. Here, I want you to smell it."

"Get it away!" he protests, as I wave the bottle under his nose. "That might be fine for a secular man, but it's too sensual for someone with a vocation."

"Sensual" is the worst word he knows. I actually called him a sensualist once, meaning simply that he liked food, music, fine wine, jazz, and cascading lace all over his body, and he nearly cried. It obsessed him for weeks. *What do you mean I am a sensualist,* he would burst out at me, bothered, from time to time as we sat with our books.

A PACKAGE IS WAITING for him on the bottom stair; it's a present from his father. He slits it open and lifts out a mason jar full of grass, containing a picture of him kneeling on an altar in gold vestments and a card that says PURIFY AND CLEANSE. I feel justified in saying it is the greatest gift anyone has ever received. It's better than the stuffed-cat radio by far. It sounds like a craft project you would read about in one of those pastel magazines for women on Valium, but I've been assured that the seminarian's father is a butch and monosyllabic man who built himself a pizza oven in his own backyard.

"Am I supposed to open it?" he wonders, turning it over in his hands. "Is it, like, an art installation?"

I have no idea. "Are you sure the grass isn't weed?" I ask. "It would be such a waste if that jar were full of weed and we didn't open it because we thought it was art."

"Weed has ruined lives," he reprimands me, but he doesn't allow it to interfere with his holiday mood. He surveys the shining apparition of the tree with satisfaction. It is hung with modest white lights and red candles and special candy canes made by superannuated German confectioners. The angel of messages is perched on top, arms held wide and sleeves flaring like bugles. All of this is as it should be, but as he looks closer, a large, horrendously wrapped package with the words "FOR HUSBAND" written on it in black marker catches his attention. "What did you get for Jason?"

"I got him . . . a trash can," I say after a short hesitation. This looks bad on paper, I know, but we're still putting every extra penny into our escape fund, and I couldn't bring myself to buy anything we didn't urgently need. "It's a pretty nice trash can. It's printed with a tree-bark design so when you use it, you can imagine that you live in the forest and are throwing your trash into a hollow log. We're going to need it when we move out."

"Why didn't you just get him what he wanted—you know, something off his Christmas list?"

I shake my head gently. "You don't understand. You can't just get Jason what he wants. The two things he desires more than anything else in the world right now are a scale that tells you the Real Age of Your Skeleton and something called a Brain-Sensing Headband."

"So you . . ."

"So I got him a trash can instead."

The seminarian steeples his fingers skeptically. You do not treasure a man by getting him a trash can for Christmas. You send him the message that husbands are garbage. You send him the message that later he might find his own dismembered pieces in it. He picks up the jar again and returns to studying it, perplexed. I can't make heads or tails of it either. If someone mailed me a jar of grass that exhorted me to PURIFY AND CLEANSE, I would probably stuff a pair of my panties in there and mail it right back to them.

"Where's J?" my father asks, swaggering belly-first around the corner with a large container of out-of-season raspberries in his hand. "Now that your mother is off gallivanting around across the country . . ." (my father has always held that the female sex's primary mode of transportation is *gallivanting*) ". . . he's gonna have to take over Laundry Patrol." He points toward a pile of underwear in the hallway that is taller than I am, that is possibly more underwear than I have ever worn in my lifetime. There is a gang of Rags loitering wetly on the top of it, wrung out from a long week of washing legs. "Tell him I'll need those in time for morning Mass," Dad says, with a note of sincere thankfulness and apology in his voice, before popping ten plump raspberries into his mouth and disappearing into his bedroom to shout at athletes who can neither hear nor respond to him. The seminarian gasps as soon as he is gone, both at the enormity of his request and the fact that I, a card-carrying woman, was not called upon to fulfill it. If I used my psychic ability to enter his head right now, I know it would be filled with the single flashing phrase *IMPENDING EMASCULATION OF MY TESTOSTERONE BROTHER* accompanied by the sound of sirens.

"Did you hear the wonderful news? Dogs can now get into heaven," Jason interrupts, bounding up from the basement after completing his daily regimen of four thousand vegetarian mind-clenches or whatever it is he does down there. He went breezing right past the pile without noticing it, and has no idea yet that he is doomed. "What?" he asks, unsettled by our silence, glancing first at one of us and then at the other, until realization sneaks up and taps him on the shoulder. "His under-wear is behind me, isn't it. All of his underwear is behind me right now." It is. "And there's Rags in there too, isn't there." Lifting his eyes, the seminarian gives Jason a look of such pained, eloquent, pure-hearted compassion that I see Christ in his face for the first time.

ORDINATION DAY IS fast approaching, which means that every so often the seminarian rushes into the room squealing, "Look at this chalice!!!" and then shows us a picture of a tall phallic cup studded with suggestive pearl droplets. He prints these pictures off the internet, and again I am seized by the desire to look at his search history: "cup for blood," "holy cup for precious blood," "what is best cup for my god," "i want to drink the crimson blood of lord," etc.

He's trying to choose between three or four different options, all of which are so crusted with ornament that they appear actually diseased, as if King Midas had contracted an STD and then foolishly touched himself. This is a decision of huge personal import, like picking your wedding china. "Which do you like best?" he asks anxiously, handing me a stack of goblet pornography and watching over my shoulder while I flick through it. What he really means is *which one is the most magical*, and he has correctly intuited that I'm the right person to ask about this. I have what you might call an overdeveloped sense of the significance of objects, which is at its keenest at Christmastime.

"I don't like any of them," I say finally. "I want you to get one where there's a dragon's hand holding the cup, and there's a trickle of blood running down between the dragon's fingers that's actually a trail of rubies, and the dragon has been to prison, and it has a tattoo on its knuckles that spells G-O-D."

"NO," he says very sternly, snatching the pictures away and pressing them to his chest. "The dragon's hand cannot hold the cup."

Time is running out. Most of the other seminarians have bought their chalices already. When they get together, they subtly compete as to whose chalice is the most valuable, the most dignified, the most impressive. Returning home after six o'clock Mass, loosening the white collar around his reddened neck, my father peruses the printouts, remarks on the choices, and mentions that his own chalice is not only "inlaid with fine amethysts of the first water," but had also been "rescued from a hoard of Nazi treasure after the Second World War." The message is quite clear: his chalice is only marginally less cool than the original Grail. He wins.

"HERE, I'VE MADE US ALL Classic Martinis," Jason announces on one of these cozy evenings, carrying in a tray and setting it down on the coffee table. He has made a touching effort to drop a curlicue of lemon rind into the bottom of each glass, so the liquid looks like a mobile citrine. The seminarian lifts his with reverence, his mind still on chalices. I sip once, and then again and again, trying to figure out why it tastes so much more uncompromising than any other martini I've ever had. Before the drink is halfway gone, I'm slithering down to the floor.

"How many shots are in these?" I ask Jason.

He calculates. "About five apiece," he says.

"Isn't that a couple of too many?"

"Oh no. It's the *classic recipe*," he insists. "This is what Julia Child drank."

I make a scoffing noise that is somewhat out of my control, like a runaway choo-choo. "Julia Child was often so drunk . . . that she tried to bake herself as a chicken on the stove."

"Would you like one more?"

"Yes, thank you," I say very politely. "It tastes like being thrown through a window."

He trots out to the kitchen and shakes up another round with audible gusto, and in about fifteen minutes the seminarian is just as incapacitated as I am. He starts telling us about "the big and gorgeous domes of Rome," and then flings open the front door and shouts into the swirling night, "IT'S THE YEAR OF THE PRIEST! IT'S THE YEAR! OF! THE PRIEST!"

"Shhh shhh shhh. Quiet now. I need to do something . . . incredibly important," I tell him, in units of varying coherency. "I need . . . to show you my beautiful stomach."

My drunkenness goes in six stages. There is Talkativeness, Dancing, Grammar Derangement, Showing You My Beautiful Stomach, Reading Your Tarot with Such Intensity That Both of Us Begin to Weep, and finally Blessed Unconsciousness. I've never hit the fourth stage so fast.

He crosses his forearms in front of his face—at last I have warranted the celibacy block! "No. No. Why would you do something like that?"

"Because Jason have roofied us," I say balefully, flipping my shirt up for one demure second.

"That doesn't give you an excuse to show your stomach."

"It gives me the excuse to do what I *want*. It's like St. Augustine always said . . . Oh God, don't make me good, not ever."

"Augustine didn't say that."

"Oh God, make me a VERY bad boy, who needs a spanking."

"No."

"Oh God, make me the member of a motorcycle gang, who has to kill an old lady for my initiation."

He claps his hands over his ears. I suspect we are not handling our liquor well, but when we turn to look at Jason, he appears to be completely unaffected. He snaps off the end of a candy cane and sucks it thoughtfully, humming "Please, Daddy (Don't Get Drunk This Christmas)" under his breath. He stares in rapt wonderment at the lights, twinkling on their green plastic vines.

"God, your mother's trees are so perfect," Jason says. "How does she make her trees so perfect?"

"Because she cares about our experience!" I yell. "Because she cares about the Christmas experience we are having here tonight!"

"What's that big package?" he asks, brightening, hoping against hope that it might contain a scale that tells him when he's going to die.

Not the big package . . . not the big package for husband! "Now listen to me very much," I say, tears of remorse beginning to stream down my face. "I am sorry to put you in the trash for God's birthday."

He has no idea what I'm talking about, but he's never let that stop him before. "Don't be sorry. It's just what God wanted," he soothes me. "Would you like another Classic Martini?"

I am long past the point of being able to feel my face. My face is not even my face anymore—it's your face. "Yes, thank you, I would LOVE one more. It tastes just like the Wonder Woman's invisible plane."

I lift my shirt up again at the seminarian, just in case he didn't get a good enough look before, and drum my fingers on it to remind him of jazz. This is my present for him—that and the bottle of Bombay gin that I set under the tree with a baby-blue bow around its neck. "Oh, isn't Christmas your FAVORITE holiday?" I ask him, with the broadness of a truly drunk person, snatching my third drink from Jason and raising it high into the air to toast its breathability.

"To be very honest with you, no, it isn't," he replies, with his handsome face downcast. "I like Easter. I like it when he is resurrected. I like when we all eat ham."

"Don't you love to get the gifts, though?" I cry, but even as I say it I know what he is thinking, what he believes. You get a gift on Easter too—a trash can that looks like a tree, to throw all your sins into.

"Christmas is lonely," he says. "You come home and the house is chilly and closed up and dark and there's no family. No one's here, your mom's not here, it's just your father and me, and we eat dumplings and watch TV. It's not like this. It's nothing like this at all."

IT IS ONE OF THOSE NIGHTS when you can feel the life in your house to be as warm as it looks from outside. The seminarian and I walk out to see if the magic still holds. The electric candles glow in the frames of the windows. The icicles hanging from the roof look so dangerous that I wish my mother could see them. We weave in and out of each other's paths, leaving one extremely intoxicated set of footprints. "Haha," I shout, spanking my hands together, "it was then that I carried you!"

The white silence is like the inside of a sleigh bell; it restores us somewhat to our minds. "It wasn't always so lonely," the seminarian says, as we smoke his brown-papered Nat Shermans. His right shoulder inches up toward his ear, the way it always does when he talks about tradition. "There used to be a system. There were women who would keep house for priests after their husbands died. It was a sort of vocation. They never married again. It was better then—there were places for people—but no one does that anymore."

A system, places for people, women who kept house for priests. In some dim corner I can still see those women, dressed in drab and black, moving on soundless rubber soles in and out of rooms, illuminated from above by light fixtures in the shape of dogwood blossoms. In their grief, nearly all of them had cut their hair. Jesus left ex-wives and widows all over the world. I remember—I was one of them.

It is probably the last conversation like this the seminarian and I will have. After his ordination, particular friendships with women will be discouraged. I understand why, but in a wider sense, it is frightening. If you are not friends with women, they are theoretical to you.

The snow falls in cartoonish heaps, and I think blurrily of how forms are destiny: how the rain is destined for its torrents and the snow for its drifts, and the poems for their sheafs and me for the poems. Something seizes me and I break into a sudden run down the silent street. "I am fast," I always insist to my husband, lying motionless and stubborn in the middle of the bed. "I used to be so fast, until I grew up and got boobs." He never believes me, but look now, I am fast again; I'm running in between the snowflakes. The unrepeating fingerprints fall all around me, into great indistinguishable peaks and slopes. The stars look like cusps, everything looks like a cusp. The streetlights still flow, the night smells like a new dime, and the mailbox seems to shine with the accumulation of all it has ever received. The seminarian is laughing and waving me toward the open door, but I am not cold and I am not coming back just yet. Places for people, wide spaces and small, little bodies floating down into their forms.

I run even toward the church, till I can see the Marian grotto hidden on one side where the garden is pinched out like a series of matches. It is almost Christmas Eve. Tomorrow, in that church, the songs I like best will flame out their brief lives, there and then gone, while the people hold soft and slumping candles under their chins and circles of cardboard catch the notes of hot wax. They will return again next year.

14

VOICE

The best way to write poetry, in my experience, is to first fail spectacularly at singing.

Because my father abused six-strings when my mother was pregnant, my sister Christina was born with a musical instrument lodged halfway down her throat. This instrument needed tending, and tuning, and practice, so for a long time when we were teenagers, we took voice lessons together. That's what we called it, just: voice.

So send yourself back to piano lessons, or flute or cello lessons, or drum corps or baton-twirling or ballet or gymnastics, or practicing free throws by yourself in a parking lot at night under the glow of a single streetlight, or throwing a tennis ball over and over at a square on a garage door. Send yourself back to the time when you practiced, when you did scales and suicides and drills, when you figured out where the sweet spot in your bat was, and your bat was your body.

Unfortunately some of us had no sweet spot at all, and I was one of them.

This was the great tragedy of my life. If I could sing, I wouldn't be here—I'd be living in an apartment in Vienna eating small cakes with my fingers and drinking cologne on purpose and petting a pale castrato on a golden couch. If I could make that white sound I wouldn't need paper. But I couldn't sing, so here I am.

I couldn't read music but music could read me. It went through me line by line and scene by scene, with one finger down the middle of the page, highlighting me recklessly. Its comprehension was so complete it was even horrifying. No meaning in me was hidden from it, but it was totally closed to me.

I didn't understand phrasing and I didn't understand breath support and I didn't understand how to not make my face look like a dead doll when I was going for a high note. Also, I didn't understand time signatures. No huge surprise for a person who is living in a world of melted clocks.

Also my sense of pitch was off. Sense of pitch is not considered one of the five. It is not even considered the sixth, somehow.

Let me be honest: my voice sounded like the final cry of someone killed by a falling piano.

But my sister could sing, she could really sing. All her words were set to music. She had height, white sound, and roundness—when she opened her mouth the forward curves of doves came out. When I listened to her, my hearing flew out of the coop of my head and then came home. I knew it was art because it drew the senses slightly out of my body, and they leaped to meet the art in the middle of the air.

Why her and not me? It probably had something to do with the fact that my sister was named after Jesus, who was constantly surrounded by harmonizing angels, and I was named after the sort of Roman politician who loved to stand up and bore everybody with long speeches.

We often sang together at church because our voices sounded related, though mine was obviously the humpbacked insane relative who lived up in the attic and only descended for meals. Still, to harmonize with her felt as transcendent as finishing a bird's sentence, or standing an inch off the ground at the butterfly house. It was an exhilaration only possible in nature.

When I sang with her I felt on the verge of physical translation. They were not words, exactly, that were coming out of us then. It was whatever words were filled with, the liquid or the plasma or the perfume of them, spilling out of us and eager to be free.

This was thrilling, because it meant there was a whole realm of existence where words were not meaningful in themselves, but rather the man-made lakes that held music.

On Tuesdays and Thursdays we took chorus together at school. Christina was two grades ahead of me and everyone stood in awe of what she could do, so I must have gotten into the chorus just on the strength of my last name.

The best singer in the chorus was not my sister, though. The best singer in the chorus was Truenessia, who took the stairs two at a time compared to the rest of us. She was tall and had close-cropped curls and tipped her face back when she sang, as if she had a flower tucked behind one ear. Truenessia told us when we couldn't hit notes to *think* our voices higher or lower—to think a second story into our sound, or a basement.

This made sense to me. Singing was full of hidden passageways, and sealed-up staircases, and secret rooms. Most of the time I couldn't find them, but once when I was doing scales a roof lifted off and my voice jumped an octave above anything. It was off the piano completely, and I sailed for a second above the city of singing. I didn't know how it had happened and I was never able to do it again. It had come from the other side of the world.

The teacher who taught chorus was a redhead with a face like a crag, windswept and stony and shaped by nature, a face that though one thousand miles away seemed to participate in Big Sur.

She carried herself as if she were fragile, as if she had more nerves to the inch than other people. She was incapable of being ridiculous, even though the whole school knew she had once dated a Ronald McDonald.

Between classes we tried to imagine this Ronald McDonald relationship. How would you even kiss Ronald McDonald without getting clown makeup all over your face? And when he looked at you with an expression of lusty intent, wouldn't you just feel like a hamburger?

The redheaded teacher sang through migraines, cramps, and all other forms of female suffering. Occasionally she crossed her arms over her belly. Occasionally she touched two fingers to her temples. She was a sharp note rather than a flat and her mouth was thinner and straighter than the bottom line of the staff.

She taught us the interior smile, since you couldn't actually smile when you were singing. You had to arrange your face as if you were smiling except completely subtract the smile. It was impossible, but singing was full of things like that. Singing was worse than Buddhism. It was no wonder so much of it was done in churches.

Here's another one: "Open up the barn door in the back of your head." This is what I'm talking about! It meant nothing but you knew exactly what it meant, same as poetry.

My redheaded teacher taught us about the great composers. Here is what I remember: Bach was a scrolled mahogany computer wearing a little wig. Mozart just farted all the time. Beethoven was deaf and had thunder for hair. Wagner was a Nazi and he had hooves instead of feet. Stravinsky bore the mark of the beast on his forehead. Aaron Copland was cut up for steaks by the National Beef Council and Tchaikovsky was a marzipan baby. John Cage had sex with a piano for five minutes in the middle of the stage at Carnegie Hall and at the end all of New York applauded.

More intriguingly, she told us the story of a man who painted a musical staff on an aquarium and put a goldfish in the aquarium and then sat in front of it with a flute and played whatever note the goldfish swam. "Oh great," I thought. "We're all goldfish, and some dick with a flute is playing every move we make."

She showed us grainy black-and-white footage of Marian Anderson performing on the steps of the Lincoln Memorial and her voice had such a marrowy, everywhere-at-once sound to it that my face twisted up listening and the wind went out of me with a whoosh. It was an awful sound, like God.

When Marian Anderson first sang for Sibelius, in the same house where he would one day burn a symphony, he cried out, "My roof is too low for you!" and called for his wife to bring champagne instead of coffee. When I read that, I remembered Truenessia standing in our midst with that same call for champagne inside her, a voice that was more than a voice, a voice that was in a duet with its own happiness. Telling us to think ourselves higher.

Our chorus had the same problem as America: too many white people. Everyone tried out, but an overwhelming majority of white girls made it every year. So the question was whose place did you take, and what was her name, and how did she sound.

I mean, I sang "I Am the Very Model of a Modern Major-General" for my audition—*in a man's key*. We weren't chosen because we were good. We were chosen because we were interchangeable, because a status quo emerged from us instead of a real song.

Once you saw these things you couldn't shut your eyes to them, and once you started thinking about them you couldn't stop—even if your understanding was poor, even if your intelligence regarding them was limited. "He had come to the stage when one realizes how difficult playing is going to be, but one cannot go back and not be musical, that is how one hears things and there is no help for it." Rebecca West said that.

After high school, I sometimes thought about Truenessia. In class, I listened to her as I might have looked at her paper: because she always had the right answer.

Though I've noticed teachers often don't like the students who always have the right answers—don't want them to raise their hands, don't want them to call out. As we practiced, I watched the line that went singing between her and my redheaded teacher, that tense and tacit agreement that Truenessia would not use her full power.

My second teacher was different. She gave me and my sister lessons in the afternoon, and she was not fragile at all. She looked like an olive or middle C, and she had a velvety plush all over her which I saw as the fat on her notes. A low, burnished, brass-lamp light came out of her, and a steady flame of song existed right at the center. She hugged us when we stepped into her house, which was washed and sunshiny and smelled of vanilla, and it was such a relief to let our sixty-pound bookbags drop down on her immaculate carpet.

I could never decide whether she was lovely herself, or whether she was just attended by lovely images. I thought of a pomegranate, a rosy skin around chambers of notes. I thought of a brocade chair, of tooled leather, a hummingbird's throat, a glowing baby grand, a gilt mirror, a gazing ball, a peacock feather, a row of encyclopedias, a red-and-gold opera house.

She looked like she knew where Prague was, which at that moment in time I did not.

When I first met her she was singing the role of Madame Flora in *The Medium*, an operatic psycho who drinks too much and thinks ghosts are trying to touch her and lets loose dramatic swollen floods of song whenever she opens her mouth. I saw her dressed for the stage, robed and tasseled and finger-cymbaled, wearing slashes of makeup across her cheeks. I pictured her in a silk turban with a jewel set in the middle of it, which was the way she looked at me.

Right away she told me I was Stuck in My Head Voice. "You're singing down into yourself," she told me. "That's why no one can hear you." The problem, of course, is that I was a writer.

Singing down into yourself was called *vocal masturbation*, and you weren't supposed to do it, even though in literature there were postmodernists running around all over the place wanking themselves into recursive frenzies and getting awards for it. In singing, though, there was no place for people who were filling whole pages with the word HAHA or not letting themselves use the letter *e* or turning to the reader and saying oh hello, I see you there, reading my book naked in your bedroom.

Being a writer meant my voice was in a different place. There was no rhyme or reason as to why I could make this sound and not the other. Always I felt that I was writing to the tune of some music that I learned very early and did not quite remember.

It was instructive not to be able to learn something. I broke my head trying to crack the problem of it. I stood next to her week after week and felt like Helen Keller, with my teacher writing a word on the palm of my hand as water ran over it, and I could not connect the two though the water was cold and clear and sometimes I came close.

She hired a soundproof room for me once, with a piano in it, and I had my lesson there. It felt completely safe, as if she had hired an eggshell to hold me, and suddenly, I was no longer afraid of what came out of my mouth. But you can't always sing in a soundproof room.

She diagnosed my sister as a lyric soprano—an angelic term, the shape and strummed color of a harp. In contrast, she suspected that I might be a "torch singer." This was a polite way of saying that in its lower registers my voice had a horny, mooing quality. My rendition of "Stormy Weather" made it clear why, in fact, my man had gone away: because he was frightened of the sounds I was making.

I thought a voice had to be about what you could do. It wasn't until I heard Billie Holiday that I realized a voice could be a collection of compensations for things you *couldn't* do. It could be an ingenuity—in the same way some writers wrote books that coursed between the boulders of what they couldn't do, and went faster, tumbled over, fell in rills and rushed breathingly over the stones.

The great singers were also the great interpreters. She had just a single octave, and she made it her lifelong subject.

I thought a voice had to be about your fluency, your dexterity, your virtuosity. But in fact your voice could be about your failings, your falterings, your physical limits. The voices that ring hardest in our heads are not the perfect voices. They are the voices with an additional dimension, which is pain.

I was sixteen years old and I wanted to die. Life was so unbearable, I had to wake up so early every morning and sit at a vandalized desk and learn about the history of Europe and the genetics of pea plants and the female reproductive system, and none of it had anything to do with me. When you cannot pinpoint a pain in your body, the whole world seems to throb with it. Trees in pain, lit windows in pain, Wednesday nights in pain. Pianos flaming with pain, and the scale sliding up into a cry.

My teacher worried about me, she thought perhaps it was something at home. "How are things . . . *at home*," she would ask, in a voice that sang with something else when she was speaking, with care.

What could I tell her? That it wasn't a home at all, but a rectory where a priest had died in bed; that his unfulfilled ghost walked the halls; that it was a hopeless house, a house that was living out a labor of hell, day after day the same struggle?

My older sister dreamed of the devil there. He swooped out of her closet on leather wings and told her he would never leave her alone. My younger sister used to sit in the bath motionless, with the water pulled up over her knees and a bar of soap in her mouth. Even today she cannot explain why.

At times the house seemed made of screaming, and I roamed it looking for a cell of silence, a single hidden rest in that thunderous and warlike score.

It was hard to be in love there, to experiment with my hair, to put posters up on the walls, to dot my *i*'s with hearts, to listen to the music I really liked. I felt too afraid to buy lipstick, I was not allowed to show my shoulders, and the only perfume I had was a sample of something called Mom Is Going to the Symphony. I lacked the courage or the knowledge to invent a self, which could have withstood this, that, anything.

I am not sure what I needed. I was as hungry as I was before I learned how to read. At one point I shaved my head, which Britney Spears later taught us was a sign of madness.

Sex would probably have helped, but the only thing I was having sex with then was the intolerable sadness of the human condition, which sucked so much in bed. It was always playing the Requiem Mass when we were doing it, and its D was very minor indeed.

I couldn't shake the feeling that I had the "Lacrimosa" stuck in my flesh instead of my head, fragmented and repeating and never quite finishing, moving my arms and legs to its rhythms. It made me walk so slowly that sometimes I forgot I was walking at all and just fell down from a standing position.

Some days I couldn't sing one note. Some days I opened my mouth to begin my exercises and an involuntary injured yowl came out, like I was the tail of a cat and someone had stepped on me. When that yowl made its appearance, my teacher would tell me to lie down on the floor and remember my breathing.

Singers were different because alone among people, they had been taught the right way to breathe. Their breath was a participation, a light lunch to give them strength, a bite of the bigger breath. You might have wanted to drop dead, but you couldn't, because music was asking you one more time to fill up your lungs the way it had taught you.

I always had trouble learning what music wanted to teach me, though. One morning I took a hundred Tylenol, having looked up "household poisons" on the internet and chosen the first one I could find. Everything grew brighter, I seemed to levitate off the bed, and then I went and told my parents, who bundled me in the car and set out for the hospital.

My father, tight about the mouth, turned back to me and said, "I just want to thank you for ruining our anniversary." I apologized, shielding my skinned eyes from the light. I had forgotten, or else I was the kind of daughter who never would have known.

When they slid the tube down my throat and began to pump the charcoal into me, I turned on my side and barfed in a single swoop of black eloquence, as if this were a film and the cinematography had suddenly transcended itself. I flowed and froze into a perfect composition. The camera, somewhere above me, connected with every point of my face.

The next morning I woke up to see three visitors standing in the doorway of my room like carolers. They were members of some religious organization, and after a brief awkward speech about how much God valued my life, they gave me what appeared to be a secondhand pink teddy bear with a light-up heart, the perfect cure for a sixteen-year-old girl who had just tried to kill herself. Examining it after they left, squeezing it so that its stupid little heart lit up again and again, I was astonished to still find myself in possession of a sense of humor.

My father came too, and sat in an unyielding metal chair against the wall and talked, his voice quieter and more targeted at me than I had ever heard it. He said, "The last time I tried to do it . . ." and the rest floated away. The gentleness of the words was so lovely, the tone, the undulations, the caress. He sounded like a wave in a woodcut.

I stayed in the hospital for a while, attending therapy with a group of other kids, including a skeletal nine-year-old with very fine fur all over her body who told me sorrowfully that she had been shut up there because she was a genius, she could make a violin do whatever she wanted.

I don't remember much about the therapy itself, except that there was a room where we were all supposed to make bad art for one hour every afternoon. The hospital was under the impression that making bad art would soothe us. The nine-year-old and I exchanged looks.

I was telling more jokes than usual, and I was wearing my glasses for once. "She's like Daria!" a boy named Patrick cried, delighted. He was there because he was obsessed with his neighbor. "I just know that she and I will always be in each other's lives," he said serenely, as we sat in a circle of chairs, and then out of nowhere he began to cry. The day I left and would not be coming back he curled up on the sofa at the back of the art room and turned his face to the wall in seeming despair, and refused to say good-bye.

There was a song in him too, the short discordant chorus of one, looping and looping until he couldn't contain it. There on the sofa, he shook.

When I came back to school a few weeks later, it was very close to Christmas and time for caroling. The nicest part of caroling was going around to all the fine rich houses of St. Louis, houses that still dreamed of a future where St. Louis was a major city, and drinking wassail and eating chestnuts and wearing black woolen coats under the snow and the stars, which fell together. That winter more than any other, I loved singing those minor-key songs: holly and ivy, three ships and three kings, all the birds I could name.

After the caroling was over, my redheaded teacher told me to think about not coming back to chorus next year, which shocked me so much that I couldn't respond. My heart flew out of me like a red cardinal, and then my parents told me we would be moving to Cincinnati that summer anyway, maybe because of what I had done, I didn't know, and that was the end of that—that was the end of singing.

Still, it was too late: voice had walked into every corner of my life; it drew my head up toward the ceiling on a string. In the clocks on my walls it kept time. "Sharp, sharp," it said when I spoke.

You know it took me so long to write this piece because I kept trying to make it beautiful and finally I just had to shake myself by the scruff of the neck until a more natural sort of grunting came out. You can't make something sound beautiful. It's either beautiful or it's not.

interesting concept

Of all the opera singers, I liked Maria Callas the most because her voice was capable of being downright appalling. If Ella Fitzgerald stole from the horns, Maria Callas stole from the barnyard—from the goose, from the hog, from the bullfrog. At times she sublimely approaches the sound of the chicken impersonator; at times a bok-bok almost emerges. On a continuum of all animal noises, she is the furthest point, which is perfection.

"Open up the barn door in the back of your head."

The funny thing was, even though my voice was so ugly, it wasn't suited to sing the ugly songs any more than the pretty ones. And after all, I did prefer the church songs that my sister and I sang at Mass on Sundays, in a small alcove full of the solemn red candles that you could light for a dollar, while my father performed the age-old ritual in a gold dress. At Midnight Mass on Christmas Eve he sang "O Holy

Night" with us. His voice was a pleasure to listen to after some priests, who sounded like all the juice had been sucked out of them by large carnal mosquitoes. Priests are the worst singers in the world, except my father.

There is something easy about singing harmony with your family— even I could do it. The sweetest part is when you come back to the home note after diverging all throughout the hymn, and you sing it in a unison that is closer than other people's. When you come back to the home note, you are hoping to achieve complete overlap. If you sing in perfect tune your sounds will disappear into each other, and for a minute you will have no sense of your own borders. You could lose yourself forever if you did this every day, but once a year on Christmas it was all right.

My teachers taught me to abandon the final consonant, so that certain songs never ended, so that you walked out of the room and into the sunlight with the song still continuing behind you.

Some unresolved chords I have heard I swear I can still feel—somewhere inside me, I am waiting for them to finish.

I left singing behind, but it does stay with you. At night, my body tries to go to the opera. On Sundays, my body tries to go to Mass.

My sister stayed on the home note, and she never walked outside of the church. She will take fresh breaths of the cathedral as long as she lives, and empty her dead breaths out into it, and in the midst of all that lofted air, her voice will keep climbing, surrounded by its angels and the arches of their wings.

Why could I never do it? Because I sang down into myself, because I was a writer.

"You must always believe that life is as extraordinary as music says it is." Rebecca West said that. You must also believe that it is as high, and as low, as strained to the breaking, and that the silence before and after it is as sweet.

More music than even music to me is what has been written about it.

Why could I never do it? Because I keep a cat. A cat is a kind of externalized thinking, another intelligence in the house, which prowls.

But some people keep a canary.

15

I AM A PRIEST FOREVER

Boys will be boys, men will also be boys, boys will be men, and men will be priests. I ought to be able to work in a reference to the seminal R&B group Boyz II Men here, but I find I'm not up to the task. Nothing could be further from their smooth, open-shirted, and mellifluous stylings than the celibate spectacle I am about to witness.

On the afternoon of the seminarian's ordination, my mother and I rush, huddling together, through the doors of the cathedral. We have to walk through a row of knights in order to get to our seats. I can't remember the name of their order, so I silently refer to them as the Knights of the Crucified Elks. Each knight is trying to have a bigger feather than all the rest. They're also wearing swords, which seems like overkill for such a peaceful celebration, until I remember that I myself could be considered an enemy infiltrator. Still, my camouflage is perfect. I am even wearing a white dress embroidered with innocent flowers, to remind everyone that some people in the world are pure.

I have snuck in contraband, in the form of a notebook. I hide it in my lap, along with a mini golf pencil. At this point, I consider myself on an anthropological mission, much like Margaret Mead. I have discovered that this makes almost anything bearable—it would have been such a salvation in my childhood to think I had been sent on a mission to *notice*. That would have turned my insubstantiality into something useful, even advantageous. But I am not here to spy, not really. I am here because I promised the seminarian that I would come.

He isn't the only one taking orders, of course. There is also Leonard, whom I have met only once; Dan, a reliable, badgerish man with a voice that sounds like it's being carried away by the wind; and Rex, who is famous for once giving a sermon called "The Pharisees Were Right." It prompted, my father acknowledged, "a number of complaints." Some elderly women who had spent their lives walking the straight and narrow were furious to discover that they could have been Pharisees this whole time.

Dan is my favorite of all the candidates, because over winter vacation he came to the rectory and drank a Classic Martini with us and then pointed to the seminarian and pronounced, "You're a . . . Temp-Taaaation to him!"

Happily, my efforts at seduction did no good. My villainy has been overcome, has been leaped like the lowest hurdle, because today these men become Christ's husbands.

THE CATHEDRAL OF THE IMMACULATE CONCEPTION is red brick with white wedding-cake trim and an ostentatious gold dome. The ceiling is painted a saturated celestial blue, with lights in it like stars. I think, as I always do in cathedrals, of what my history teacher told us about Gothic arches—that they imitated alleys of trees in the forest, and the way their branches crossed each other at the very top. Like most of the facts about history I have permanently retained, this one seems unlikely to be true.

Still, churches do resemble forests in one respect: the light in them is filtered through something else, some live leaf. The silence in them has been sifted through music. And the people standing in them do seem under a natural protection, to have come in out of the weather and taken shelter under a stone umbrella.

My mother finds us space to sit in the shadow of a marble column. A square of black cloth is pinned over her hair, its solemnity somewhat offset by a Band-Aid on her nose, where she recently had a patch of suspicious cells removed. Nothing serious, but to the Irish, as she has often warned me, the kiss of sun can all too easily become the kiss of eternal night.

She touches the Band-Aid with sudden decision. "No. I don't want to remind people of injury . . . not today," she says, and rips it off mercilessly. Then all falls quiet, and the congregation stands and turns toward the open front doors.

It's starting. The bishop just walked by carrying some sort of magical gold shepherd's crook. I wonder if he has license to hit the priests with it if they don't behave

If the whole cathedral erupted into a fight scene, you just know he would start laying people out with it left and right

Then the fake knights would come in with their swords, and then my dad would probably whip out a hidden handgun, and then church would finally be exciting

Oh god, what is this triumphal music—it sounds like the farts of a man with a French horn for his intestines

"*J'adore* the French horn," my mother murmurs, amid the holy blasts. I am less appreciative of its grandeur, possibly because I am a heathen. Jason's father is a French horn player, and one Christmas he gave us a CD of songs he had recorded called *Horn of Praise*. Several years later, it was followed with *Horn of Praise II*. Perhaps the mad impulse to praise with horns is endemic to all Christianity.

A litany of clergymen begins to march down the aisle, led by a boy swinging a censer that pumps blue smoke. Bobbing along in the slow procession are my father and the candidates, all of whom are wearing white robes and black shoes and that special scrubbed aura that suggests they put soap in their own mouths when they are naughty. Alongside them, dozens of other men flow up to the altar and mill around, performing various occult tasks. One of them is decorated with much more lace than the others, gouts and gouts of it, frothing all over him like pony sweat.

"Get a load of Father Doily over there," I remark to my mother. "Now there's a priest who really loves lace."

"That's because he's Hispanic," she whispers. I didn't even know that was a stereotype.

It would be nice if they had a ceremony like this for accountants, or firefighters, or tree surgeons. Imagine if to become a plumber, you had to lie flat on your face in the toilet section of a hardware store while all the senior plumbers swung plungers around you

Or if a zookeeper had to get blasted by a trunkful of elephant water before he could begin his duties, or if clowns all had to cram themselves into a special car, or if old magicians had to shave intricate goatees on the young ones

I mean, even the president doesn't swear on a Bible this hard

If a cathedral is a spiraling, infinite library of human prayers, it is also a palace of free association. I have not felt the pleasure of letting my mind wander within the walls of one for a long time. First things first, I think, and set myself to studying the stained-glass windows. I am seated next to a tall rectangular one that depicts the crucifixion, all done in ruby and sapphire, with a black sky like a lowered eyebrow. Underneath Jesus' body are the words "IT IS CONSUMMATED." A few pews down, there is another that depicts Jesus being heavily messed with by a crowd of his haters. That one reads, "HE WAS SUBJECT TO THEM." Above the altar is a large rose window that looks like the universe's final orifice, dilated beyond human imagining.

I know how they are put together, because my father used to make them, before the pain in his back became so bad that he had to give it up. Clad in a disintegrating T-shirt and a pair of his billowing bengal-striped Zubaz, he would bend over his worktable in the garage and drag an X-Acto knife against the sheets of glass, which were opaquely swirled like candy, but which let the light flood through when you held them up. The knife made a shrill sound as it scored, and then he would tap-tap-tap the puzzle pieces out, with a sound more satisfying than a bone breaking, and join them together with soft bits of lead. Gradually they added up to abstract pictures: flames and stone tablets and pale extended feet. I was fascinated. I sat for hours with him among the raw elements, breathing in that ancient, mythic smell of what, of Roman glass ground under the heel, and before that the sparkling sands, and waited for the moment when my father held his work up to the sun. I felt the windows stood very thinly between me and art—they were not art themselves, but I could see art through them if I squinted, somewhere far off in the distance.

Across town was another workshop, the opposite of my father's in every way. It belonged to my heathen uncle, whose hair was as long as Jesus' hair, and whose jeans fit better than other people's because he was a Modern Artist. All day he painted slick staring eyeballs, and screaming mouths around rows of television-shaped teeth, and carbonated dots in flying formation. He never spoke to me of painting, or theory, or how to look at things—it was enough for me just to know that he was there, that he had a studio in his house that was full of "good light," that it was possible. No one had to tell me what "good light" meant. It was a little bit prouder because it was being put to a purpose; it was pure and clear and watery and went gladly into harness, like water on the wheel being turned into power. It was his and his to use, the way the silence in my room was mine. I could not tell then whether the pictures of my heathen uncle were any good or not. I did know they were different from my father's wine, scroll, and sky-colored windows. When I thought of being away from my own house, I thought of being in that other workshop, where the paint was still wet and everything smelled new. I could not decide whether I liked that smell better than the ancient one. I wondered if at some point I would have to choose.

THE PRIESTS ARE kissing books constantly, with wet, juicy, open-mouthed kisses. This is the only part of the ceremony I understand.

Hand signals fly back and forth, candles are lit and extinguished, bells are rung, cloth is touched with insane reverence, and the choir keeps bursting into a demented round that sounds like a mummy trying to unwrap itself while wearing mittens. Latin streams from every mouth, and I recall the long-ago morning when I showed the seminarian a poem of mine that had just appeared in *The New Yorker*—a poem that contained two instances of the word "vagina."

"This brings us one step closer to an issue of *The New Yorker* that is ENTIRELY composed of the word 'vagina,' repeated ten thousand times," I said, cackling, rubbing my hands together with maniacal greed.

He rolled his eyes. "Do you even know what vagina means," he asked me.

I did, but it was better in these instances to play innocent. "It's sort of like a pussy, isn't it?"

"It means 'scabbard' in Latin."

"Pussies aren't in Latin," I told him.

My father strode colossally into the room then, and looked over the poem and congratulated me, even as he declared that it was "part of *The New Yorker*'s mission to abolish age-of-consent laws." I have no idea where he got this notion. There is something about hearing him trot out one of these new, astonishing conspiracies that must be like a mother hearing her toddler use a word she never suspected was in his vocabulary.

"What do you mean?" I asked.

"Mark my words," he said, cryptic as God's own sphinx, stopping just short of putting a finger over his lips, and then vanished up the stairs like a vapor.

I don't mean to be rude, but these ceremonies were probably a lot more uplifting back in the Middle Ages, when everyone was always about to die from a disease they got from touching rats

They keep playing a song called "You Are a Priest Forever." It is, and I do not exaggerate, as catchy as hell. Somebody should try to sell cars with this jingle

Is there a note of subtle menace in it, though? You are a priest FOR-EVER. If you try to be a priest for just a short while, we will have you killed

I've figured out that if I say "me too" after everything the bishop says, I will get to be a priest also. Major loophole, boys. Major loophole

The boys in their snowy robes wait, for a moment that may prove to pale in comparison to the one when they were first summoned: at night, in their beds; in chapel, at prayer; outdoors, under a sky that rang like a bell and then cracked. Eating pizza, with a girl who wore the same perfume as his mother. A catastrophe has brought them all here, the catastrophe of being called. I think of that Buster Keaton stunt where the wall collapses and he finds himself standing in the open window of the upper room, not merely unharmed but chosen. After that, you must live the rest of your life differently, carrying that open window around with you always, amid the whoosh of everything else in the world falling.

The boys stand, then kneel down, then lie on the floor, then stand again, all the while getting their heads touched. The bishop touches the candidates' heads so thoroughly that I start to worry for their brains. Then the other priests walk by and touch their heads too, for good measure, and then they help them get dressed in new clothes and then kiss them on the necks to let them know that the new clothes look good. It's essentially a makeover montage, with the added disturbing implication that they're not allowed to take these outfits off for the rest of their lives. "And you felt this," I say to each man as he passes, "and you felt this, and you." Ending with my father, "And you felt this too."

"YOU ARE A PRIEST FOREVER," the choir shrieks again.

"Thanks," I say under my breath.

Everyone always thinks that their religious rituals are the last word in dignity, but that if they slipped into another house of worship they would find a bunch of brainwashed idiots acting ridiculous. But I can tell something is happening now because my mother is crying, silvered streaks next to the injured nose, and so, when I find him among the crush of men at the front, is my father. The seminarian takes a handkerchief out of his sleeve and dabs his black buttonhole eyes, which are fastened at last. He and the other candidates present themselves, a row of fresh haircuts. All at once, a hundred cameras flash.

Is it possible to pin the moment when power descends, is bestowed, is transferred from one hand to another? It does not come down as a dove, but as a lick of fire, a language the powerful speak to each other. But careful, let it fall in the wrong place and the whole cathedral goes up with a roar.

A REAL OBSERVATION suddenly interrupts the flow of toy ones. I recognize an elderly priest in the moving mass on the altar as a man who used to come over to our house. He was for a while my father's particular friend. I did not like the way he looked; his skin was too pale and soft, like underbelly, and he had a mocking walrus mustache, and once he made fun of Walt Whitman right to my face. My little brother was five, six, seven. He was towheaded and charming, and the priest used to sit him on his lap and stroke his hair intently and give him garnet sips of wine. He crooned my brother's name in a velvety voice, reciting it like poetry, and flicked his eyes at my mother as if daring her to stop him. Already I had learned to recognize the ones who hated women, from the way they treated my mother.

"Young children need to be touched," he said, in that voice that meant he hated her and also something else.

There are small pockets in civilization, between words of conversation and everyday gestures, where secrecy lives. The priest fell dreamily, happily, into the alternate universe of the wine, where it was warm. He held my brother on his lap. The fevered lamplight shone around him. A sky rose up behind my eyes when I looked at him, a wide sky of clear and ruthless seeing, with a short stunted tree of compassion twisting in the middle of it. A tree that seemed to belong to someplace else, to Jerusalem. He drank and drank, his walrus mustache growing more and more ironic, laughing off my mother's protests in a way that made my stomach climb down a flight of stairs; until finally, pink-cheeked and furious, she succeeded in banning him from the house.

When I learned he and the seminarian are close acquaintances, I felt that ancient and instinctual alarm. Late one night after everyone else had gone to bed, I told him about those visits, and for a brief space he seemed to receive it. I showed him the family picture of us in that rectory, laughing and clowning in front of a Christmas tree, but I could not put into words the strangest part: how the priest grew younger and younger as he did it, until by the end he looked like a boy too, young and happy, who had sent away for something in the mail, and now, after a long wait, it had finally arrived.

"He was sent away for counseling years later," I say, "to Arizona or Texas or someplace in the Southwest. One of those dry places where people start over. All I heard was that he was *drinking too much* and *acting inappropriately*, whatever that means. I don't know." That was the frustration—there were your impressions, and there were the euphemisms and rumors and scraps of information that surrounded them, but never the sense that you knew anything concrete, and always the sense that it would be much more irresponsible for you to speak up about it than to be quiet; after all, you *didn't really know*. The seminarian stared fixedly at the side of my face and took short shallow breaths, and began, "I have heard some things," and then went and shut himself in his room.

But the next day he returned to me, determined. "No, I don't think that could be right," he said, "because . . ."

And you feel what you have seen set neatly aside, in that tall pile where no one looks, marked LAUNDRY. And you feel foolish, and perhaps even wicked, for having mentioned it at all.

Again on the altar, the mass of men moves as one body. And I chant to myself *Who is protected, who is protected?*

SOMEONE IS PRAYING NOW, calling in a loud voice for God to help the poor, the victims of prejudice, the unborn. He places a ringing emphasis on the word "unborn" that he does not place on "poor" or "victims of prejudice." A sort of breathlessness enters my head, as if I just overheard my name, and with a concerted effort I stop listening. I go sideways; I let myself drift.

The old impressions return: that you are floating in the jelly of a clock, that you are inside a bird's backbone, that your head has gone an

octave up and your body an octave down. That you are physically com-
pelled to stand and kneel with the rest of the people, that you are required to answer with everyone else. Religion trains you like roses—it
installs automation in the arms and legs, even in the mouth. Or as Jason
once asserted, with his trademark mix of authority and malapropism,
"They're priming you like Chekhov's dogs. To hear the gunshot and
drool."

I do not take Communion, but the mere word brings the taste back
to me. In childhood, we used to eat unblessed hosts by the fistful, not
distinguishing much between them and my mother's Health Crisps.
They came in sturdy plastic buckets that you could wedge between your
legs, and the white discs on white discs gave the look of riches. They
tasted like the second dimension, and vaguely like the black leather of
my father's car seats. There was a cross on each that you could feel with
your tongue. Ten seconds, and it would melt into nothing—no calories
even, just a moment of texture.

Later, I would sit in empty churches and keep the Eucharist company. This was pleasant; it was communing with an idea. It was much
like a girl spending a long afternoon brushing her hair and polishing
her nails and looking at herself in the mirror—marveling at herself,
except I was marveling at my mind, at my ability to swoon or be astonished, at my capacity to understand metaphor better than I understood
anything else. I was combing my brain down to my feet. Of course I
could have sat in that place and kept company with any object that
shone as the end point of so much human thought. I could have sat there
and kept company with a copy of *King Lear*, and later, that is what I
would do.

Still, there was such a perfect privacy to those hours, such an enthrallment, such a feeling that the outside world was black-and-white and bloodless compared to the rainbow in the church, that I can understand a little why these men are here. I understand, too, that some people flee to that perfect privacy because of what they must hide.

"Wow," says the baby behind me, a sweet and sober redhead whose parents have stayed with us at the rectory once or twice. "Oh, WOW," he says over and over, the word climbing higher into music, until his mother carries him out.

THE PROCESSION PASSES AGAIN, with a sound like snakes' lingerie, and then it is over. As we turn to leave, one of the Knights of the Crucified Elks approaches me. "I saw you writing in that notebook there," he says in a booming, unionized voice. "What were you writing down?"

His interest verges on propriety. He takes a friendly step closer, begins to reach. He might have the largest feather of all.

"Oh, she's always journaling," my mother trills, fast on her feet, whirling me past him protectively. "Ever since she was a child."

Don't mess with me, knight, or my mom will snatch your hat. As soon as we pass him, I turn to her in disbelief. "Was that guy about to take my notebook? What was he going to do, throw it up into the air and slice it in half with his sword?"

"Maybe he knew who you were," she says, steering me by my elbow toward the door. "Maybe he knew you were a debauched writer."

"Oh, that's rich," I say, starting to laugh. "Scratch the most debauched writer on the planet, scratch a Parisian who wrote about whips and chains and dungeon masters named Gaston, and find a person who was raised in the Catholic Church."

. . .

THE WHOLE CONGREGATION WALKS in a body through the drizzle. My mother and I share an umbrella; a car on the slick road honks at us. The celebration is not yet over—we have to go congratulate the new priests and be blessed by them.

Do you know that when a new priest blesses you for the very first time, you have to kneel down in front of him and kiss the palms of his hands? "Oh, disgusting, DISGUSTING," I wail as I fold myself down on the portable kneeler in front of the former seminarian, whom I will never refer to as Father. "The patriarchy must be crushed in all its forms. How is it that my research has brought me here? I'm GLAD you never get to have sex. I hope that you can see all twelve of my gray hairs from up there and are reminded that witches exist. I—"

"Oh, be quiet," he says, and holds my head in this weird way like he's about to crush it, and says some run-together intimate sentence, and then presents me with a holy card. At first I do not feel different, but then I realize it has made me more hilarious.

"I licked your hand, dude," I tell him when I stand up, and he wipes it on his gorgeous outfit.

In the corner are Leonard's female relatives, stamping and doing handclaps, their head wraps forming a yellow rose. They are here from Nigeria. Leonard's nephew pinwheels through the room in a great ecstasy. A new suit, a trip across the sea—he is bursting out of his outlines. It wouldn't surprise me if he grew an inch in the night. He nearly runs, with that gleeful noticing look in his eyes which means he's going to grow up to be good at jokes.

Children, as usual, are the cure for fine ironic feelings. I think how it might have been to travel to another continent to watch my father be ordained, and how it might have meant something different to me then—how the ceremony might have seemed part of the horizon's broadness, or a tangerine sunrise through a plane window, rather than that relentless narrowing to a point.

The nephew waits in turn to be blessed by his uncle, who now has that power. His face is expectant, it is open like a door. And who knows what feels narrow or wide to him now, or what will.

16

ABORTION BARBIE

MISSOURI, 1985

The alphabet had been radicalized; it marched for me now. The words in their order marched. This meant that I knew how to read. This meant that I could read the signs. They said ABORTION STOPS A BEATING HEART and IT'S A CHILD, NOT A CHOICE. Some of the signs had pictures on them too, always the same picture, a picture of a fetus turned to the side with its thumb touching its lips and a human rope floating out of its belly and a pulse of black omniscience for an eye. The fetus was the suffused red lit-up color you saw behind your eyelids, or when you put your hand over a flashlight. But I did not say fetus, I was told never to say that, they had told me to call it a baby.

There was no difference between born and unborn, they told me, they were just different rooms of the same house.

We had stepped outside into the light. It was morning and we had set up camp on the sidewalks all around the clinic. If you looked at the sidewalks closely, you could see flecks of quartz and mica, and sometimes two names inside a heart, and if you paid attention you often found a penny. I was masterful at finding pennies because I was always looking down. We sat on folding chairs and rummaged in a cooler for cold drinks and fanned our faces, probably with the literature. My mother told me to stay close and not wander. I was not the kind to wander anyway, not into this kind of a crowd, which had a strong thrumming bloodstream that might carry you off. It was not like any crowd I had met before. The energy was high, but it felt like the distinct opposite of a parade. We were waiting for something to happen, but I couldn't tell what. Ribbons of people moved through and among us with greater purpose, but I couldn't tell where they were going. My father was here too, but I couldn't see him.

"Why are we here?" I asked my mother, just like that, as children sometimes will when they need to get the story going. She hesitated, and then her voice rang hard out of her red head, somewhere between me and the sun. "Because these people kill babies," she said. The sentence was full of determination, as if she had made the decision to be open with me, to speak to me as an adult. I felt the shock of cold water. I said, "White babies?" because there was a book in one of our bookcases that told how babies were thrown off the sides of ships on their way over from Africa, and I must have been able to read, because I had read that.

"All babies," she responded. "Black, white, red, yellow babies. Purple babies," she added wildly, to show how far these people would go, after something that didn't even exist, but I had seen purple babies: my little brother Paul went purple when he cried. He was flushed purple now, in the sun; like everything else in the world, the sun seemed to have it out for him personally. I looked up at him. His head lolled on my mother's shoulder and a spit-up rag was tucked under his chin. Something loud and rushing had happened to my hearing—it was full, I couldn't hear anything more. *These people kill babies.* I looked at him until my eyes got full too and the sense of it shook me by the shoulders. My brother was a baby. Why did we bring him here, if these people wanted to murder him? Had she gone crazy, had everyone gone crazy?

In my head I asked, "How do they kill them?"

In my head she answered, "They take them away from their mothers," and tightened her arms around him.

That was the beginning: until I was much older, I thought my brother was a bright and moving target. I thought people followed us and kept him in their sights. Whenever we were in crowds, I felt them slipping through spaces with their eyes on my brother, wearing disguises and clothes that would blend, hunting him. We had been careless and now they were after him. That he was never captured was due to my vigilance, my alertness, my awareness that they were on the family scent, that they would stop at nothing. I should have asked who—who were these people, what did they look like, why did they do it—but she might not have been able to answer. If they were as she described them, could they even have human faces? If the enemy was so different from us, how could they walk on two legs?

The atmosphere was blue and shining and loaded with something like bullets. After a moment, I understood that it was us. It was our faces, our eyes, it was the ejection of breath from our mouths. It was copper-tipped and ready, it was us. All around the clinic, we were everywhere. We glittered. Girls and their mothers walked past us with their heads down, and I was not a girl and her mother, I was something else. I remember being held up in the air among the signs, and the merciless interpretation of the sunshine beating down. The signs would not stop talking, now that I knew how to read; they would not stop saying ABOR-TION STOPS A BEATING HEART and IT'S A CHILD, NOT A CHOICE and EVERY CHILD IS A WANTED CHILD. What the sentences were trying to tell me was that the truth was in turns of phrase. The slogan that reaches across all movements is this: if you arrange the words neatly enough, people will understand. There was one that sounded prettier, BEFORE I FORMED YOU IN THE WOMB I KNEW YOU, and that must have come from somewhere else.

The signs would not stop talking and the picture with one eye wouldn't stop staring. It looked the way the drumming in your ears felt when all the blood had rushed to your head. It was screaming with oxy-gen and solar orange, like something out in the night that needed to arrive to us. It was suspended, even though it must have already been born, two or five or even ten years ago. I closed my eyes and willed it to arrive, saw a flash of my little brother bobbing in the blackness, felt a wave of dizziness and opened them again. I was waiting for something to happen.

My father was sitting in a folding chair in front of the clinic's doors, with his legs apart and his hands folded, waiting. The focus of the crowd intensified and poured toward him, as if this were church, as if he were starring in a passion play. There was a sudden whirlwind of efficient movement around him, it was the police, he was standing up peacefully, they were turning him around by the shoulders, they were putting hand-cuffs on him, they were leading him away, and red white and blue lights were going up. He had been arrested, I understood, and something else: he had gone there intending to be arrested. He was not the only one. There were a few other people with him, though I hadn't really paid much attention to them. One of them was a nun. I heard it whispered admiringly that she had been arrested twenty-five times. I heard it whis-pered that she refused to eat and they had to put a feeding tube in her. I looked back at my brother just in time to see him spit up on my mother's shoulder. His hair swirled out from his cowlick like a fingerprint, as if it were intended, as if it were someone's design.

LATE THAT SAME AFTERNOON, we went to pick him up from jail— not a scary place at all, just a square place piled with paperwork. There were nameplates on the men's desks, with the names printed in gold. It was crowded with the same beige metal and sharp corners and fat bellies in white shirts that I would later encounter in schools, and had the same smell of petty bureaucracy that stacked paper up even in your nostrils.

Where were the criminals? I wondered. Where were the murderers? Hadn't they caught any of them? The word "murderers" had floated above the crowd outside the clinic, heated, urgent, so maybe they were all still loose. I saw only sharp corners and my father, who looked none the worse for his imprisonment. His collar opened its little white window on his throat, and he squared his shoulders at us and looked proud. Was jail something you could just try on for a while, like a robe, like a vestment? He had been given only a dry bologna sandwich and it tasted like sand, that was the first thing he told us—you know men, the saying went, always thinking of their stomachs.

I examined him carefully to see if he was different. He looked just the same only more so, as if he'd gotten a good watering. His face was serene. He felt complete. He had said his piece with his whole black-and-white body, while other bodies slipped by him one by one and he did not listen or could not hear. I thought of the way the handcuffs shone in the sun as if they had just been poured, and were cooling around his wrists for the first time. I considered the cell and thought its emptiness had a certain appeal. My father was the sort of person who liked to be alone in a little belly with his thoughts, with his own heartbeat booming everywhere around him, and so was I. We were people made of isolate particles. We drove home with him and he told us about jail.

I sat next to my brother and listened, and I heard that rushing in my head again, but this time I knew what it was: blood moving in and out of human shapes across the universe. Into and out of Patricias, into and out of Pauls. One could empty at any moment. A new one could fill.

My mother must have seen something in my face afterwards, the way I hovered over my brother and kept close to her in crowds, because she never took me back to the clinic again. She was a kind woman. She was other things too, but she was kind. The feeling did not leave for a long while, the feeling that death was after my brother, and then I forgot it, and remembered it only when we grew up and he went overseas with a gun in his hand and the merciless sun on the family face, though that is a different story.

YOU LOVE YOUR MOTHER most when you're hip-height and can still hide in her skirts. In the churches, from behind my mother's skirts, I watched the women. They held third, fourth, fifth babies in their arms. Sometimes they balanced one baby against the round belly of another. They walked more slowly than the rest of us, knee-deep in some meadow, and had a certain physical serenity, as if they'd handed their lives over totally to biology. They were happy the way crabgrass is happy, doing what they were designed to do, at large in the world, elsewhere called a weed, but they didn't care. It was the look of vegetable love, growing wild over the kingdom of God. It was the look of bodily lushness, which takes in air and multiplies it and gives it back somehow greener. Their cheeks and lips were naked, and something else in their faces was even nakeder, some longing and some fulfillment lying skin to skin and side by side.

The natural order is a powerful narcotic. I don't mean this in the sense of any opiate of the masses. If you sneer at religion as the opiate of the masses, you must sneer also at the brain, because the receptors are there. You must sneer at the body, which knows how to feel that bliss. What I mean is, a sweet look of lying down in poppy fields, of feeling control finally by giving over control, a look of wild and then tame relinquishment. In the mirror, I examined my face for signs of my mother and saw something else.

It's not that they thought women were mere incubators—the men might have thought that, but not the women. The women were in love with the body's seduction of itself, they bent backwards to it, they danced in their own arms and danced beautifully and looked down on anyone who didn't. They dipped low, almost to the floor, they swirled their skirts when they weren't wearing any, they felt a hand on their lower backs and moved with it. What it was, was a sense of pride. They wanted to be more of their noun than other women, as John Wayne was more of a man.

We are the ones, they often said among themselves, at kitchen tables and over cups of tea, who really respect women, who really understand them. The opposite of machismo is marianismo. You know, sometimes you run across a word that is meant for you, is part of the currency of your country. When I saw that word "marianismo" for the first time, I put it in my pocket. It was exact change in the form of a concept and I knew I would need it someday.

And when these women were depressed, it was elemental—it belonged to the older, blacker blood, it was an overspill of salinity that was trying to get back to the sea. And when one of these women committed suicide, as they sometimes did, that was elemental too, there was no equivocation and they left themselves no out, it was suicide the way a man would do it. But here I find myself tempted to make the words march.

The fact is that mostly those women looked content, unless they weren't, until they weren't. In my mother, you had a woman who had never had a difficult pregnancy, never had a miscarriage, who could conceive of nothing else, no other idea: why would you not want children? Her milk always came in, as reliable as my books. There was no twisted branch inside her, only apples. She never had the feeling of a child going wrong inside her body, which she paid for later, maybe, with the feeling of a child going wrong outside of it. Helplessness, helplessness. I was hers, and then I was not. Later I would be hers again.

She was once slapped in a grocery store by a complete stranger, a woman who spat at her about overpopulation, who said, "How can you do this, when children are starving, starving . . ." I looked up at her uncomprehendingly; I think I was there. I was not starving. I was in the grocery store.

AND HOW IS THIS the same mother as the mother of my other stories? And how is this small, frightened speaker the same self? But my father's house has many mansions.

YOU WILL HAVE ONE MEMORY where your mother and father are strangers, where they do not fit the story at all. They are too tall, their faces are distorted, they move in the middle of some spine-chilling scene, suddenly there is nothing funny or cozy or domesticated about them. There will be one deep-set square inch of the brain where they stand up next to each other and are as primally shocking to you as motherhood and fatherhood must have been to them.

Sometimes when you looked at them you could tell how frightened they were to see you walking around outside of them. They practically bled where you had been taken out. They didn't just want to protect you now, or flank you on both sides into the future. They wanted to keep traveling back to the night you were born and make sure you got there safe every time. They wanted to tie off every reality where you didn't get born like an umbilical cord. When they talked about abortion the verbs they used were "sucked," "scraped," "ripped," "vacuumed out," and when they said them, it was plainer than plain that they were talking about you, and the violent rushing in the gut they felt when they thought about your absence. The possibility that you might not have existed was so vast and you were so small—they held you in their arms and thought of large and minute laws, past, present, and future laws that would force the world to let you through, that would force whatever government there was to let you enter the country, the state, the city, and finally the little four-cornered house, and finally your mother's body, and finally your own. That was what it was.

MY SISTER HAS THE NEWEST BABY in the world now, and she gave her an old name, Etheldreda, the name of some Middle English crone that you would go to for a packet of herbs, who lives alone in the thickest part of the forest among dried lavenders and chamomiles and mustards. When I am with my sister's children, something happens to time and suddenly we are playing together against it, with an instinct I never experience elsewhere. When I'm bouncing the baby, spinning her in circles, lying on my back and raising her up and down for kisses, time simply stops, it can't make a move against me as long as she's there. Her personality is lined up inside her intact, the way you're born with all the eggs you'll ever get. I think, "So appleness and aboutness, you have those too. Some quality goes through to the core, and that is you. Wheatness, wineness, stoneness." There's a wholesome feeling in the bones that ought to be ground up for loaves of bread, something golden. A reflex reaches out of my hand sometimes and catches her before I even know she's falling. There is a call that rings in the hindbrain, that says come back to your senses, come back to all five of them, and after that come to the sixth. But I cannot, or I will not.

The twinge you are feeling right now is the twinge of wondering whether I am really right-thinking, whether I am really on the right side when it comes to this subject. I put that twinge in because I sometimes feel it myself. But after all that, you must understand I had to leave right-thinkingness behind.

THERE IS A SPACE above Missouri that is crowded with prayers for the unborn, just as there is a space above Las Vegas that is flocked full of magicians' doves. In the 1970s and 1980s, in the Midwest, Catholic rules-lawyering met with Protestant fire-breathing and gave birth to something new. It was the Movement, and for a while our whole lives were tied up with it. The air of a subculture is a different air; it has words in it, even messages. It is harder to breathe, but it gives purpose to every part of you, every cell. It propels you forward, it works through you, your eyes produce a spotlight wherever they fall—a hot white beam of accusing clarity—and everything you look at is bathed in it.

There is a picture, as I have mentioned, of my father at a pro-life Halloween party in the early eighties, dressed as Dracula and pretending to bite the necks of other pro-lifers. You are not alone in thinking that this sounds like the worst Halloween party anyone ever had. We had pro-life bumper stickers on our car, and pro-life pamphlets scattered among our books. My older sister cried each year on her birthday because it fell on the anniversary of *Roe v. Wade*—that was the sort of fact we knew, even as children. We were forbidden to put quarters into March of Dimes candy machines, because the March of Dimes wanted to eliminate birth defects, and the only way to do that, the logic went, was to eliminate all the babies who had them. Remember those little silver foot pins that people wore in the eighties, intended to remind you just how small a pair of feet could be? We had so many of those around our house, in junk drawers and change dishes, that one time I swallowed one and we had to wait for two days to see if it would pass through me intact. Like a penny, and it was currency too.

We patronized pro-life businesses, which in the Midwest, back then, was easy to do. It was possible to buy a pro-life pizza, despite the fact that a pizza is by its very definition made out of choices. In my mother's closet I can still find hangers with pro-life messages printed on them. The Midwest, contrary to popular opinion, does not lack a sense of irony. It might have too much of one.

It's the habit of most movements to characterize the opposition as infinitely stupid and infinitely wicked all at the same time, and ours was no exception. What did the enemy look like? A typical story might feature a large woman in a sweatshirt going to the hospital with stomach pains, and the doctor telling her it was because she was giving birth right that very minute. "And thank God," the person telling the story would say, campfire shadows leaping up their face, "because she was one

249

of the leading feminists of the day, and she would have aborted the child without hesitation." It was accepted wisdom that the average feminist couldn't tell bad indigestion from a head emerging between her legs, and that therefore the country was overrun with women in big shirts who didn't know they were pregnant. This is the only thing that strikes me as funny now, the feminists in big shirts. Back then, though, it never occurred to me to question any of these stories. It was always my religion to believe anything anyone told me.

"How would you feel if you aborted . . .

". . . Einstein?" they would whirl around and demand, when they were feeling especially rhetorical. Poor Einstein got aborted so often in those arguments—he was the bomb to end all bombs. If that didn't work, what if it had been Jesus? If that didn't work, what if it had been you?

Facts and figures were handed around: fingers at this many weeks, heartbeat at this many weeks, brain activity at this many weeks. The size of a berry, a plum, a cantaloupe. Now it could feel pain, now it was dreaming, now it could survive on its own outside the womb. Facts crowded the world, like the dead and the living. These things were facts. But what else was?

AT THE KITCHEN TABLES, over tea, the women would dream up the worst possible scenarios and then at the end they would say, in the alto tones of a martyr, "Well, I would keep the child." Always *I would keep the child*, with the flame-circled air of a person setting her jaw and throwing her head back and making the heroic choice. But what they were asking was for there to be no choice at all. That was the country they wanted.

When the men walked in on these low susurrating conversations, they looked unnerved, as if they suspected us of trying to decide something in their absence. When they walked out again, we resumed. What if, and what if?

"What if it was your own grandfather?"

"What if you were twelve years old?"

"What if the baby's head was twice the normal size? What if there was something wrong with it?"

"Well, I would keep the child."

And even, "What if you knew it would kill you?"

And the answer, "Then I would die," while we, the children who would be left behind, watched from the corners of the room.

THEN I WOULD DIE. Good sentences repeated themselves for me, and that was a good sentence. It got its teeth on some soft part of you and just bit. Why, these women are wild, I marveled. What it meant was that all civilization left the body when a child was born, that the city and all its government were neatly ejected from a woman and she reverted to feral woods again. It meant that childbirth turned a mother into something with twenty claws, and she would turn them on herself if she had to.

THAT ISN'T THE END. The end is that we took in a woman named Barbie. Barbie was pregnant, and she wanted an abortion, but my father talked her out of it. She was alone in the world and poor; she didn't think she could take care of a child. We could help, he must have said. We would help her through it. And so she lived with us as long as her state of grace lasted, talking on our beige phone, curling the cord between her fingers. Her back was always to me, her hair plummeting down between her shoulder blades as if her beauty had nowhere else to go and had jumped the cliff of her. It hung in free fall, and she cradled the phone against her ear and talked. Once my mother asked her to babysit me and my sister Christina for an afternoon, and after a long look of assessment she shrugged and left us alone and walked down to the corner store to get some Twinkies. She was nineteen years old. She stayed with us and got big as houses, and then she had her baby, and we never really heard from her again.

What happened to Barbie? I was told we had helped her, that we had rescued her from an enormity she didn't really want to commit, from the shame, the guilt, the rushing vacuum. "But where is she now?" I asked much later, when the story began to seem strange, unfinished, organized around its missing pieces. "When is the last time anyone talked to Barbie?" On the beige phone she liked so much, curling the cord between her fingers? What was her baby called? No one seemed to know. After she disappeared, we moved into the enormous rectory that we all thought of as the mansion, and for years I felt we had shut her in one of the innumerable rooms, where she still lived and where we never visited. The thought persisted that I might open a door to her one day. It is far worse to be haunted by a living person, carrying her baby in her arms.

THAT IS HOW I RECALL IT, but I know I must have the details wrong because I always have the details wrong, or else I have the details right but nothing else. I work up the nerve to ask my mother about it. We're sitting in a little hole called The Peanut after the seminarian's long-awaited ordination, wearing dresses fit for the cathedral and improbably eating chicken wings. I took notes all throughout the ordination and I want to take more now; I am in that noticing and setting-down mood where the day is your dog and sits up begging for attention. "Did Barbie have long hair?" I ask. "When I try to picture her I can only see her back, and I'm sitting at the kitchen table and watching her talk on the phone."

She nods. "Long blond hair. She was beautiful—she looked like a Barbie, actually. But she was an alley cat. She would go out on the weekends and just pick up men." She looks around the bar and focuses on a regular slumped over and sleeping next to an empty pitcher of beer. "She would pick up a man in a place like this. She didn't care at all."

"How did Dad find her? He didn't stop her on the way into the clinic, did he?" I worry that he might have taken her by the arm or kept her from entering the doors, even though I know that wouldn't have been his style.

"Oh, everyone in the pro-life movement knew about Barbie." She lowers her voice as though speaking of the dead. "Barbie was a repeat offender."

I turn this over in my mind: repeat offender. A police-station phrase, a phrase that puts someone in cuffs. She neatens her pile of bones and drinks water. "Alley cat and repeat offender," I think.

"It wasn't her first abortion. It was her third or fourth, and she had other living children too."

Where were they? Where was the rest of her family? Why were we her refuge, and were we a refuge at all? "Who was she always talking to on the phone?"

"Usually her grandmother. Her grandmother was a drunk and she used to call us in the middle of the night, ranting, making no sense." I think about asking where Barbie's mother was, but I forget. I think about asking what her baby's name was, but I forget that too, or maybe my mom doesn't know it—maybe she hasn't known it for a long time. We don't sound like ourselves. We've taken up the rhythms of a gentle interrogation. On the wall behind her is tacked up a poster of a big-headed alien with black eyes, and it stares steadily at me.

"The baby lived with us too, you know, for a few months after he was born."

I didn't know. I feel a fierce desire for reparations for him; I hope that after all that, he was born one of those geniuses of lovability who sometimes show up on earth; I hope he only ever heard the word "no" when it was good for him.

"It wasn't just Barbie, either. We had another woman living with us at the same time. Do you remember Maria?" As soon as she says it I can see her face: round and rosy and bent over her daughter, who had dark silky monkey hair all over her head. She had gotten pregnant by a Lutheran church leader and he wanted her to have an abortion, he pressed and pressed her to do it, so she fled to our house. "We did help," she repeats, "we did do some good."

She smiles her thinking-of-babies smile. "I took a picture of all three of them once, did you ever see that picture? Paul and Barbie's baby and Maria's baby. They were all sitting in your dad's lap." I have seen that picture—he's wearing his collar and his hair is in black orbit around his head and he's chomping his mouth open at the babies, who are all wearing white dresses and looking redder than they were when they were born, because now they had a reason to be angry: they had been baptized. I'm wearing a white dress too and I haven't spilled a thing.

The house must have been like a women's commune. It must have been nice, everyone taking turns with the dishes, rocking each other's babies interchangeably, overt sunset colors of estrogen pumping through the air. Though probably it was more like Barbie eating Twinkies with her bare feet up on the kitchen table, and Maria walking strange halls at night, homesick for a married man, picking up the phone to call him and then setting it back in the cradle again. We moved away, my mother said, and didn't leave Barbie our number. There was a reason—her voice tightens and ascends—"we couldn't let her know where we were." But her grandmother found it somehow and called us one night, drunk, repeating, "You didn't help her, you didn't help, you said you were going to help her and you didn't."

Right then Jason calls to tell me he just found three copies of my new book in the bookstore downtown. He sends me a picture of them all fanned out and I show my mother. "Can you believe it!" she says, shining with pride and hot sauce, and the smile on her face is the thinking-of-babies smile.

ON THE DRIVE BACK HOME from The Peanut, she tries to articulate some feeling about the movement. "The way those people used language—" She breaks off. "It was like they were using language just for each other. They said things that sounded like regular English, but they meant something secret, something only people in the group could understand."

"Those are called dog whistles," I tell her.

"There's a word for it?"

I had the same reaction when I first heard it. To this day, I'm always shocked to find out there is a word for something, as if I spent my first seven years in the forest sleeping next to a bone.

"I told him I would never take you back to the clinic," she says, because that is how these talks always end. "I didn't know where it had gone wrong, but I could see how frightened you were."

"How old was I?"

"Oh, you were still a baby yourself," she says, surprised. "Three or maybe four. I had you there in a stroller."

My mother drops me off at home and kisses me good-bye and I walk around the house and start writing outside in the still green backyard, a place where biology has pooled too, and a sound is coming diagonally to my ear that's like a baby's cry. But then so many things in nature sound like a baby's cry.

OF COURSE I GREW UP and got married, and for all these ten years there hasn't been the sight nor the sign of a child about me, and I'm not sure what kind of justice that is, poetic or otherwise. Sometimes my sister recommends me special vitamins and raspberry leaf teas, but so far I haven't minded. The slogans are what stick with me the most. They hit almost in the same spot poetry did, with a ring of perfect sense, of revelation, each slogan looked like the moment the clouds broke apart. I thought they were true because I could understand them perfectly, but as you grow up, you begin to understand something else. You understand it the first time you sit alone in the doctor's office, full from head to toe with specifically female blood, struck in your very center with specifically female pain. Some new realization comes out to its fingertips, grows fingernails. You understand it the first time something goes uncannily wrong inside you, or the first time something goes uncannily right. Something had gone uncannily right with Barbie, she had *fallen pregnant*, as they say in England, she had put fruit out as easily as a red berry bush. A woman's body always stands on the outskirts of the town, verging on uncivilization. A thin paper gown is all that separates it from the wilderness. Half of its whole being is devoted to remembering how to live in the woods. This is why Witch, this is why Whore, this is why Unlucky and this is why Unclean. This is why attempts to govern the female body always have the feeling of a last resort, because the female body is fundamentally ungovernable. Barbie, the neatest, tannest, blondest doll who ever existed. Barbie, from the Greek, meaning foreign or strange.

17

MISSOURI GOTHIC

Once a month, I dream that I am back inside the mansion with all my high school friends, and a masked man is picking us off one by one. The mansion, as my mind conjures it, is a boxed infinity that contains all my different houses. A hundred childhood rooms unfold in it, one after another, and the dream ends with me backed into a closet of the rectory we lived in when I was a teenager, the one next to the church called Our Lady of Mercy, unable to move even a muscle. My friends are long gone, and I am alone with him, whoever he is, whatever he wants. Then a carbonated feeling in the head, and my body streams upward, and I wake.

The longer we stay, the more often the dreams come. If the lunacy of the rectory is closing in on Jason, it is doing something equally strange to me: I am turning to vapor. If I seem colorless and receding, a background character in my own life who simply receives what happens to her, it is because I am vanishing again, the way I did when I was young. It is such an annihilating sensation that sometimes I think, just a gentle push and I would fall back into the old faith; I would believe all of it again, everything.

"I don't know how you survive them," Jason says the morning after one of these nightmares, over an egg-white omelet called the Triathlete. "You can't even watch movies where moms and dads fight. You get scared by the sound of violins."

"Tense violins, that are playing as a girl walks through the woods to her certain death," I say, pouring cream into the coffee that helps me stay so nervous. "Besides, you got scared once when you looked down, saw your shadow, and thought it was *a little child hugging your leg.*"

"Both of us are easily frightened," he acknowledges. "It's why our marriage is so successful."

"Tell the cook there are nightshades in this," my mother instructs the waitress, handing back a plate containing a single deadly potato. "One bite of a nightshade, and every joint in my body will become inflamed."

"Is the mansion still there?" I ask my mother, as Jason offers her half of his Triathlete and a piece of dry wheat toast. She looks at him with love; he is so healthy.

"Of course," she says. "I could take you up there to visit it, but I don't think we would be allowed inside. It's a Home for Troubled Nuns now." She squeezes her fist and says, "I'll give *them* trouble." No one is sure why she hates nuns so much, though she has alluded to certain sinister teachers from the past, presiding over classrooms in black habits. When I asked her about it once, she said darkly, "Sister liked to spank," and then refused to elaborate further.

That weekend, we drive the three hours from Kansas City to St. Louis to investigate, and find the fabled mansion sitting on top of its steep sledding hill, still guarded by its epiphanic oak. It's built of brown brick and is surprisingly modernist; it looks like the clash of two rhombuses. I creep around the corner and try to peer into the kitchen, where my mother used to pour iced tea on my Cheerios in the morning, but can see only glass reflecting other glass. A flash slides by inside, and I run away before the Troubled Nuns can get us. "Gun it!" I shriek, and Jason and I leap into the getaway car. Mom peels out on the road with nun-despising glee, as if to say *Who's getting spanked now, Sister?*

I do not ask if we can visit the rectory where the nightmares always end, the one across town at Our Lady of Mercy. Every step and square foot of it is painted on the inside of my eyelids, and has been ever since the first night I spent there, alone with my sister Christina and my father in the pitch-black of its basement. It was the height of dead-aired August in 1994, and our family was moving back to St. Louis after five years in Cincinnati. The three of us had driven out a week ahead of everyone else so we could unload boxes and furniture and get things in order at the new parish, and Dad had used this rare opportunity of complete freedom from my mother's civilizing influence to show us *The Exorcist* for the first time.

Perhaps he saw it as a tender rite of passage—it was, after all, the same film that had converted him on that paranoid submarine so long ago. He popped the tape into the VCR and settled down beside us on the sofa, stretching out so expansively that I had to shift half of my sitting apparatus onto Christina's lap. The most frightening theme music I had ever heard began to play, strongly suggesting that a green demon had entered a synthesizer and was thrashing around in there, refusing to leave. As the glow of tween possession began to warm my father's face, he said, with every appearance of perfect happiness, "Now here's what you need to know. This story is absolutely true, it happened right here, right in St. Louis, and it will one day happen again. Maybe to one of you, or to one of your friends."

There are downsides to believing everything that everyone tells you, but I had not discovered this yet. Terrorized, I scooted the other half of my sitting apparatus onto long-suffering Christina, who groaned with something more than fear. He continued. "This was not a *psychological disturbance*. This was not *puberty*. Don't listen to the *shrinks*. This was the presence of evil, pure and simple. The wing where that kid was kept is permanently fifteen degrees colder than the rest of the hospital. A priest I know who was allowed access to the case file *threw up* as soon as he set eyes on it and was never afterward able to speak as to its contents."

"You're going to die up there," the possessed girl said on-screen, in that strange, empty-drawer tone of someone whose words were not her own. My father chuckled with narrative satisfaction and rammed a handful of potato chips into his mouth. "Now get a load of this," he said. "She's about to pee on the carpet."

The true story ran mercilessly in its course; it overflowed its banks and threatened to sweep me away. After a while, it occurred to me hazily to wonder how I was still alive, since I hadn't breathed in more than an hour. My father attempted to mute the line "Your mother sucks cocks in hell!" but hit the wrong button on the remote and actually ended up blasting it at maximum volume. By the time the credits rolled, my sister and I were so paralyzed that we couldn't even get up to brush our teeth. We slept on the foldout sofa bed that night clutching each other, muttering what must have been prayers, trying to drown out the occult creakings and soft, unholy speeches of this new place. At four in the morning, I woke to hear her singing in the tiny bathroom, valiantly and loudly, in the face of onrushing darkness just like a Christian soldier. I wish I could remember the song.

. . .

WE HAD ARRIVED BACK in North County just as everyone else was fleeing it, in a mass exodus that seemed almost biblical. The airport had grand ideas of expansion and was buying up swaths of small, boxy houses in the surrounding suburbs. My father's church in Hazelwood was too underpopulated to support a school—schools seem somehow to die at my father's touch—so we attended St. Lawrence the Martyr in neighboring Bridgeton, which would lose more than two thousand homes and a third of its population in the next decade. Kinloch, a historically black town that had flourished on the other side of the airport for a century, was being razed, and its displaced families were moving in reluctant procession to Berkeley, Florissant, Ferguson.

Any attempt I made now to dissect that atmosphere would be slicing with a scalpel my twelve-year-old self did not have. All I understood then was the feeling of doom, that certainty that the last days were stepping toward me and had knowledge of my name. Above me and always, the sky roared in its loud blue suit like a preacher. The airfields were so close that if you got your courage up, you could walk to the weedy fringe of them and watch the bolted silver bellies go by overhead, spiriting people other places.

Mostly I did not get my courage up. The year before, a girl named Cassidy Senter had vanished on her way to a friend's house, and her bludgeoned body was found wrapped in comforters, her jeans pulled down over her ankles. She was the latest in a string of North County girls who had been plucked up by God knows who and sometimes set down again, sometimes not. *The New York Times* wrote a story about it called "A Town in Terror as Children Disappear," which began:

Ten miles from the hustle and horrors of big-city life in St. Louis, some of the streets twist and dip like a country road, and the fields and woods nearby remind everyone of what once was.

But these days there is plenty of heartbreak and fear in these suburbs to remind everyone of what now is.

Someone is stealing and killing children.

That's a hell of a lede. If my mother hadn't hated *The New York Times* even more than she hated nuns, I might have suspected her of writing it.

Before my father took over, the rectory had been inhabited by an ancient priest who left an upstairs closet stocked with poker chips and rhinestone-colored schnapps. The legend was that he died in his bed, staring at the ceiling until it broke into clouds, and then became a chill presence that squeaked open the closet door and drank Sour Apple Pucker in the night. The level of the Razzmatazz and the Hot Damn! never went down, but the Sour Apple Pucker sank by gulps. "Girl. That place was HAWNTED," Mary tells me when I ask her what she remembers of that era. "Hawnty-hawnty. Big ol' ghosts. Guzzling that nasty Jesus juice." Then, after a moment of reflection, "Either that or Paul was drinking it."

I had my own room for the first time since the mansion, a basement room with a wide window that gave me an excellent view of the neighbors. Mom had instructed us never to interact with them because they were "a family of drug dealers, whose daughter calls me a bitch whenever she sees me." This sounded like a promising premise for a sitcom. The Drug Family had pale, scrappy fights in the front yard where they rolled flamboyantly across the hoods of each other's cars while emitting rebel yells. "Bitch!" a voice would call out if my mother happened to emerge from the front door while they were in the thick of it.

"Don't worry, I'm on the case," she said grimly, and assured us that she was both "spying on them through bird-watching binoculars" and "keeping a daily log of their activities," including the comings and go-ings of the bad daughter, who wriggled out of her window on Friday and Saturday nights, disregarding the warnings that at any time she might disappear into thin air.

She was the only one who dared. Children were gap teeth in the landscape, missing wherever I looked. I never heard anyone chanting *Cinderella dressed in yella* or the contained splat of a basketball. If I did venture somewhere on my own, an anonymous car would often crawl alongside me until I reached my destination. The neighborhood was nearly silent, as if it had been blanketed in snow, as if it had been swad-dled up in something. Nobody went outside. We went to the house of the prophet instead.

THE PROPHET'S NAME WAS BILLY, and the first thing you heard as you approached his house was singing. It floated through the ceiling in a ring and gave the low, humble roof a halo. Christina and I were late for the meeting, as usual, so we hurried across the lawn and eased open the door, which was never locked. At once our shoulders squared and our faces went under the same blank, oval spell, which waited to be rushed full of something else, like eggs.

When Billy first formed the youth group, he had christened it God's Gang. This was the mid-1980s, mind, a time when parents believed that gang members were tiptoeing into the suburbs at night and singing,

"When a CRIP is a CRIP he's a CRIP all the WAY," at their children's open windows until the children sleepwalked outside with their arms straight out in front of them and murmured, "Now is the time for me to join a gang." Teenagers especially must be kept off the streets, or they would go mental from peer pressure and begin worshipping at the church of crime. Either join the Gang of God or else find yourself a member of the Drug Family, visibly dusted with crack, wrestling your own brother on the hood of an El Camino while my mother watched through binoculars.

I stepped behind my sister into the basement, which was 40 percent shag carpet and 60 percent Bible verses. This proved the prophet's Protestant background. Bible verses were . . . fine, but we secretly thought they would be more effective if they bled when you read them, just as we thought the commandments ought to shriek when they were broken. When I wasn't swooning over the Psalms, which were poetry, my own Bible study mostly consisted of reading and rereading all the stories about whores, and the donkey emissions that they desired, and wondering who was Oholibah and why the *heck* were her breasts so round.

In the far corner, we saw a group of teenagers with their eyes closed and their plucked-chicken arms raised, singing, with the peculiar naked look of people whose souls had risen to the surface and were breaking through in patches. The voices rose yellow and dizzy and yearning, straw spun only halfway to gold, and the circle opened in two places and we joined them. My sister's voice lifted above the others in a pretty heaven. "The Lord is my shepherd, I shall not want" was printed on a picture of lilies above her head, but we were here because we wanted something terribly—even if just to be elsewhere, away from our own homes.

The singing portion lasted about twenty minutes, and we usually wrapped it up with "Bananas for the Lord," which consisted of a single verse, repeated faster and faster until the circle broke into laughter.

He's a peach of a savior
He's the apple of my eye
He prunes away the branches
When the branches get too high
He bears his fruit in season and his love will never die
And that's why I'm bananas for the Lord!

"Why on earth did you keep going?" Jason occasionally wonders, appalled at the idea of me down in that basement Wednesday after Wednesday for five years, proclaiming that I was Bananas for the Lord. "My youth group wasn't like that. It was mostly just an excuse for kids to fingerbang each other in the backs of church buses."

"Well, they had soda there," I say lamely. "And no one stopped going once they had started. Or if they did, no one noticed they were gone."

He bursts into a Christian rap and I join him; sadly, we remember every single word. ("CHARM is DECEITFUL and BEAUTY is VAIN! A woman who fears the Lord, she AIN'T PLAYIN'!") We know the genre so well that we're unbeatable at that game where you flip through radio stations and guess within five seconds whether a song is Christian, usually because they use some gross hopeful chord or a word like "arise."

The truth is that I have searched myself and still I do not know. Sometimes I suspect I went because I so loved to sing, and where else could I in all my imperfection do it?

. . .

"EVER SINCE I WAS A CHILD," the prophet said, "I've been afraid of very beautiful people."

I looked around the circle and was reassured. "Very beautiful people" were not a big danger here. Everyone who attended was a sibling or a cousin, so that our faces repeated each other with bland variation, like casseroles. In order not to tempt each other with our bodies, everyone wore plaid shirts over T-shirts. Our jeans fell in cascades, our center-parted hair fell in cascades, we flowed like the water out of Jesus' side. We pronounced "milk" as "melk," "mostaccioli" as "muskacholi"; we had a talent for ecstasy and we were in this together.

"The devil can work through *perfection*," the prophet said, with a televangelical thrust of one hip.

I called Billy the prophet because he looked like the Old Testament. He had the profile of a promontory, with crazed eagles of belief wheeling majestically off his forehead and cheekbones. His eyes were a fixed and staring blue, and shed a fanatic starlight. It was plausible that he had grown up in a town with no dancing. There was something thumping, something plain-pine-church, something snake-handling about him. Once, we had heard, a burglar broke into his home and Billy sat him down and testified to him about Jesus until the burglar wept. He walked out of the house forgiven and free, and as high off the ground as the Good Thief.

"The devil can work through perfect *symmetry*," he continued.

I exchanged glances with my friend Angela, who was drawing something unchristian on the hem of her jeans with black ink. She listened to the kind of music where people screamed, but still she served the Lord.

"I have no idea," she whispered. We loved Billy, but sometimes it seemed like he came from another planet.

When he had finished enlightening us about how symmetrical faces were the devil's playground, he asked us to welcome the main speaker, and I braced myself. The quality of our speakers was unpredictable. The best, by far, had been a woman with a side ponytail who cried as she told us about a therapy session where she had beaten a pillow labeled with the words "MY MOTHER" to symbolic death with a Wiffle-ball bat. Her teenage son, sitting in the circle, let his lank corn-tassel hair swing forward and twirled his guitar pick between his fingers as she spoke. The principal of my grade school came too, and cried as she confessed that she had slapped her daughter hard across the cheek that morning— but when she dropped to her knees to pray about it, she saw a rich, throbbing, near-black red, and knew that God had carried her into his hot aorta to forgive her. Her teenage daughter, sitting in the circle, summoned perfect anonymity into every line and curve of herself and crossed her long, knifelike, lifeguarding legs. It was a blessing, then, that my father hated happy-clapping so much. It meant I would never see him up there talking about me.

Most often, though, our speakers were well-scrubbed virgins in their twenties and thirties who were saving themselves for soulmates they hadn't met yet, which became more poignant as the seasons passed and they kept returning. Could that happen to us? we wondered. Because we were saving ourselves too—the majority of us kept virginity pledges in our wallets that mimicked the look of business cards, and said "True Love Waits" on the back. I carried one myself, not feeling the need to disclose that I had long ago sacrificed my herman to a deep end.

This week we were treated to an earnest male virgin in Dockers, who looked like a spaniel standing on hind legs. He was one of the ones who was so determined to give it to us straight that he sometimes said things like "Did God create the anus to be a pleasure source? Yeah. Absolutely. In His infinite wisdom, He did." Right now he was explaining in patient detail that you could get AIDS from kissing if the person you kissed had flossed too hard that morning, and if you had also flossed too hard that morning, so that the two of you were bleeding freely into each other's mouths in a dark Sadean parody of kissing.

"WANNA RISK IT?" the virgin yelled, and I blushed for him. At least he hadn't sat in a chair backwards, like the last one.

The boys stared into the wells of their guitars and plucked stray chords, while the girls kept very still and somehow folded themselves tinier and tinier, like those notes we passed in class that told you who you were going to marry. Across the room, Christina sat next to her boyfriend, whose front tooth was dead and the color of fresh concrete.

"Well," the boyfriend deadpanned, "I'm never flossing *again*," so that the whole room broke into laughter the way earlier it had broken into song. Christina pressed closer to him; they were saving themselves for each other. Next to me, Angela's laughter turned to the habitual barking cough that dragged along the ground like a length of chain, and she tugged her plaid sleeves down over the words she sometimes carved into her arms. "HURT," the word said this week, though razors are imprecise, and it looked a little more like "HUNT."

There was a girl with a black widow's peak and a lovely froggy voice who wore larger T-shirts than the rest of us, and she sometimes sobbed uncontrollably throughout these talks, her friends leaning hard on either side of her as if trying to dive down into her heart, telling her *there there* with their entire bodies—because, if I have not said it, these people's veins ran with kindness, and they wanted to do right by each other.

Sometimes an adult came and prayed over her. Her father had gone to prison for sneaking into her bedroom at night while everyone else was sleeping—he was drunk, everyone said—and had been released again before we came. I did not know about it then, so I wondered why she cried. Perhaps, I thought, she felt guilty.

But always, the talk would continue, about how premarital sex was like using a dirty toothbrush or drinking a cup of spit. How sex was a fire that belonged in a fireplace, but if it got out of control, it would burn the house down. How bodies, once given to each other, were never really separate again. Not often, but sometimes, the girl cried, and people gathered around her and laid their healing hands.

Once freed, the girl's father returned to our fall festivals and fish fries as if nothing had happened, a pillar of the church restored to its place. I see ice-pick scars along his cheekbone, I see the same widow's peak, I see even a shining leather belt. I see him in the gym at St. Lawrence the Martyr, smiling down at the spectacle of our Halloween party, with his large handsome head full of howling black space and the red Mars light of what he had done in the center. His wife stood by; she had not left him. She had prayed, she said, and God had told her to forgive.

Say instead that the wife had prayed, and God had told her to scoop up her children and run, run. Where would she have gone, and how would her family have lived? There were so many of them, and the littlest baby's palate was cleft clear up to the nostrils. The cleft glistened; it made his smile somehow sweeter. He cooed through it, rocked in one of his sisters' arms.

St. Lawrence the Martyr was said to have been roasted over coals, and halfway through he called out to his torturers, "Turn me over, turn me over, I'm done on this side!" That is the kind of story we were told, and those were the saints who watched over us.

. . .

AT THE END, we joined hands and prayed for our friends who were battling demons, temptation, and brain tumors. Then everyone who had been blessed with the gift of tongues opened their mouths and dismantled the language, tore down everything residential, until there was no trace of its civilization left, just a pile of shocked components. And with those built their tower to the moon.

"*Sham-a-lam-a-ding-dong*," the boy next to me murmured, his hand sweating wildly in mine. Each week I listened with helpless fascination, my hand in the grip of someone who was approaching definite scat territory. Whenever I had tried it, embarrassment had overwhelmed me— it felt like I was sticking my finger down English's throat. Why would tongues come on command, I wondered, when no other gift of language did? And why would I willingly demolish something I spent so much of my time putting together? If I had had a broader sense of literary technique, I might have seen the possibility in such a scene, have associated it with automatic writing or cut-up text or poets in candlelit circles allowing spirits to speak through them, freeing themselves from meaning in order to find it, but I was so naturally reverential where words were concerned that all I could see was people tumbling down the house where I lived.

After the meeting, I drank a can of Wild Cherry Pepsi and walked in aimless loops through the crowd, among boys discussing their pet snakes and girls pressing books into each other's hands with millennial urgency. Angela had just lent me one about a band of people struggling to survive during the End Times who oozed a black goo out of their chests when they fornicated, which ruined all their shirts. She promised me it would be awesome. That was the word we repeated above all others: *awesome*, we said, awesome.

When almost everyone had gone, I stepped with my rib cage aching into what felt like the entire night, sitting in a black cube on one man's front lawn. All up and down the street I could see a loose constellation of those yellow ribbons that people tied around the trees in their front yards to protest something called *eminent domain*, which to my ears sounded like another name for God.

My sister walked ahead of me in a trance of human and higher love, seeming to hover over the grass. My mother was waiting for us at the curb, reading a copy of *Prevention* and marveling at the healing properties of various superfruits that "Bananas for the Lord" had not yet discovered. I passed two boys playing Hacky Sack, their skills honed to astounding sharpness by countless hours of Christian skanking, and discussing their eventual plans to acquire Komodo dragons, through illegal means if necessary. "Awesome," the one boy said to the other, "that is truly awesome." It was a word that sought to split the human atom, a word that contained its own cloud. The dragons, I knew, had grown huge on their closed and isolated island, until they almost counted as another species.

THE TIGHTEST, MOST SELF-INVOLVED KNOT is connected to strings that go everywhere. When Michael Brown is murdered, a few miles away from where we used to gather, I will watch the videos and study the photos and recognize the subtlest twitch of wind in the trees, the midday slap of sun on the pavement, the mobile shadows and the angles of the stop signs. The police, underneath their black riot gear, will look like the boys I went to school with.

And when I see that strong, surging flux of teenagers in the streets, kerchiefs tied over their faces to protect them from tear gas and lit by flares against the backdrop of American flags, I will fill at once with thudding dread and think, I wonder if they are sick too. They must have fished and waded in the creeks and played pickup games on those dirt lots. Their basements must have flooded in springtime. As they march against a swarm of more imminent dangers, I will wonder if they know, because we did not.

We prayed so much, and were so determined to carry our crosses with good grace, that sometimes we took our suffering for granted. As an outsider, though, I was occasionally uneasy: why were so many of us limping, feeble, milk-white, ill? There were half a dozen kids among my acquaintance whose growth had been stunted by rheumatoid arthritis, who had fragile walks and pink pinpoints on their knees and knuckles like outrageous emeralds. One boy's eyes were so clouded with it that he was nearly blind; the blue of his irises had a heavenly look. Asthma and infertility and rare cancer clusters, little girls with cysts all over their ovaries. A preponderance of twins, often one sickly and one well. Rashes of stillbirths in nearby St. Charles, which was where we lived when we attended those weekend protests, carrying those signs that said DO YOU HEAR THE SILENT SCREAM? in horror handwriting that appeared to drip blood. Babies born missing eyes, missing ears, conjoined. No one knew why.

I never recall seeing a single CAUTION sign or canary-yellow triangle, though five minutes' research reveals that the poison was everywhere, stashed at storage sites and piled out in the open. This is where they purified the uranium used in the bombs that were dropped on Hiroshima and Nagasaki, a fact so hidden that even my father, with his abiding interest in world war, was not aware of it. The local landfill contained

8,700 tons of radioactive waste, loosely mixed with topsoil and dumped there in the wake of the Manhattan Project. In Coldwater Creek, which had decades ago been contaminated with uranium, thorium, and radium, people reported seeing two-headed snakes winding with the current and crystalline crawfish snapping clear pincers. The water traveled through Florissant and Hazelwood and curved in a sweeping arc above Berkeley, Black Jack, and Ferguson. The state health department has acknowledged cancer rates are high in these areas, but suggested the residents would be healthier if they ate a salad once in a while—though some of the families who were hit the hardest were the ones who ate vegetables out of backyard gardens.

I will think of the call that came from the Marines when my brother Paul was training at Parris Island, informing us that his jaw had been completely hollowed out by a cyst, I will think of the parathyroid tumor that lopped the top octave off my sister's transcendental voice, I will think of my mother's crabbed hands and my own childlessness. It was in this place, after Paul was born asthmatic, jaundiced, and crusted with eczema, that my mother first embarked on her frenzied, all-consuming hobby of keeping us healthy, saving our lives.

BUT WE COULD BE CURED of anything, we knew. Some of us had made pilgrimages to Fátima and seen the base-metal crucifixes of our rosaries turn precious. Others had bathed in the waters of Lourdes. Miracles came to the little villagers, and so they could come to us.

And to believe with that kind of wholeheartedness, I can describe only from a distance, as you might describe a city on fire.

It felt: like the axis of the earth exited through my feet. Like I had grown a steeple. Like getting stopped at the top of a Ferris wheel, alone in my seat and exhilarated, one sandal hanging off the tip of my toe. Like the sunlight flashing off one of my facets or the water of me coming to a boil. Unhinged in the highest sense, so that my whole front door was gone, and the wind of what may come blew through. A church silence, a church stillness, reverberant with the last notes of the organ, filled with sustain multiplied into eternity. I was saved, set apart, snatched off the streets. The halo was a flaming hoop I had leaped through. I was on the other side.

Everything signified. Everything I looked at was designed for my eyes. The fabric of existence was cut to fit me; all ceilings were as tall as I was high; each book in the library fell open and let the word "rapture" leap toward me. The greatest gift of rapture was that it existed independent of the intellect; I needed no education to feel it. It was a capability, and born in the body when I was born—a reflex that sprang back gold against the hammer. We held hands and closed our eyes and felt our bones glow, and when there was pain, we offered it up.

I never wanted to write about any of this particularly, but when I began, my ink was suddenly liquid, like the dried blood in the glass vial. The conviction that we were part of a pattern is still so powerful I cannot shake it; these are the pages where it is hardest to tease out what is connected and what is not. And even now I could not tell you which curves of that circle were harm and which were haven. I know the house was always open. I know the prophet welcomed strangers there for decades, offering them food, offering them drink.

"I NEVER LIKED IT," my mother tells us on the way back from St. Louis. "I never liked that Gang. You know, every time Billy saw your father, he told him he was *praying for God to open his heart*. That's worse than giving him a book about the universe."

But no matter what I write now, I fit there. I did somehow fit. I did not have the right clothes, I did not have the right information, I had long ago grown timid in the face of my father's thunder. The horizon was limited, so my thoughts went perpendicular. My thoughts shot up and up, and my body chased after them, fizzing high over the sad and secretive rooftops, the swelled baptizing rivers, the emptying streets and soon-to-be-abandoned church spires of my town. I looked down on it all as I evaporated upward, and around me swirled the blue skirts of the patron saints, the poured-out martyrs, the powerless ladies of mercy, who watched over and could do nothing.

After 9/11, air traffic plummeted so sharply that the new runway fell into disuse and was soon seen for what it was: a great folly, a delusion of grandeur. Kinloch was gutted for nothing, and its community driven out to the hostile wilds of white suburbs, all for nothing. As of this writing, the Bridgeton landfill is smoldering underground, and the fumes of it are so overpowering that often children cannot play outside. My mother sometimes sends me articles from her nemesis *The New York Times* about what will happen if the fire reaches the radioactive waste at the nearby West Lake Landfill; it is creeping closer every day. The contaminated creek still winds through those counties, many of them poor and some growing poorer. I believe a great number of people do not know, as we did not. I believe most could not leave if they did.

"What are you afraid of?" we once asked a pale, eyeglassed boy who came every week, who cried within that ring in the prophet's basement and could not stop. "What are you afraid of?" we asked him, in a single voice grown strong on singing, our hands raised above his head and our fingers turned to blazing rays. *"Of . . . being . . . possessed,"* he sobbed out to us, ashamed, collapsing suddenly as if he were centered around a dark star, and we saw ourselves at once in the mirror of him, clutched with the same terror of being howled full of black wingbeats and wind and other will, of the forces we could not control. Yet even as we were afraid, what a thrill to feel ourselves fought over by light and darkness, desired with equal fierceness by high wild heaven and the leaping flames.

The house of the prophet was taken up into the sky by the airport, which is what it had wanted all along. My friends and our pattern were scattered. I could not visit even if I tried—those suburbs are just erased, nothing there, all trees now. I have seen pictures, and it is green, green, old-names-of-dinosaurs green. It looks like the planet after people are gone.

But locked into the circle, laying hands on each other, it did not seem likely that we would ever leave. Our work was there, and our rearranged language, and our shared songs. We used to walk up to strangers sometimes, ones who appeared in our sight with an unmistakable bold outline, and deliver them the message and say, "It was laid on my heart to tell you this." We used to say that and mean it.

18

POWER AND LIGHT

Darrell is dying, but we don't know that yet. For now, he seems like the only normal person here.

I'm carrying a bowl of grapes through a sea of twenty-five seminarians, which parts to let me through. I recommend doing this any time you want to feel like a symbol. As their faces turn toward me, I can sense myself streamlining down to the neat, empty, skirted shape that lets people know they're going into the right bathroom. My lordly father, who is presiding in a folding chair at the front of the room, catches sight of me and cries out, delighted, "You look like a goddess of the harvest!" We never could control what comes out of our mouths, which means that most of the time we say stupid things and then sometimes something beautiful pops out, whole, intact, and sweet, like a piece of fruit in reverse. How nice of him to say "goddess of the harvest" instead of "the little daughter who went down into the underworld." I curtsy to him formally and set the bowl next to the cheese and crackers, the tubs of ice and bottled beer, the chilled white wine. The seminarians circle the tables while they wait; they are hungry. They have been locked in a stone tower all semester, inhaling one another's arguments and exhaling their shared conclusions. The food at the seminary isn't good, they have informed me, and the daughter of the cook dresses sluttier than the Book of Revelation.

My own skirt might be too short. I keep tugging it down to fingertip length, the old school rule. I step away from the grapes and the men descend.

EVERY YEAR MY MOTHER cooks gumbo for the seminarians. Don't ask me how this tradition got started. It's just more proof that my father associates spirituality with shrimp. The gumbo is not authentic, exactly— if my mom ever saw a bayou, she would shout "DROWNING HAZARD!" and "WATERY GRAVE!" as loud as she could till men came to drain it, and that would be the end of Louisiana—but it's at least respectful. There are no tomatoes in it. All morning she's been chopping vegetables for the trinity (celery, onion, and bell pepper), but her hands are so knotted with arthritis that it's taken her twice as long as usual, and my father is losing his patience. I've come to placate everyone with snacks.

It's always strange to encounter words like "trinity" and "mercy" and "infinite" outside the dictionary of the church. Seeing them in the wild is like seeing a teacher outside of school, dressed in normal clothes. It must be how people feel when they come to our house and see the priest wearing nothing but an enormous pair of boxer shorts. I survey the room: shaggy seminarians, short and bald seminarians, virgin seminarians, older and wiser seminarians, a seminarian who converted from Judaism, seminarians from overseas, two seminarians wearing free

T-shirts they got at a Christian car wash, six corn-fed seminarians from the Midwest.

We're gathered in the narthex of Christ the King. "Narthex" is a word that never fails to make me laugh, because it sounds like a poison chamber or the foyer of a mastermind's lair. The narthex is another in-between place—not outdoors and not fully a church yet. Historically the narthex was the place where people who weren't allowed in the real church could go, and now we are here.

The front window looks out on the bus stop, that will take you across town. Whenever I glance across the street, it seems to be surrounded by a sphere of rain. Sometimes, when that sphere is raining harder than usual, the mothers who are waiting for the bus step inside the narthex with their little children and stand there until the subtle currents of "Do you belong here?" carry them out again. Then they take their children by the hand and collect themselves for a moment outside, under the shelter of the statue of Jesus that looks like it's made of endless breadsticks, and cross to the other side.

ON AN EASEL are pinned stacks of pictures of all the seminarians, smiling, with white windows at their throats and their names underneath. You're supposed to take a picture of a seminarian and pray for him every night. The most handsome seminarians are almost gone, a few unfortunates have hardly been touched. I examine each one in turn and try to find its counterpart in the room, but it's hard to tell them apart—their faces are too smooth and too ancient at the same time. They appear to be missing their beards. They look like Civil War reenactors who are reverse-aging into babies.

The ceiling is low, and the lights flicker fluorescently and emit an insect whine. The whole place smells like where coffee goes to die. Even what comes out of the taps is suspect, as if it might have caught a blessing from the holy water. There's a book on the communal bookshelf called *Sometimes God Has a Kid's Face*, and a few steadfastly inartistic paintings hang on the walls: velvet-skinned saints, guardian angels guiding children over bridges, Last Suppers that look like dogs playing poker. Through a window in a side door I can peer into the church itself, which I have only ever heard described as ugly, as ugly beyond belief.

Christ the King is so ugly that my father is trying to rip its guts out. He calls the altar the big rock candy mountain and he hates it so much that as soon as he's able to raise the money he's going to tear it out and put in a new one. The steps are slippery and circular and people always trip going up and down them—it's going to kill someone someday, he says of the big rock candy mountain. He can barely make it up those stairs on his knee replacements; my mother fears he is going to fall.

On my way out the doors, I walk past the holy water and almost dip my hand in to genuflect and make the sign of the cross. Memories of religion reside mostly in the body, as if it's a light gold sport that you played during childhood in a vacant lot. Your hands and the hands of your friends all moving together within some larger organism, the comfortable and gold-oiled grooves of your position, the hope that this time the ball will disappear over the fence and never be seen again; God had taken it.

BACK AT THE RECTORY, the gumbo is simmering on the stove, in the battered aluminum stockpot that my mother uses to cook for crowds. It's the color of the flood and everything is swept up in it. I stir it with a wooden spoon and discover that her arthritis isn't the only reason the chopping took so long: each piece of celery or onion or bell pepper is exactly the same size, almost supernaturally so. My mother and I are after perfection. We are seeking a particular click in the head. We share the feeling that if we hang a picture or set a sentence down just right, we will instantly and painlessly ascend to the next level. We will be recognized, and the time we spent will be multiplied into forever and given back to us.

"Yes, I *am* OCD," my mother confessed to me once. "Obsessive-compulsive . . . [long pause] . . . DIVAAAAAA!"

She adds the shrimp at last, waits for them to just turn pink, and we carry the gumbo and the ground sassafras and the white rice over to the church. The phrase "like white on rice" used to obsess me. I couldn't understand what it meant, but I knew it held some sort of key, and when I unlocked it, I would understand something about language. Like white on rice. Like *white* on *rice*. The meaning flickered on, two steps ahead of me.

"What took so long?" my father asks when we finally arrive, but he knows, he isn't really angry. Without even bothering to listen, my mother goes straight over to the refrigerator, and without ceremony, begins stabbing a block of ice in the freezer. "I told them about this refrigerator!" she repeats as she stabs, her voice barely able to contain her joy. The knife is a full six inches long and the arc of her arm is swift and merciless. She looks like she's avenging someone's death, as she so often does, and the final element of the scene clicks into place for me: yes, this is it, I'm home.

THE DAY IS CLEARHEADED; it thinks of us. The sphere across the street still rains. The sphere in here is filled with the old, cloistered, rosewood-scented air of a thousand years ago. All the seminarians line up to spoon out rice and gumbo, and then file back to their round tables to hunch over their bowls and eat. In between bites, they tighten their circles and argue in their private language, one that has been formulated to settle the biggest of big questions.

Darrell walks through the doors carrying two angular bags of trash, lets the sun in for a second, and then exits out the other side. He is dying, but we don't know that yet. For now he seems like the only person here who isn't standing with one foot in the afterlife, who isn't trying to rush heaven before his time.

Darrell is one of the handymen. He works under a man named Chuck, a screaming male tornado who leaves general destruction in his wake. The sounds of crashing bottles and power tools accompany Chuck wherever he goes; he moves in a whirl of nails and wrenches and loud invective; he is a force that could rip gates off their hinges. He sees it as his duty to shout at Darrell. Darrell sees it as his duty to withstand.

I'M STANDING AWKWARDLY by the trash when Darrell comes to get it again. How can one roomful of people generate so much garbage? He looks at me a little bit sideways, because there is the risk, in this place, that if you look someone full in the face, you might see the starkest, most brutal Old Testament verse written there, like CIRCUMCISE YOUR CHILD ON TOP OF A MOUNTAINTOP WHILE A RAM WATCHES, and by then you're caught, it's too late to look away again and pretend you didn't notice. He doesn't know if I'm one of them or not. He asks me where I'm from, and I start to talk too much about Georgia.

"You ever watch *The Real Housewives*?" he asks me hopefully.

"Is that the show where insane blond women are always pointing really long fingernails at each other while holding glasses of champagne? And then one of them yells a catchphrase like *Girl, don't even start with me, because I'm a bitch on wheels and I just stopped at the gas station!*"

"That's exactly the one." He laughs, and it's the first laugh I've heard in ages that is set loose from theology and participating in the world. It almost seems to be in a different key, glad and major after so much minor. "Anyway, there are some Real Housewives down in Atlanta, and they might be the craziest ones."

Finally, someone with a functioning sense of who is crazy and who is not. I edge toward the tubs of ice. "You want a beer, Darrell?" I ask.

"I don't drink," he tells me, a solemn spark in his eye, as if maybe he really does, or maybe he really did, and then tells me the best place to go downtown for dancing. "You gotta go to the Power & Light District," he says, which sounds weirdly religious, as if it had been named by a youth pastor, and then he slams his fist into his palm and calls it out again, louder, "Power & Light!"

THE SICKNESS IS IN HIM, healthy in itself, flourishing, like a sunflower that turns its head to something we can't see. It grows up on a resilient stalk and does not leave him. It is happening so fast, the footage speeds up, it rustles taller and taller. For the last six months, he has confided to the secretaries, he can't keep on weight no matter what he does. The women in the office adore him, and urge him to go to the doctor, but some men won't go to the doctor for anything: it can only be bad news. He is dying and we don't know that yet, but maybe he does.

When I was a girl, I thought so hard about the saints who stayed young in glass coffins, paused waxy and glowing in their incorrupt bodies. Were the sicknesses preserved inside them too? The tumors, the epilepsies, the common colds? The little cavities in the teeth, the holy anorexias? If they died hungry, did they stay that way? If they died angry, could they keep it?

He doesn't look skinny to me, he seems as solid and ongoing as anyone here. But it is hard, while people walk among us, to imagine their absence; while they are present, they are a bread that is passed and passed among us and never comes to an end.

NOW THE PARTY is almost over, and my mother and I are sitting at our own table, blooming from the wine and laughing at jokes that no one else here would find funny, and chatting with the few seminarians who have remembered to thank her. The seminarians from other countries, she has observed, are the only ones who thank her every time. Everyone else assumes she just comes with the church. I see Darrell bouncing on the balls of his feet in a corner, his attention searching the floor so he doesn't accidentally catch the eye of some wild-haired prophet who wants to drag him out to a conversational desert and share his rhetorical locusts with him. For a split second I wonder, "Why is he still here," and then realize that he has to stay until everyone is gone. My mother beckons to him from across the room. "Darrell, come eat," she calls out, serene. Her voice is finally musical when she is offering something to someone, though most of the time we beg her not to sing. "Sit down a minute and eat," and Darrell sits down to eat my mother's shy, by-the-book, fish-out-of-water gumbo.

. . .

DEATH IS CLOSER TO CHURCHES, in both obvious and invisible ways. Death is in the pews every week and puts its dim money in the collection basket and walks out every Sunday with a different family on its arm, gallant and black-suited, opening the doors for them and ushering them through. People who are closer to the beginning and the end have a place in churches: they orbit around them, held by some force. The boy who rakes our leaves and shovels our snow recently lost his mother. The woman who teaches music to sixth-graders stepped in front of a train. The man who lives next door is missing something in his throat, so his wife never eats solid food in front of him, out of a feeling of solidarity. There is always a phone call in the middle of the night. There has always been an accident. There is always something unfixable wrong with a baby. And a voice is saying, "Please come."

After Mass, I would often pass by the living room where I was not allowed and see my father talking, talking, talking to shadow figures with their backs turned to me. They were in need. They had runaway sons and pregnant daughters; they had absent husbands and alienated wives. They had, at the end, terminal diagnoses. The living room was the church, as much as the building next door. Sunday after Sunday in our living room sat the unthinkable and spoke to my father.

That room was smaller on the inside than the outside. As soon as you stepped across the threshold, the world shrank down to an abnormal cell. The information in the air was all black news, as the information in a kitchen is all cups of flour and snips of herbs and someone cares for you. A hush was settled over the carpet like the first dusting of a snow-storm, the one that shows whether it will stick or not, and it sank soft into the night-blue cushions of the couch. During the week we never went in there—it was too frightening. You could still see the prints where the people had been.

As long as I lived in my father's house, I remembered to set a place at the dinner table for the unthinkable, to include it in the conversation, to pass the bread to it and refill its red wine, but I've been away so long that I've forgotten. I have to learn how to do it again.

Being next to the church also meant that sometimes a stranger knocks on the door at three o'clock in the morning, asking for five dollars for gas, his children are waiting in a locked car off a shoulder of the highway, there were always children waiting just outside the picture, five dollars. We couldn't say yes that often because then they would all come; they all needed help, every one. Need in the human being is a natural state. Need water, need food, need green money, need meaning, need touch and need talk, need I don't know what. If we said yes to one, then a man might show up at the house the next night, hungry for a conversation about what happens when you die. My father always answered the door, and spoke in a low paternal voice that was soothing to me even through the walls, but he could not always help.

What calls a person to a life-and-death job, a middle-of-the-night job, an edge-of-the-cliff job? My father lounged horizontal at home, and sent us up and down the stairs to fetch for him, but when the call came at three in the morning, he was up and out the door without the smallest sigh or protest, to serve the unthinkable, to read the ritual words to it, to plump the pillow under its head. His Last Rites kit sat on the stairs just by the front door: a square plastic bottle of holy water and a smaller one of golden oil, called chrism, and a round metal box with a simple cross on top that held the host. It was a source of fascination to me—an elevated survival kit, with a space allotted for each precise instrument you might need in the fight against death. The holy water didn't smell any different from regular water, but the chrism smelled as if it had been wrung out of olives in the Holy Land. We called it Last Rites, but the Eastern Orthodox had a similar ritual called The Office at the Parting of the Soul from the Body When a Man Has Suffered for a Long Time, and I liked that better, because I liked words.

I WAS RAISED to think about the body. The body hung off a piece of carpentry at the front of the church; all my attention poured toward it. There was nothing else to look at, nothing in the world. The ribs heaved, the chin touched the chest, the hair stiffened with sweat and the last words were nailed to his lips. The color of wood, but we called him white. If I stared long enough, my head would unfocus and my borders would expand up and out, up into the spires and out toward the wide walls, and I would start to feel the church was my body and I was a small pulsing red point of pain in it.

After I received Communion, I knelt down in the pew and watched. The people who were sick often went last, in wheelchairs and on walkers and assisted by their daughters. On Good Friday, a man hauled himself down the aisle on two crutches to kiss the foot of the cross. He had waited till the very end so he wouldn't hold up the line, and I never saw anything so dogged. His own feet dragged, seemingly useless. His legs twisted down like a flag from the hip. The seconds were slower in his service and the organ kept going as long as he moved and the spotlight of personhood shone on him, and all of us watched the body.

. . .

THE PEOPLE WHO DO odd jobs around churches are the ones who really need the work. The job is five dollars in the middle of the night—it's a wife and children waiting just off the shoulder of the highway. It's a past that swallowed a person up and spat him back out here, naked and with nothing to his name.

We have always had a handyman, someone to fix, patch, rewire, uproot, tear down and nail up. He comes with the church, like Jesus, and he always has that same smell of hardware stores and the mustaches of uncles. A faint beerishness, a knowledge of sports, a body that expands to fill the space. He comes when my mother calls, because if she cannot put her mark on these anonymous places, how can she ever feel at home? This is the first I can recall us having two, though. Maybe they both needed the job, so much that it had to be multiplied like loaves.

I wake on weekend mornings to hear Darrell mowing the back lawn while Whimsy barks joyfully and frisks around his legs, and every so often he comes into the house to help move my father's bed up or down the stairs—whenever the pain in my father's back becomes unbearable, he decides a change of scenery will do the trick. If Chuck is accompanied everywhere by the sounds of indiscriminate hammering, Darrell is attended by his adjectives, all of which are bright spots in the language. His patience, my mother tells me, is infinite. But what would happen to him if it weren't?

When I ask my mother why Chuck hasn't been fired, her mouth sews itself into a straight line. "I wish he would be. I hate the way he talks to me," she says. "I hate the way he talks to Darrell. Bellows at him, treats him like a child, just blows up at him for any old thing."

I know he would never talk to Darrell that way if he weren't black, the same way he would never talk to my mother that way if she weren't a woman. I'm so afraid of Chuck that every time I hear him blasting through the door, shouting "MAINTENANCE!" at the top of his lungs, I race into my room to avoid encountering him. Whenever the call comes, "ANYBODY HOME," I whisper "no" to myself and run upstairs. The whole duration of my stay passes without me ever catching a glimpse of him. As I describe Chuck now, he is faceless, just six feet of sounds and their effects. And once or twice I hear Darrell's voice swept up in the velocity of his like a piece of paper, saying, "You know that won't help anything. Yelling like that isn't going to do *anything*."

Sometimes I even find myself crouching, staring out the side window at the blue sky, silent and still and spelling out M-I-S-S-I-S-S-I-P-P-I in my head the way I did when I was small. I listen for the slam that means he is gone. No one's home, I'm not home, there's no one here. You can be so objective, finally, when you feel like you don't have a body at all.

I RECOGNIZE THIS AS BLUSTER, because my father is a blusterer. If you have a blusterer in your house, you must treat him as the weather, capable of gathering himself in a second and storming. If a blusterer does harm, it is as the weather does harm: by flattening and blowing down. This is more a feature of fathers, I have found. God too spoke out of the whirlwind.

Sometimes the bluster is even funny. Every so often, during his rages, my father would yell "HOMEY DON'T PLAY THAT" at the top of his lungs, to demonstrate how much he would not accept the bullcrap of whatever was going on. No one knew where he had picked it up. Did he stay up late and watch *In Living Color* after we were in bed? He pointed at us and shouted it, HOMEY DON'T PLAY THAT, like it was one of the commandments. Who was homey? Was he homey, or was it God? Did homey signify some sort of respect for the natural order, which we were disregarding through our actions? Our Homey, who art in Heaven, hallowed be thy name. Thy kingdom come, you do not play that, on earth as it is in Heaven.

There was something about me specifically that made my father angry. It had to do with my head, and what was in it. It had to do with what I'm doing right now: sitting outside the circle in silence and sifting the scene through my right eye. He used to say, "I've forgotten more than you'll ever know," which puzzled me. Didn't that still mean that neither of us knew it?

"Don't look at me like that," even my mother would cry sometimes. "Don't you dare look at me like *that*."

"I'm not looking like anything," I would protest, and I didn't think I was. "I'm not doing anything," and I was certain I wasn't. Still I stood there, as if to prove some point about immovability and irresistible force, and looked. My mother always turned away first, but my father never did. The staring reached out of me and the stared-at reached out of him, and somehow we met there, two powers of the air.

"I know everything you're thinking," he would say to me, like a hypnotist. "Everything that's in your mind. You're never, ever going to say something I'm not expecting, because you're exactly like me." This should have been laughable—most of what I thought was so strange, and my father could neither make a good joke nor properly compare a crescent moon to a fingernail clipping to save his life. Still, he carried the pulpit in front of him always, and his voice rang out and reverberated in the dome of my skull: *I know everything about you, I see everything about you, looking at you is just like looking in a mirror.* When I stared back at him, it was not to be defiant, but to insist that I was not simply the image of everything he hated about himself and was powerless to change, that my face was distinct from his, was mine.

He hasn't lost his temper with me once since I moved back, though. The knowledge that someone is writing about him has wrought a curious change in my father. "I think he's being more patient with me because you're always watching," my mother has confided, and when she asks him if he's worried about how he'll be depicted, he tells her gently that I can write what I want, because people belong to themselves. Some calm has entered him, some rough chop around him has smoothed. When he walks home after Mass one Sunday afternoon and sees me reading under the cool forgiving oak in the front yard, he laughs and calls out, "I never thought it would be so much fun to have you home. It's so nice when your kids grow up and you don't have to kill them anymore."

"Y'ALL AREN'T CATHOLIC, ARE YOU?" Darrell asks Jason one night, when Jason is shooting baskets in the church parking lot, in a circle of burnt-orange glow.

"Oh my GOD no," Jason says, pronouncing the word "God" with the proper fervency for the first time in his life.

"Because the people around here can be *really Catholic*," Darrell says, with a force of understatement that could shoot a rocket to the moon.

"They talk about the bishop all the time," Jason says, defeated. The two men share a moment of sympathetic understanding, surely asking themselves: how did we end up here? Then, as if to insist on their citizenship in a wider, brighter, less cross-carrying world, one not weeping

to the rhythms of Gregorian chant, Darrell asks if we've gone dancing yet—in that real night where lives are streaming and loosed, their
bodies hanging from them by a single stitch, just up the road at Power &
Light.

CHUCK BLOWS UP AGAIN—over nothing, my mother tells me, over
absolutely nothing. I picture him building to an actual physical explosion, puffing suddenly into a fight cloud, flinging words and gestures
and hot breath outward in every direction. "That won't help," Darrell
repeats to him, the phrases well-worn as beads. "That won't do anything." One of the faithful secretaries has had enough, and when she
hears about it, she corners Chuck and shouts at him, "You better watch
out, or else Darrell is going to have your job and be living in your house,"
and suddenly I've rounded the corner on a panoramic view—could that
be true? Could Darrell move into the handyman's house, maybe have
his son over, maybe see his mother there? I don't have a house either, and
I don't know that I ever will, and a house seems like the ultimate acre to
me, the place where you can finally live a real life.

The worst part, my mother has confided, about being married to a
priest is that she must float from place to place; the bricks are never hers
and she is never home. So when she moves into a new rectory, she calls
the handyman over, gives him a list, begins telling him the things to do
that will make it seem like she belongs there. It will be this way as long
as my father is alive. When he passes away, she will be turned out with
nothing: no house, no retirement, and no money, just an armful of
screaming guitars.

"I think it's the last straw this time," my mother says about Chuck,
though she admits that hardly anyone ever gets fired around churches,

no matter what they do. Still, she is hopeful that a reckoning is coming, that things will be put right, valleys exalted and mountains made low.

BUT OVER LUNCH ONE DAY, just before I leave on my book tour, my mother tells me that Darrell is dying. Her sentences are flat with resignation, already stepping in rhythm toward the horizon, and there isn't a breath of the glee she sometimes takes in relating some distant disaster, that unconscious glee that can only mean "It wasn't us this time, it wasn't our family, I counted the heads and we are safe."

The cancer started in the liver and now it's everywhere. Metastatic, and I think of that definition of the word "flashover": *the point at which a fire in a room becomes a room on fire.* He is wasted, the kind of wasting that makes every joint stand out bare in all its brass mechanism, like a doorknob waiting to be turned. He doesn't want visitors, he doesn't want his son to come, he doesn't want anyone to see him like this. They think he only has about a month. My mother offers no other baroque details: no color of, no size of, no pain scale. Only that: a month. If she isn't crying now, she will be as soon as she's alone. Her father died of cancer, it went to his brain, at the end he didn't even know who she was.

Whenever someone says the word "month" to me, I call up an empty square filled with other empty squares, days and hours and minutes, bricks on bricks spiraling inward, pinwheel and diamond and herringbone patterns marching smaller and smaller to some vanishing point. And when she calls, not even two weeks later, to tell me he's gone, I see a tall wall of those bricks knocked down and him striding out free with the real day pouring past him, all hours and minutes and seconds in a red rubble at his feet, the whole church of time torn down.

He was only thirty-eight, my mother tells me chokingly. She says, "It was not fair."

THERE IS TALK of holding the funeral service at Christ the King. If there isn't any money, we'll raise it, since money is the one thing we can raise, up to save us with its arms held wide. But Darrell was a Baptist, he has his own church. The funeral will be held there. "It's in a bad part of town," my mother falters. "Dad doesn't think I should go," and suddenly I'm angry. "Bullets go flying in that neighborhood," she tells me, in the voice she uses to echo my father, who believes in bad neighborhoods with as much conviction as he believes in the Sermon on the Mount.

"Bullets go flying in every neighborhood," I say stupidly, and I am talking about the random, which ricochets down every street, but both of us understand she will not go.

Instead, my father says a memorial Mass, because we do what is within our power. My mother asks me to come, but I can't bring myself to do it. There is something I cannot stomach about those prayers for *the faithful departed*—they are so final, they freeze a person at the moment of their leaving. A real life walks out, and a door in our imagination closes. That's that, we tell ourselves, it couldn't have happened any other way. Nothing we could have done, no flowers we could have heaped on them while they were still among us.

DEATH IS ONE of those subjects where it's worse to be glib than to be bad. When you set out to write about death, your limits are in front of you like a kind of mortality. You can go that far and no farther, and you can see nothing beyond. There is no great, grand, thunderclap ending except the thing itself.

When I was a child, I always hated being used in my father's sermons, shrunk to a symbol to illustrate some larger lesson, flattened out to give other people comfort or instruction or even a laugh. It did some violence to my third dimension; it made it difficult for me to breathe. "That's not me," I would think, listening to some fable where a stick figure of myself moved automatically toward a punishing moral. "That has nothing to do with me at all." If I had a soul, I thought, it was that resistance, which would never let another human being have the last word on me.

This is what it is to write about people who are alive and then, sometimes, people who are dead. To say that his eyes were clear as agates, that his voice was a gravelly baritone, to surround him with the right adjectives and set him into the story—all this is an attempt to fit him in the glass box of a good sentence so everyone can see what he means. But it won't work, the words can't hold him, and I am glad.

The desire to describe voice, gesture, skin color, is a desire to eat, take over, make into part of the pattern. I am happy every time to see a writer fail at this. I am happy every time to see real personhood resist our tricks. I am happy to see bodies insist that they are not shut up in this book, they are elsewhere. The tomb is empty, rejoice, he is not here.

MY FATHER COMES HOME from work and he is exhausted. He winces as he walks on his knee replacements, he hunches under extra weight, feeling always the subterranean throb of his back, sometimes exhaling a distressing sound of pure suffering—never the word "God," but close: *gad*. It was always this way. He came home and there was nothing left except a desire to be alone with himself, so he could regenerate the language he needed to speak universally. There is a certain fatigue that comes from always presiding over the baptisms, the weddings, and the burials—the three ceremonies where you are most certain to encounter poetry, even if it is present nowhere else in your life.

A truce, then, between me and my father's house. I was not made in his likeness, but I have chosen something of his same extremity, his willingness to be available for the questions that knock on the door in the middle of the night. His voice inside the verses was so sweeping, his judgment from the pulpit so black-and-white, that it was hard not to inherit them. It was hard not to inherit the desire to stand over the deceased and say something, and it was impossible, finally, not to inherit his anger. As long as I lived under his roof, I told myself that I had no temper, that I would never speak that knot of heat I felt so often in my throat, forced down into my rib cage, sent flowing into my fingertips. But I belong to myself now, and I can admit it. When I sit down at the desk, the anger radiates out of me in great bronze spikes, like holiness in the old paintings, and a sermon rises up in me as if it had been waiting for breath, and puts itself together bone to bone.

I'M NOT INTERESTED in heaven unless my anger gets to go there too. I'm not interested in a happy eternity unless I get to spend an eternity on anger first. Let me speak for the meek and say that we don't want the earth, if that's where all the bodies are buried. If we are resurrected at the end of the world, I want us to assemble with a military click, I want us to come together as an army against what happened to us here. I want us to bring down the enemy of our suffering once and for all, and I want us to loot the pockets, and I want us to take baths in the blood.

What do I want? I want him to have a job, and be living in your house. I want us to stop selling heaven as the home we don't get here. I want an afterlife for my anger; I want levitation, perfection, and white wings for it, and I want an afterlife for my question, which is an answer.

But for now the question just hangs in the middle of the air, halfway up the blue sky, the long unbroken mosquito whine of a why, and the only thing that answers is the voice of my father, saying what he always said, saying the same thing your father always said: "Life isn't fair, nobody ever said it was going to be, who told you that."

19

INTERIOR CASTLE

My grandfather George Lockwood built houses, the sort of quick-and-ready houses that made the country ugly. When we at last move out of the rectory, nine months after we first stepped over its doorstep, it is into a house that reminds me of these. It is forty miles away from Kansas City, in a small town of aspiring radicals called Lawrence. Forty miles is an excellent distance to be from your parents: close enough for your mother to bring you an "extra" sour cream apple pie that she "accidentally" made by "mistake," but far enough away that it feels like real life—despite the fact that your closest neighbor is a hippie with waist-length white dreads who grows lettuces for his job.

You want my mother on your side during a post-apocalyptic war for resources, and you also want her with you when you move. She acquires superhuman strength during these times, like the women who lift cars off babies. In a way, that's what she's doing, except the car also contains all the literature the baby has ever owned, the contents of its closets, and all its freaky baby makeup.

As Jason carries boxes of long-lost books through the front door and I group them on the shelves according to mood—archipelagoes of books about islands, obscene books piled willy-nilly on top of each other, stories of parallel worlds set side by side—Mom disappears into the dirtiest holes of the house she can find and rejoices in them like Pigpen's mother giving him his annual bath.

"BLACK MOLD!" she shrieks as she scrubs the bathroom, and then, "No. No, it's just some filth that somebody tracked in."

Just before she leaves, with a cardboard box of cleaning products under one arm, she turns sober. "I just want to warn you," she says, with the seriousness of someone about to tell me that my father is not my real father. "Meadow mice may be a HUGE problem for you here." She points at the window of my new study, which shows a panorama of the wind-warped backyard. We have nearly an acre, with a fire pit and a picnic bench and a pyramid of chopped wood, which crawls with brown recluses. "You're really verging on the wilderness."

She glances at my desk, which Jason has just finished setting up against the back wall, where I'll have an unimpeded view of the hordes of meadow mice attempting to encroach on my domain. "Be sure to sit up straight when you're working, Tricia, or else you'll get a Dowager's Hump."

She is right, though, about the wilderness. The first morning in the new house, I wake at dawn, make myself a cup of tea in my special personalized mug that says DOUG on it, and walk into the study to see the branches filled with glossy black squirrels in perpetual motion, gamboling up and down like scraps of shadow. A bobcat patrols the corner of our yard between a jogging trail and the forest, I make friends with a large sensual skunk named Big Boy, and one night a mole, that most agoraphobic of creatures, tunnels his way into our basement, creeps up the stairs, and scratches at the basement door for me to let him out. Even the stars out here are fierce, like points of fangs, like my thoughts.

"Look what I found in the garden," Jason says after a weekend afternoon of yard work, and presents me with three huge quartz crystals, clear and cloudy and clotted with dirt. I wash them in a bowl of warm water and add them to my collection, which is ranged in bits and pieces all across the windowsill.

"WHAT ARE THE COMMANDMENTS?" Jason asks me before he leaves for work, holding a brown paper bag full of fruit in one hand, because living with my mother made him fat.

"Drink water. I am not Lawrence of Arabia's camel," I recite. "One hundred pretzels is not a meal. If I start thinking about penguins, I'm too cold. If I start thinking about hell, I'm too hot. Too much coffee has made lab rabbits explode. If I find myself reading the Wikipedia entry for 'Death,' step away from the internet."

"And?"

"And I am the only zoo animal currently living who has the key to my own cage. Open it and go outside."

WHEN I WAS A CHILD I lived in the woods, where my friends and I occupied ourselves with a game called Rooms. It never occurred to us to call the game anything else, though I was supposedly famous for my imagination. The woods were on an empty lot next to our two-story brick house and they were full of peat-brown, barky vines that grew sinuous along the ground like free foundations. It was a mystical game, but also a practical one: the Rooms existed already among the trees and it was our job to recognize them. We dragged mud-caked rocks up from the creek bed and built walls where we felt walls to be, and paced discerningly around our perimeters and ripped away screens of leaves where we felt windows were. It was always very clear where the door was; it seemed to stand in the air. We entered each other's Rooms with a grand twisting gesture, to give the door the luxurious feeling of having a knob, and stepped exaggeratedly over the threshold, to give ourselves the luxurious feeling of coming in out of the wild.

They were an arbitrary form that nonetheless felt ordained, like a sonnet. I always chose the ones that would hold the narrowest beds, the cells. I lined them with emerald-green cushions of moss and sat among mulching leaves and cutouts of sunlight in the middle of them, long after my friends had gone home, reveling in a feeling of totally transparent walls and a roof I could leave through.

I wonder what would happen if I went outside and tried the game again, just to see if I still have the knack, but in the end I stay confined in my study. Confinement is different, after all, when it's your idea. I draw my knees up to my chin and look at the books stacked all around me, thinking, "Who does a story belong to? Is this one mine?"

IT IS IMPOSSIBLE to think about literary seclusion without thinking of Dickinson writing, "I had a terror—since September—I could tell to none—and so I sing, as the Boy does by the Burying Ground—because I am afraid—"

People like to speculate about the cause of this terror, assuming it came from outside her own body. *Emily Dickinson: Scared by a Big Dog in Her Prime? Emily Dickinson: She Saw One Penis and Renounced Human Society.* Instead, I like to speculate about the slim, dangling rope she threw across that terror, with a basket at the end filled with little cakes for children. I like to imagine, too, that she sent down cracked-out poems along with them, mostly pertaining to baked goods:

> Heaven—Was a Sugar Cube
> Baby took a Taste
> Just—as Pearls—of Cherubim
> Bit into the Christ

People assume that the shutting-up made her smaller. But locking yourself up can be a way to shrink the castle down to your size, and to expand your body toward the wider limits of the walls, until you are rooted at the foundation, see sideways out the glass, and do your highest thinking with the smoke that leaves the chimney. And still, through the window, you can send out sweets. Emily did not show her face to the children, only the hands and arms that set down the poems. What if she wanted simply to reveal, and not to be exposed? What counts as hiding, and what counts as devoted contemplation?

There is a place near our gray-and-white house that reminds me of her. It's a museum of miniatures, where you can see the whole imagined spectrum of human habitation for five dollars. The building is Spanish-style, with a roof of undulant red tiles that blends into a broader roof of leaves. The first time I visit, I race around like a giant gobbling local villages in order to see it all. The best is the violin shop in the hollowed-out body of a fiddle, and the miniature jewelry store where a woman in a fox stole is considering a diamond ring, and the miniature dollhouse workshop that makes the whole enterprise self-aware. Also the food—tin-scaled fish slit down their bellies, quails waiting to be plucked, glistening tiny hams in crumbs of brown sugar and bunches of radiant grapes. There are rings of keys, scrimshaws and sextants in salty sea captains' parlors, empty cradles and blue willow china. Teakettles. Desks for writing letters. Vials of perfume and shadow boxes of speckled birds' eggs and inkwells that will never diminish. I am in the house of nouns here, and it fills me with the conviction that good books sometimes give: that life can be holdable in the hand, examined down to the dog hairs, eaten with the eyes and understood.

"Everything looks just like everything," Jason exclaims, wheeling from case to case in a frenzy, wondering how the artists have shrunk domesticity to the last detail. The only thing that isn't convincing is the people. Somehow they can never get the people quite right—something about them cannot be nailed down.

"Do you think you could get really into dollhouses?" I ask him, as he peers into a sitting room and squeals over an infinitesimal stained-glass window.

He responds instantly. "Yeah. Dollhouses for Men. *It's Good to Be a Small Man.*"

HOW DID I BECOME a person who almost never left the house? Until I was twelve I lived as an element of nature, tending to my untamed Rooms, wading through creeks and waist-high grasses, and bicycling diagonally across vacant lots long after the sun had flamed down. All the while I collected: unsplit geodes with their lunar skins, horn corals with mushroom frills at the top, shivered green glass and grocery lists and bottle caps not yet flattened into the second dimension. Collecting was a mad instinct to own the world. If I had to go inside at all, I wanted to bring the whole outdoors with me and hold my own context in my hand.

Then, when we moved to the neighborhood in St. Louis that was piece by piece being lifted into the sky, where girls were in danger and no one played after dark, the most curious thing happened: I felt the slow clank of a metal shutter coming down, being lowered by some unseen hand until there was only a stripe of light underneath, and that was the news from outside. I was thirteen, and it was beyond my strength to raise it again. How to go back: to that diagonal flight across fields, that confident pocketing of everything I surveyed? How to remember that easy, bone-deep assumption that the world is for you too?

I know all women are supposed to be strong enough now to strangle presidents and patriarchies between their powerful thighs, but it doesn't work that way. Many of us were actually affected, by male systems and male anger, in ways we cannot always articulate or overcome. Sometimes, when the ceiling seems especially low and the past especially close, I think to myself, *I did not make it out.* I am still there in that place of diminishment, where that voice an octave deeper than mine is telling me what I am. Before I turned thirteen, I had never been part of the class that my father called empty-headed and addressed as "dollface," that our church seemed to see as just bodies. I was simply myself, unique and irreducible. Suddenly I became female, and it was as if a telescope I had been looking through—with a clear eye, up at an unbounded night of stars—had been viciously turned on me. I went to a pinpoint. *Does God exist* was never a question for me then; *do I exist* took up the whole of my mind.

I did not make it out, but this does. Art goes outside, even if we don't; it fills the whole air, though we cannot raise our voices. This is the secret: when I encounter myself on the page, I am shocked at how forceful I seem. On the page I am strong, because that is where I put my strength. On the page I am everything that I am not, because that is where I put myself. I am no longer whispering through the small skirted shape of a keyhole: the door is knocked down and the roof is blown off and I am aimed once more at the entire wide night.

ONE AFTERNOON I am sick in bed and my father calls to ask me how I am. I try not to let him hear my surprise, since he usually calls us only on our birthdays, to sing, "Happy birthday to you, you belong in a zoo, you look like a monkey, and you smell like one too."

"Feel better, Bit," he tells me in a gentle voice, like a bear that has swallowed a songbird. "Try not to write anything obscene today."

"Too late," I say, glancing at my laptop, where I'm sketching out the memory of our first road trip. I hang up the phone and begin to laugh, remembering the sight of him at the wheel in his Psychotic State T-shirt, the same shirt I would later inherit and wear all through high school. Thinking if I could write him how he really is, I would be the greatest genius on earth. If I could see it as clear as it really was, and show it to you how it really happened.

When I was very little, we drove a window all the way to California together. It was my first time away from my mother, and from the tragic look on her face as she waved good-bye to the van, I could tell she entertained absolutely no hope of me ever being returned in one piece. Dad assured her it would be good for me to experience something of the world, and strapped me in tightly next to his project, which was six feet long and depicted the Last Supper. Judas, crudely geometric but recognizable, leaned toward Jesus even knowing he would betray him. All the way to California, I looked through the richness of that scene at the abundance of the country. The country was wheat and wine. I had a bag of grapes in my lap, and they shone with veins when I held them up to the light, just as the stained glass did. The perpetual meal was laid out, always in the process of being eaten. It was enough, the story promised, to feed us all forever.

"Pork rind?" my father offered from the front seat. I took one and held that up to the light too. It was transparent and bubbled and the color of an earlobe. Pork rinds were our favorite snack at that time, though I would soon give them up, after learning they were made of skin.

"That's the stuff," he said. "Kill Porky, bay-bee." The radio was blasting the insanely juicy bass line of "Heart of the Sunrise," which was one of his anthems. His seat belt hung free, and the minivan ate the miles. Three of the grapes in my bag had turned into raisins, which seemed like a revelation.

"Dad, I have to go," I said.

He himself had not peed in eight hours, and viewed this as a moral achievement on par with fasting, wearing a hair shirt, or whatever the hell it was that Joan of Arc did. "You know what to do," he told me, and pointed to the plastic baby potty in the side of the van.

The test had come. I unbuckled from my seat and looked pleadingly at the Jesus of the Last Supper, who was said to save people by offering himself in their place. I tugged down my elastic-waisted shorts, which were the exact shade of indigestion medicine, and began to hunker down. At that precise moment, my father swerved into the next lane with the satanic decisiveness of a man committing vehicular homicide, I was thrown in all my glory against the clear glass of the side window, and the bare bottom of a tiny child became visible to a long line of truckers making their way down the interstate.

"Ahahaha!" my father laughed, a wild laugh, the laugh of a man who has taken on himself the task of driving a bucket of pee and a church window across the country, and though my face had flushed deeper than the oval in Jesus' cup, I knew we must have been thinking the same thing: wouldn't *that* make a story for the people back home.

I stumbled back to my seat and buckled myself in. Who does a story belong to, the one I rode beside? Neither my father nor I could really claim it. It belonged to some church far off in the distance, which neither of us had ever seen. It would be installed in a stone wall, where it would glow over the good people like an agate slice. Flat faces, flat loaves, flat halos, flat savior and flat sinners, a cross section of what actually happened. Didn't it? Couldn't it have?

The next morning, in a sunny bungalow in San Diego, I felt the earth move underneath me and in me: a slight shift, a rumble, two inches more into the blue sea. A cross went crooked on the bare wall above me; my heart went crooked inside my chest. It felt so private that I was sure it belonged to me alone, until I went out to eat cereal in a strange kitchen and my father told me there had been an earthquake, that all of us had been through it, separate and marveling, on the earth that we shared. A good thing they hadn't installed the window yet, I thought, because it could have cracked, been unpuzzled into its hundred original pieces, dividing Christ from his followers and Christ from his betrayer—and after everything had settled, I knew there wasn't anybody in the world who could look at that jumble of bright color on the floor and put it all back together again, bit by bit and just as it was.

FOR THE FIRST FEW WEEKS, Jason and I bask in the glow of being recently reunited with a whole marriage's worth of shared belongings and private speech. There are moments when we feel something is missing, but we soon realize it is either (a) guitar or (b) meat smell. The meat smell I re-create by roasting haunches and cooking complex ochre-red stews, and Jason makes up for the lack of guitar sounds with piercing falsetto Neil Young impressions. From time to time I even leave a Rag of my own in one of our sinks, wet and haunting, to remind us of where we came from.

We don't have to talk about the bishop anymore, or the robes and crosses and chalices, but still we do. We are part of that circle now, for better or worse. The latest topic of gossip is the epic triptych that my father has commissioned to hang above the altar, to make his hopelessly modern church appear more traditional. When it is delivered, and my father unveils it to us on one of our weekend visits with shy pride, we are shocked to discover that the artist has painted Jesus wearing literal Pampers. Tens of thousands of dollars, for a picture of the incarnate word in a diaper.

"Tell me about when you stopped going to church," I ask Jason later that night, though he has told me before. We are in bed, in the grip of that marvelous aloneness that I can hardly bring myself to believe. My head is tucked against his chest, and his breath stirs the most counter-clockwise of my cowlicks.

"I must have been twelve or thirteen. I just told my father I wasn't going anymore. We were unloading the dishwasher, it was a very domestic scene. We didn't fight or anything. He said, 'Well, if it isn't true, why would so many people have died for it?' With this checkmate look on his face.

"I felt so sorry to have to say it. I said, 'Dad, people have died for *every* religion.'"

"And then he was quiet," I finish.

He is quiet. "When did you stop believing?" he asks in return, though he knows there wasn't one moment.

"It just seeped out of me, after I left the house. It was like forgetting a language you spoke a long time ago, when you were a child." That is not quite right, though—I did not forget so much as turn it inside out, repurpose it, and occasionally use it to tell jokes like "Jesus is SUCH a manger babe" and "God got so many abs that he look like a corncob." People do sometimes accuse me of blasphemy, which is understandable and which is their right. But to me, it is not blasphemy, it is my idiom. It's my way of still participating in the language I was raised inside, which despite all renunciation will always be mine. The word "God" does not fall out of the vocabulary, as the sun does not fall out of the sky; the shapes of the stories remain, as do their revelations. I was never fluent in tongues back when it mattered, but when I am left to myself, out come all the old worshipped words, those fondled verses tumbling on verses, onto the page which can hold and forgive them.

I sometimes wish my childhood had been less obsessed with the question of why we are here. But that must be the question of any childhood. To write about your mother and father is to tell the story of your own close call, to count all the ways you never should have existed. To write about home is to write about how you dropped from space, dragging ellipses behind you like a comet, and how you entered your country and state and city, and finally your four-cornered house, and finally your mother's body and finally your own. From the galaxy to the grain and back again. From the fingerprint to the grand design. Despite all the conspiracies of the universe, we are here; every moment we are here we arrive.

WHEN I WAS SEVENTEEN, and nearing the beginning of the madness that would carry me away from singing and God's Gang and that neighborhood that had such a grip on us, I went to visit the Carmelites, one of the last cloistered orders. The convent was bare, pale linen and sandal-wood and linoleum, with sketches of trees outside the windows. It smelled of both human and historical age. I imagined the nuns ate penny-tasting lentils and coarse bread for dinner, sitting together at long knotholed tables, while prayers bumped gently at the ceilings of their heads like loosed helium balloons. They were called *contemplatives* for a reason. I imagined them drinking clearer water than mine, and eating fruit that was outlined like the apples of Cézanne. They were light with the power of owning nothing, because they renounced their possessions as the priests did not.

I went to chapel with them, where I knelt and cried in front of the host. How could I not, when it was so blank and complete, when it tasted so of paper? It was the page that said everything. After we filed out again, a particular nun approached me. She seemed, despite her strictures and her rope sandals and the unremitting brownness of her clothes, to be in charge of her own life. I remembered how my father, whenever he met a nun who might be described as a feminist, would say, "Bit, she's just mad she couldn't be a priest." Then he would reassure me that it would never happen, not as long as the church stood plumb on its foundation, because he and his people were Christ figures and Christ was a man.

But I did not want to be a priest. I was the same as most girls who wished themselves in a convent: I wanted to be where I could think, and where not just anyone could look at me. I wanted to sleep in a bed that was just big enough for me and my own salvation. I wanted to choose constraint and be freed by it, after constraint was all that had ever been offered to me.

It was cold, though it was not winter, and something howled outside, not wind. It was unbelief, which could not get at us, not here. The sun had set while we were kneeling in the chapel, and the darkness smelled of curled leaf tips and keys. The window behind the nun was a scrubbed square of onyx, like the stone in a ring you might kiss.

She took my hand and peered up. A sweep of black hair had escaped her habit. She must have been able to see something in me—that I was in the *process of discernment*, as they said. I could feel that I looked like the first tall stripe from a paint roller covered in white, wet and weirdly shining and desperate to change the whole room.

"And for you, I think, a religious life," she said, a calm certainty all over her crisscrossed face. She didn't even bother with a question mark. My calling was so obvious; it was written all over me. Two years later, I would be living in my own convent as an order of one, typing poetry in the deep glowing hours to a stranger. Four close walls and cathedral space within, arriving with a rush to myself every moment.

I turned back to the priest who had driven me there over back nowhere roads on a school night. He was the director of vocations, and was rumored to be in possession of a piece of the One True Cross. He jangled a handful of metal deep in his pocket, with the formidable key to the cathedral singing somewhere in the sound, and blinked his black pebble eyes, which still counted among my collection. Two years later, he would be locked up, in a smaller, starker cell than these. I told him I was ready to go home.

20

ISLAND TIME

promised myself that when it was all over, if I had a little money, I would take my mother to Key West. "Do you think Dad would want to go too?" I asked her, but she was dubious. He mostly stays in his room during vacations, and the man's feelings about Florida are complicated. On the one hand, it is the natural habitat of ships, salt air, and jumbo shrimps; on the other hand, it is the nation's wang, on which lives the Homosexual Mouse of Disney. "Key West is the worst of all, to him," my mother told me. "He thinks it's one of those places where it's legal for people to have naked parades."

I'm not sure when we set our hearts on it—late at night in the stopped white clock of a Midwest winter, perhaps, while snow laughed around the house. The wind that flew over to us from Kansas always seemed angry that it no longer had a sea to beat around, to whip up, to form. It must have sent into our ears the thought of going there. Key West in my memory was faint gold, ink-outlined, and had an overspilling treasure chest open at the middle of it, as if it were drawn on a kidskin map I had carried folded in my pocket since forever. We talked about it for a year, not really believing it would happen, but then I sold my book and bought three tickets and told my mother she would sit next to the window on the way.

"Oh!" She clasped her hands over the travel guide we were perusing, with its glossy pictures of lighthouses and men in go-go shorts. "The only time I've ever seen the tropics is when I went on the Republican Cruise."

Oh my god, I had almost forgotten about the Republican Cruise. Soon after I ran away with Jason, my father took it into his head that my mother deserved a holiday—on a neoconservative ocean liner. The featured speaker was to be a woman who once wrote a whole book defending the internment of the Japanese during World War II. The food, we are left to assume, was the flesh of the poor, grilled to order. Shortly before they were set to depart, however, Mom took to her bed, pale and fighting for air.

It was not that my mother seemed physically indestructible. She frequently reminded us that she could be killed by so little as a bite of apple, because what was a healthy snack to others was a lethal poison to her. She did seem indomitable, though, powering through life on caffeine and a desire to mother the world, never held back by her limited body. It was stunning to see her felled, breathless, struggling as if she were on top of a mountain, subjected by doctors to dozens of baffled tests. It turned out to be histoplasmosis, also known as Darling's disease, which is caused by a fungus that lives in bird and bat droppings and mostly attacks the lungs. She was exposed while cleaning out the barns and attics at the old family farm with her usual terrifying thoroughness. "Imagine," she said, on receiving the diagnosis, "that the whole time I was scrubbing, I was also breathing toxic spores."

When I came back to visit her in the hospital, I kept sending my glance up to the ceiling, to make sure there were no cracks in the plaster. A world without Karen was not really imaginable. How would the rest of us remember to be careful? Where would alertness go, where discernment, where extreme pleasure in the colored silks and cottons of existence? Where the ability to choose the best peach, would it be returned to the tree? Where would the 20/20 vision and the red hair go? Would they be released out to the wild again—back out to the crispness of the view, and the wind that wanted something to run its hands through? No, it was not really to be thought of, so we spoke of other things. Sitting at her bedside, one hand on each thigh, my father said worriedly, "I just hope you're well enough to go on the Republican Cruise."

"Don't worry about me, Greg," she croaked, raising barely one white-capped wave in the sheet. The lack of feistiness was what really concerned us. When my mother cannot summon the strength to contradict, argue, or shout medical acronyms at you, the situation is serious. Gradually, however, her old self began to stir and grow strong, and soon she was back to interrupting everything we said with the joyful, life-affirming word NO. She recovered just in the nick of time, though she was never able to gasp as deeply as she had before, and sailed the Republican seas with my father at her side.

Later she would look back and reflect, "I was so lucky to get one really rare, deadly illness in my life—AND I got to make puns about it, since it was the batshit disease."

"Maybe one day you'll get an illness so rare they'll name it after you," I said.

She searched the horizon dreamily. "That would be nice."

. . .

THE NIGHT BEFORE HER BIRTHDAY, we pack our suitcases and speed to Kansas City and sleep over at the rectory in the upstairs room—a necessity, since we'll need to wake at the break of dawn in order to catch our flight. I despise the dawn more than any other time, and wish that I were able to "break it" once and for all, but when the alarm rings I actually tumble out of bed in my eagerness to rise up and start walking around the clock. The year has been long. I feel like a single particle standing in the middle of my own ghost, I resemble a log of haunted cookie dough, and I need to be cured of myself. Mom and Jason, when I greet them downstairs, look just the same, pale and expectant and munching tropical nut mixes to get themselves in the mood. "Have a good time, baby!" my father calls out cheerfully as we leave. "Protect your mother from the lesbians!"

As if. That would be against my code. Besides, she's not in any danger. If my mother took the Gay Inkblot Test, all she would see is roadkill.

On the plane, my mother studies the safety card for a long time—perhaps too long. She lavishes especial attention on a picture of a baby wearing a life preserver, thrashing its fat helpless arms. She sets her lips in a determined line. That cartoon baby isn't going to drown if SHE has anything to say about it, and when she gets it back on land, she's going to make it lose weight. In the row in front of us, a man opens up a book called *Bait for Satan* and settles into his reading with a contented sigh. Satan will not bite his worm today. My mother sits next to the window for the whole flight, gazing down raptly, waiting, waiting, and then tragedy strikes: the first glimpse of the warm and glittering gulf makes her realize she has to go to the bathroom. "Welcome to my life," she says, lurching down the aisle—not sarcastic at all, as if she really is welcoming us to it.

THE BEACH HOUSE is very near the ocean, and decorated in all the shades of feminine hygiene. A picture of a phantasmagoric grouper, arching his back in salty ecstasy and pinning us with one sequin eye, fills almost one entire wall. It satisfies all our desires, our hopes, our fantasies—all except the soap.

"Do NOT use the soap in here," my mother says, hunched insanely at the kitchen sink. "It has torn apart my hands."

We orient ourselves at once to the fish market and the wine shop. The shy realization comes to us that we are allowed to eat outside, and after that we plan picnics on the porch every night, with oranges and crackers and conch ceviche. "Can you recommend something?" my mother asks the man at the wine shop counter, with an air of conspiracy. "Something crisp and not too sweet. My palate has changed somewhat over the years—Veuve Clicquot tastes like shit to me now." We carry all our purchases home past the boatyards, where the sails are as white and pointed as a pine forest cut out of paper, and past the performance artists who balance upside down on unicycles and spit fire.

"Why is it so free," my mother wonders.

"It's the southernmost point of the United States," I tell her. "We're on the verge of escaping our borders and pitching headfirst into the sea. It's why people come here to write novels and be gay."

When she calls up my father the second evening and tells him how scented the breeze is and how succulent the seafood, his voice turns hard-edged. He is already missing that unifying force that keeps his life sound, sweet, and together; that spirit at work in his universe like a god of love. "You're not making me feel very good right now," he snaps across space and time, and she hastens to hang up the phone, her cheeks reddened and her eyes very bright. Something in her face falls, and Jason and I busy ourselves building it back up again with jokes, just as my brothers and sisters and I did when we were young. Scooting closer to her on the couch, putting my head on her shoulder, I am visited by the same minor despair I have felt so often before. "I can only write down what you say," I tell my father silently, tired of editing him with such childlike vigilance, of choosing only the quotes that show his brightest side. "Please, give me something. Be a human being."

"You know how he is," my mother says, almost to herself. "He likes me to be there."

WE WALK MILE AFTER MILE on lengthening legs, as if released from cages. Jason and my mother have convinced themselves that there is an Ernest Hemingway look-alike convention in town this week, and they can't be talked out of it. "Look at all the men with big white beards!" they gesture frantically as we pass the overflowing bars on Duval Street.

"I think that's just because they're old," I say, with tact. And possibly drunk as well, and asking women to call them Papa. Still, in this beating sun, it's good to think about the nearly stupid genius of Hemingway, who had the moral sound of a man who had memorized the Bible. When I see him, I do not see him at any of his masculine tasks—not shooting elephants or skinning leopards or running with the black lathering bulls. I picture him with an airy crystal box in front of him, the shape of a pulpit or a coffin, and all his books emerging through that, and coming out the rectangle that books should be.

One jumbo Hemingway, rollicking down the middle of the side-walk, nearly sends me crashing into a store window. Straightening myself against the glass, I behold a T-shirt printed with a yellow dog licking his own rectum, underlined with the legend I CAN'T BELIEVE IT'S NOT BUTTER! Who says all the great writers are dead? My mother scans the various T-shirt slogans with fierce distaste, recalling the PLEASE BLOW ME debacle of yesteryear and wishing for her scissors. Another Hemingway sashays by and gives me an exaggerated, painful-looking wink, as if a fishing hook just flew into his open eye.

"Why not a Wallace Stevens look-alike convention? Why not a hundred lesbians dressed as Elizabeth Bishop?" I grumble. But no, it's Hemingway who's everywhere, dogging our steps, smiling back at us from every grizzled head. In the gift shop of the treasure museum, among the blurred pewter pieces of eight and fake emeralds with cool blue fire at their hearts, I pick up a book of Hemingway quotes about writing—displayed between a book of Hemingway quotes about fishing and a book of Hemingway quotes about big-game hunting; apparently the man never uttered anything but quotes—and read:

Forget your personal tragedy. We are all bitched from the start and you especially have to be hurt like hell before you can write seriously.

I laugh out loud. Bitched from the start. Good old Hemingway. The old motherbitching tit-sucker of a she-bastard, or whatever the hell he would say.

"This is what happens when the president makes cigars legal," my mother says, shaking her head at yet another Hemingway as he shoulders past us, not dead at all, put back together by that firm restoring wind from off the sea. I do not tell her that Hemingway smoked a pipe, not cigars. I also do not tell her that he learned to write those bold declarative sentences at *The Kansas City Star*.

Better to visit a writer's house or a writer's grave? I have always wondered. I have no idea where Hemingway is buried (in a bear's stomach, maybe?), but the house is here: terraced, fanned by palms, overrun by six-toed cats. The walls are white space and the windows let the air in and the guides set down one true sentence after another. People crowd up the stairs to his study and snap identical pictures of the place the thinking happened; there has never been a room so haunted by the specter of a human head. When we walk out through the iron gates, we see a woman across the street selling drilled coconuts under the shade of an umbrella. They cost four dollars apiece, and we buy two of them, not realizing that they're bottomless and we won't reach the end of them no matter how much we drink of their light, astringent juice. As we take our first sips from red straws, the woman tells us that coconut water is the "universal donor, and is used for blood transfusions in times of war!" Improbable, but of course it turns out to be true.

WHEN WE LIVED in the Sailfish Capital of the World, Jason and I used to drive down to the Keys whenever we could scratch together the money, once every year or so. Those were some of the first vacations we ever took alone. Next to the sea we were submerged, and what we said in the middle of the night did not matter, it was just breathing half turned into language, silvery bubbles that wobbled up through the depths. It was liminal, it felt liminal—we washed in and out between two states, back and forth through an arch of marble, slow-moving flesh, mermaid hair, hips that went with the waves. Now, in the middle of the night, I listen to the quiet roar and think how Jason once called long hair "mermaid disease," and smile. A rain sketches softly down. I love the water.

ON WEDNESDAY AFTERNOON, we drive to the beach. My mother never swims, so I bring along one of the romance novels from the vacation house, called *If He's Dangerous*. A man who might be dangerous, but you won't know whether he is or not unless you read the book? It's written to order for her. She regards the nearly nude Scotsman on the cover with disgust, and then her phone rings. She picks it up and purpose floods back into her face; someone needs her.

"Listen, Christi. Listen to me," she says after a long minute. "Do you know how many kids don't want to be potty-trained because they're afraid of pooping snakes?" Another minute. "More than you could ever guess." Laughing, Jason and I escape toward the white and musical line of the tide.

The light on the water is insubstantial as phosphenes. It recalls the pressure of fingertips on closed eyelids, and the appearance of the bright and ordered components of the universe, which turn and whirl and fit their teeth into each other. About a hundred feet out, there is a loose assembly of people standing on an island of piled-up coral. When they're not upright they're on all fours, peering down into the tide pools. Jason and I swim to join them, and find that they're mostly children, clambering over the rocks like monkeys. Their instincts radiate out from their bodies. They do not fall, they do not slip. They are balanced by their vanished tails.

The leader is a teenager in a bright swimsuit, with reddish-brown hair straggling down her neck like kelp. She put on mascara this morning and now her eyes are ringed with it. She greets me with her hands on her hips.

"You have a long arm," she observes. "Can you reach down between the rocks and grab those goggles?"

I'm gratified she noticed—my long arms are my one beauty. After a short hesitation, I squat hulkingly on the jagged gray edge of the island and reach down until I feel my fingertips brush something man-made.

"Hey!" I say, and offer them back to the boy who lost them.

"Hey!" he answers, happy.

"I am from Toronto," the girl tells me, "and those kids over there are from Hershey, Pennsylvania." The boy whose goggles I rescued informs me that the whole town smells like cocoa beans when the wind is up. Savannah used to smell of paper being pressed, a much redder smell than you might expect, a smell like canned blood.

It is unexpected, but we don't fall either. Perhaps we are met halfway by the large secret brains mounded here and there on the rocks, glowing with their green ideas. Certainly there are brains in nature. Certainly sometimes they reach out and do our thinking for us. We clamber as nimbly as the children. The dead coral stamps pink symbols on the palms of our hands and the soles of our feet. Great gray fans spread out in it, and small single-chambered personalities. Each floweret represents a breath. I am working out a way to describe the living black and moss and jade of the reef underwater, like a sea turtle's back. If I were experimental, I would write the story by listing one unbelievable color after another: blue, blue, blue, pink and gold and bronze for flesh, a lemon-yellow twist, a deep rich darkening into black, and then the white of the moon pouring down.

"If you look down there, you can see a crab," the girl announces, and sure enough, the tip of the crab's claw is pointing at us like a ruby solitaire. She shows us spiny purple urchins and fish striped with tigerish yellow, and tells us there was even a rumor of stingrays earlier. "Give me your hand," she says, and helps me toward her, and her hand feels smooth and strong and porous. I see at once that she belongs to the tribe of Interested People. She has no self-consciousness; there are facts to find out.

"Where are you from?" she asks me, frank sunlight on her face, but that's a question I haven't been able to answer all week long.

On the beach is a long line of girls flipping themselves from heads to tails like doubloons. My mother used to call them "sun worshippers," and I took that literally—I believed to a ripe old age that sun worshipping was still a religion. My mother kneels next to them in her flowered swimsuit, taking picture after picture of the sea. What she wants is to be left alone to take one thousand pictures of a beautiful thing, and then, to round out her happiness, one unflattering shot of her child's ass.

"My mom is over there too," the girl says, waving a vague hand toward the pine-protected stretch of sand, as if it's the land that's shifting, inconstant, and slippery, and not the sea. Why aren't you on the beach getting a tan? I want to ask her, but I wouldn't have been either. I'd have been out here too, with the rocks and the things that become rocks, out in the mindless liquid center of a minute, between the back and forth of the breeze, between the immediate and the longing for permanence, the gulls and the hot stones, the feathers that want to become fossils.

The girl stands very straight at the top of the pile and surveys everything around her with the fresh completeness of a discoverer, who has just felt the right key slide into her lock, the last piece pressed into her jigsaw. She stands and speaks with the sunlight fearlessly. Her ear, tilted up to it, is transparent. She bends toward the water, to get a closer look at some flashing silver school, and I watch her all the while in silence.

Part of what you have to figure out in this life is, Who would I be if I hadn't been frightened? What hurt me, and what would I be if it hadn't?

Next to me, Jason blinks, and I see the artificial lens in his left eye sparking like a mermaid scale, a point of contact between the seen and unseen world. I drop into the multicolored water, here cold, there warm, and float on my back until I cannot feel myself. The sun, when it is so direct, has something to tell you. But find a fluent current, and it will let you speak.

WE'VE BROUGHT ALONG another picnic—firm mahi-mahi starred with cilantro, roasted pork with caramelized onions, prawns on a fluffy split roll—and begin setting the food out on a table under the fine-needled pines. "You want a pineapple juice?" I ask my mother, pulling a can out of my bag.

She gives me the keen look of a king whose taster has just dropped dead from poison. "Tricia. When you were on the elimination diet, the day that you had pineapple, most of you wet the bed." She pauses. "I almost wet the bed myself."

She begins scrolling through the pictures she took of us exploring the coral island—two hundred of them, according to her count. "Here's a GREAT one of you from behind," she says with excitement, and shows me a picture that might as well have been taken on a whale cruise, so violently is my tail punishing the water. Just above me, in a turquoise the color of heaven, bent over and dead center, is the interested girl's butt.

We sit sipping heinous coladas out of coconuts under the lizardy dapple of the trees for the rest of the afternoon. Then, just as we're leaving the beach, I spy an iguana flickering his way up a trunk, darting here and there between the lips of the leaves, quick as his own tongue. My mother drops all her belongings and spends the next twenty minutes clicking her long black camera at him. He likes a high-pitched singing that Jason makes, and turns his head down to us and blinks one gold eye. Isak Dinesen wrote:

> *Once I shot an Iguana. I thought that I should be able to make some pretty things from his skin. A strange thing happened then, that I have never afterwards forgotten. As I went up to him, where he was lying dead upon his stone, and actually while I was walking the few steps, he faded and grew pale, all colour died out of him as in one long sigh, and by the time that I touched him he was grey and dull like a lump of concrete. It was the live impetuous blood pulsating within the animal, which had radiated out all that glow and splendour. Now that the flame was put out, and the soul had flown, the Iguana was as dead as a sandbag.*

He is, for us, the only iguana that has ever existed. We must have him, and we do. But the thing that sighs out all its color here is not the iguana itself, which you can picture down to the last green enamel scale, but my mother's jewel-like joy as she shot him—badly, badly, badly, and then finally, just as he was. The photo, when we marvel at it later, sees everything there is to see about him, knows everything there is to know. His own gold lens looks back and acknowledges her. She, too, had been an Interested Person. She, too, was called back to it in paradise.

IT IS OUR LAST NIGHT, and my mother is drinking champagne. It rises glittering to the top of her head like a tiara, something gold and incorruptible set free from the Spanish galleons. Her benevolence shines on everyone; it is motherhood itself. "All children are my sons!" she cries. "That are men. They're really children between the ears, and yet physically they're men!"

When her champagne runs out, I give her a taste of my vodka. "Tastes like jet fool," she says, practically spitting. She sits with it for a while, feeling the burn, and then ventures, "This is not affecting me at all, though maybe it is making me psychic."

"Can you read Jason's mind?"

She turns the full fire hose of her power on him. "Yes I can. I think he's contemplating. I think he's meditating. He's monknatious. He processes and he takes it in, sunrise to sunset. He's not time-pressured. On a scale of ten, he's sixty-six and two-thirds of not caring. Wait a minute, is he writing down everything I say?"

"I am," he says, "because it is literature."

"Do you want another drink?" I ask her, because why slow a woman when she's on a roll?

"No I DON'T want another drink. It's calories. It's dehydration potential." Then, drunkenly, "I love language!"

BEFORE WE DRIVE to the airport, we stop by the Basilica of St. Mary Star of the Sea. It is bleached as a conch, and the side doors are all flung open so the stroke of a crosswind can enter. It's a kind, ministering wind that suggests someone is combing your hair, though mine has been short since I was thirteen.

At the front of the church, there is a doll of Christ dressed in a long dress like the baby Hemingway, promising to deliver us from the condition of being bitched from the start. Look-alikes even here. He gets a

much prettier dress than his mother, but she gets to be Star of the Sea.
Some corner of my memory has stored the fact that that fine name, *Stella
Maris,* is the result of a transcription error. St. Jerome called her *Stilla
Maris*, which means drop of the sea, not star. Later someone wrote it
down wrong, as someone is always doing.

Outside, we wander over a series of rosy circles in the grass. "They
are a rosary," my mother says after a minute, surprised. "You're supposed to step on one and say a prayer, and step on the next and say another," and sure enough, there is a knot of people making a steady
pilgrimage from stone to stone and reciting together in the same voice. I
could join them; I still remember how a rosary is said.

To escape them, we step into the nuns' courtyard, and my mother
breathes not one word of her avowed hatred. She walks around taking
pictures of the Stations of the Cross, which are mosaic scenes with gilt
skies. At the center of the courtyard is a fountain, with an overblown
white rose floating just at the lip of it. Jason gazes at the fountain with
sudden desire. "I'm tempted to splash fountain water on my head," he
says. "Would that be all right?"

"Oh, I don't know . . ." I begin, worrying that the Drop of the Sea
might not like it.

"Of course, of course!" my mother laughs, and he dips his hand and
sprinkles his bald head all over.

"That's the most religious thing I've ever done," he says with satisfaction, "but really it's just because I was hot."

Religion flows to every corner here, as it does in every place. In the
Audubon House, I read the story of a pirate who claimed to have been
converted by doves, whose long liquid cooing throughout the night
awakened in him thoughts of his sins. Though perhaps he simply liked

listening to them, and thought he might hear them better in heaven than elsewhere.

WE LIFT UP over the water and fly home, tanned and drowsy and our limbs loosened. When we arrive on the doorstep of the rectory, it's just chiming midnight, and we tiptoe inside, not sure if my father is sleeping. The scene, as we expected, is one of chaos. The smell of hamburger is so intense and penetrating that it might be a government tactic to flush cult members out of a building. My father's sacred gowns and underwear are flung everywhere. The dining room looks like a dog just opened a birthday present in it. An enormous cardboard box lies dismembered on the floor just a few steps from where it must have been delivered.

"Greg?" Mom calls up the stairs, tentative. "What's this package?"

"IT'S THE MONSTRANCE FROM LONDON!" he shouts with considerable finality, and then we hear the surreptitious closing of a door.

Jason's eyes light up; he thinks he said MONSTER. A religion centered around a MONSTER FROM LONDON might be one he could finally get behind.

"No, no," I tell him, "a monstrance is a sort of twenty-four-karat-gold sunburst that holds the body of the Lord." There's a window at the center and a thousand rays reach out of it in every direction, so it stands on the altar like a permanent dawn. The word "monstrance" means "to show," and when I read it, up rises that round image of the bread through the glass—bread that my own father has consecrated, at the climax of a metaphor that is more than a metaphor, at the moment where real time intersects with eternity. How to explain this moment to someone who never believed it, could never believe it? That bells ring, that the universe kneels, that *what happened* enters into the house of *what is always happening*, and sits with it together and eats at its table.

"How much," Jason wonders in a whisper, and, "Where did he get the money," but we don't ask him those questions anymore. The size of the box, the wild rips in the cardboard, the far-flungedness of the newspaper packing all tell us that this one must be a beauty—and there is hardly enough gold in the world, after all, for something that holds a slice of the mystery.

"No matter what you do, do not go into the bathroom," my mother interrupts, bustling past us with a pile of Rags and throwing them straightaway into the trash can. "Something might be dead in there."

Silence upon silence from upstairs. Then, like music over the closing credits, the most objectionable American guitar riff I've ever heard begins to somersault down the steps, shirtless and wearing the tightest possible jeans, signaling that it's time for us to leave.

"Isn't he even going to say hello? Or good-bye? Safe travels? Sleep tight?" Jason asks, as puzzled by this as he is by the twenty-four-karat monster. "Isn't he going to come downstairs at all?"

I repeat the same sentence that ran unbidden through my head the night my mother called him: *I can only write down what you say, what you do.* Please give me something, anything: a crumb of the bread that you stand in front of the people and change, a word of the absolution that flows out of you toward anyone who needs it. Forget your gold sunburst and come downstairs, I think, but whole Bibles have been written about the man who wasn't there, who appeared for some and never others, who was thunder in a cloud.

"He is who he is and that's all he's ever gonna be," my mother says, picking up pieces of revenge garbage with a pair of tongs, and it sounds so much like a fresh, confused entry in the litany of names of God that

I almost laugh. "He alone is his very being, and he is of himself everything that he is," I think, and am somehow comforted. Who among us is not the great I AM? Who among us doesn't live in a nightgown or some other bare-ass outfit at the center of his own wide sky—shining, unchanging, without beginning or end, a word in the east and a body in the west? A people who cannot change, crying out to a power who does not: *please*, and *come downstairs*, and *be a human being.* As soon as I have unpacked and showered off a bright blue week's worth of salt, I know I will absent myself just as he is doing right now; I know I will shut myself up again as if to pray, alone with my shapes and my symbols and my self, calling on the message to appear in my midst, to walk toward me looking terrible and saying be not afraid.

"Is that Cheap Trick?" Jason exclaims. I startle, thinking he is referring to my internal rhetoric, until the words "I want you to want me" come floating down over the screech of the guitars, and it's impossible not to hear it as coming from heaven, impossible not to hear it as God's own song.

"Oh, it was *so fun*," my mother whispers, holding me. Then she walks with us to the doorway and waves to us until we disappear, standing outlined at the center of a warm gold page, her face appearing to pour forth light.

AS WE SET OFF on the road that stretches home, my petition is forgotten, my *Please, give me something.* Radiance still sits in my skin, warm color still pulses in me, and I understand that what I have is enough. The afterimage of the rectory flashes behind my eyes, the white door open and beckoning me inside, the steps leading to that eternal upstairs where I could stay as long as I needed. It was an idyll, of course it was an idyll. A family never recognizes its own idylls while it's living them, while it's all spread out on the red-and-white checked cloth, while the picnic basket is still open and before the ants have found the sugar, when everyone is still lying in the light with their hearts peeled and in loose sweet segments, doing one long Sunday's worth of nothing. It recognizes them later, when people are gone, or moved away, or colder toward each other. This is about that idyll, and I began it in that grass-green clearing of time, and I am giving it no chance to grow cold. This is about the moment when I walked into the house, and they were there, as they had always been there, as they would not always be. This is about how happy they were when they saw me, how the sun rose in their faces, how it was another day.

ACKNOWLEDGMENTS

A thousand thanks to the people who made this book possible: To my tigress of an agent, Mollie Glick, and to my editor, Paul Slovak, who is as graceful and insightful with prose as he is with poetry. To the team at Riverhead, particularly Geoff Kloske and Jynne Martin, who sent me whiskey after I was robbed. To Helen Yentus for her work on the jacket. And to Megan Lynch, who championed this book in the first place.

Thanks to my parents, who supported me even as I wrote down everything they did, and to the seminarian, who took everything in the greatest good humor. To my brothers and sisters, who answered my dozens of questions and who propped up my memory where it failed. To the people who read this work in different drafts: Greg, Michelle, Sasha, Jesse.

Thanks to Jason, who is afraid of both "blood" and "sharp things going into people," yet who gave me huge courage in that house full of crucifixes. To my writing companion Alice, who passed away soon after I turned in my finished draft.

My especial and boundless gratitude to all those who donated so that Jason could get new eyes.

Finally, to my nieces and nephews Wolfgang, Aria, Seraphina, John Paul, Gigi, Gabe, Dreda, and Veronica—I thought you might like to see your names in a real book, as I would have liked it when I was young.